MOUTHFUL
OF
ROCKS

Modern Adventures in the
French Foreign Legion

CHRISTIAN JENNINGS

THE ATLANTIC MONTHLY PRESS
NEW YORK

•

First published in Great Britain in 1989 by Bloomsbury
Publishing Ltd.
First Atlantic Monthly Press edition, October 1989
Printed in the United States of America

Library of Congress Cataloging-in-Publication Data

Jennings, Christian.
    Mouthful of rocks : modern adventures in the French foreign
legion / Christian Jennings.—1st Atlantic Monthly Press ed.
    Reprint. Originally published: London : Bloomsbury Pub.,
1989.
    ISBN 0–87113–340–7
    1. Jennings, Christian. 2. France. Armée de terre. Légion
étrangère—Biography. 3. Soldiers—France—Biography. I. Title.
U55.J46A3 1989   355'.0092—dc20   89-37593

The Atlantic Monthly Press
19 Union Square West
New York, NY 10003

FIRST PRINTING

CONTENTS

Acknowledgments are due to many people but I am most grateful to my parents for putting up with so much for so long. Thanks to Frances Coady and Caroline Dawnay. And thanks to Mike Petty and everybody at Bloomsbury, especially Asheley McCracken.

THIS IS FOR SAL AND JAMIE

All the names given in these pages are fictitious, as, apart from two, the men who feature in this book are still serving in the French Foreign Legion.
This is how it was and this is what happened.

Soldiers and women. That's how the world is. Any other role is temporary. Any other role is a gesture.

Jeanette Winterson, *The Passion*

MOUTHFUL
OF
ROCKS

— 1 —

NORSEMAN ON THE TRAIN

The Gendarme on duty at Boulogne Police Station looked surprised when I said that I had come to join the French Foreign Legion. I had stepped straight off the ferry from Dover and had nothing in my pockets except a disposable razor and my toothbrush. I told him that I was English, an ex-paratrooper and that I had come to be a legionnaire.

He took my passport off me and told me to sit down on a bench set against the wall; I picked up a magazine and read it while he checked my details. He handed me some leaflets and magazines about the French Army, one of which was *Képi Blanc*, the monthly journal of the Foreign Legion. On the cover was a picture of two legionnaires with shaven heads staring over the battlements of a fort in Chad, where in that summer of 1984 the Legion was assisting the government in their low-key war against Libyan-backed rebels. Having looked at my passport, the Gendarme made a telephone call during which he turned to look at me, spelling out my name and saying that I was English and a former paratrooper. Then he walked over and told me that a Corporal from the Foreign Legion recruiting office at Lille would come to pick me up in two hours; until then I was free to go for a walk and get something to eat.

I went outside and stood in front of the police station, which was set on a hill. I had woken up as the ferry was docking, feeling bad-breathed and half drunk, and had walked off the ramp, shown my passport at customs and asked where the police station was. I was directed up through the town, past some municipal gardens to a small building set back from the road. From where I stood outside it I could see the Channel and the town of Boulogne set around the port. I turned right and walked up to a crossroads where two shops and a bar were open; I couldn't go in because I had no money, so I continued up the road. On top of the hill was a wood of beech trees surrounded by a stone wall; I climbed the wall and found that underneath the trees were hundreds of moss-covered gravestones of soldiers from Napoleon's Imperial Army who had died of disease while waiting to invade England. In the middle of the wood was an obelisk commemorating the Emperor. I sat on it and smoked a cigarette before falling asleep in the long grass. For some reason I felt detached from all that was going on, presumably because I was tired and drunk. When I opened my eyes, it had got colder, so I stood up, brushed off my blazer and set off back to the Gendarmerie. As I approached it I noticed a beige Renault outside with military markings. The Legion had arrived.

Earlier that morning I had awoken lying on the grass underneath an oak tree in Regent's Park. Pushing myself up off the wet ground, I brushed the twigs and earth off my trousers while I checked my pockets. My passport was wet and creased from where I had lain on it all night; but it was there. One side of my trousers was soaked with dew, and there were mud stains on my shoes; my hair was short and stood up on end, and there was a leaf in my ear. It was 7.00 am and I was very cold.

That summer of 1984 was very hot, with successive weeks of clear skies and sunny days, but so early in the morning there was mist in the air and the grass was still wet. I lit up a Rothmans as I walked jerkily over the park, shivering, the cigarette rushed to my head and I felt better as I drew on it strongly, cupping the end in the palm of my grubby hand. There was dirt underneath my fingernails and my hangover was worse than normal, as the result of weeks of drinking throbbed through my head and churned my stomach. There was nobody in the park at that time and I walked quickly through the dew, my feet soaked before I had gone ten yards, a trail of sliding tracks behind me on the grass. I headed for the tube station at Baker Street and turned down my collar as I came into the Marylebone Road. A man wearing an anorak was walking his dog, and the terrier trundled past me on its lead as I rubbed my hands together, trying to keep warm. I leant back and looked at the seat of my trousers, checking that I had brushed off the mud; I wanted to make the transition from somebody who had just slept rough to somebody who looked as though he was out for an early walk. I had only to make it to Dover and then I could sleep on the ferry to France. I had £30 in crushed fivers and damp change sitting in my pockets, and all I needed to buy with it was the train ticket to Dover, a toothbrush and some beer. I counted on being able to dodge my way on to the ferry and I didn't think I would need any money once I got to France.

I fell asleep on the Circle Line and had to retrack from South Kensington to Victoria, curled up in a corner seat in the warm tube. The train for Dover left at 11.00 am so I bought a copy of *Soldier* magazine and leafed through the photos of happy-looking squaddies as I drank a cup of British Rail coffee, which tasted hot and disgusting. I hoped that the off-licence opened soon because the journey to Dover could only be improved by getting drunk; besides, a few cans of lager helped me through the morning pretty well, and killed off hunger till late afternoon. I had another coffee; I was confused, irritable and dizzy as I stood by the buffet and watched the station cleaners, suddenly desperate to be on my way before tiredness made me change my mind. I had come this far and was determined to make it to France.

As soon as the off-licence opened I bought a dozen cans of Norseman lager, hefting the packs under my arm as I went off to find a quiet corner of the station where I could guzzle them in peace. I was on my sixth one by 10.30 am, sitting behind a luggage trolley with my head against the wall. I felt much better. I got on the train and settled myself in a corner compartment with my back to the engine, feeling pissed and happy as the carriages rolled out of Victoria towards Clapham Junction and the South Coast.

I couldn't wait to get to Boulogne. I was going to join the French Foreign Legion. I didn't know quite where or how or with whom but I was going to turn in at the Gendarmerie and take it from there. They would know. This was the most dramatic move I had made in all my twenty-two years, and, buoyed up by ten cans of lager, I was convinced it was a good idea.

I had enough remaining money for a proper ticket, and I bought a toothbrush as well. It was lunchtime so I bought a packet of Jaffa Cakes and more lager, which I drank while waiting for the ferry to start boarding. I ate the biscuits in one go and walked on to the boat, climbing up the decks to stand at the back. The ferry turned into the sluggish waters of the Channel. I went down to the washroom to get a drink of water, and to have a shave; I didn't want to turn up at Boulogne Police Station looking scruffy. Fortunately a lorry driver was washing in the basin, so while he went off to have a shit in one of the cabinets, I rifled his spongebag and pinched a disposable razor. Scurrying aft, I had a fast shave, using the pink slime from the soap-dispenser to lather my face. Later I watched as the white cliffs of Dover diminished in the ship's wake, before going downstairs to get some sleep. I wondered how long it would be before I saw England again.

I was working in a heart clinic off Harley Street as a receptionist and delivery boy when I decided to join the French Foreign Legion. My job was to answer the telephone and welcome the patients, who were mainly wealthy Greeks and Arabs who came to have check-ups and electrocardiograms. I would open the door to them and check their names off in the appointment book, often unable to converse because of the language barrier. They were referred to the clinic by their doctors in Greece or the Middle East, and looked horrified when I said there was no lift and they had to walk down seventeen stairs to the basement. The closest I came to anything clinical was watching a nurse shave the chest of a Lebanese businessman, so that she could attach the electrodes required for an ECG – I held the kidney dish into which the used razor was deposited. I was having a spell as a civilian after leaving the Territorial Army in mild disgrace.

I had initially become interested in things military through my father, who had served in the Cavalry in World War Two. His tank had been in an encounter with a German howitzer and he had been badly burnt, his face, hands and arms requiring extensive plastic surgery, although he went on to run a preparatory school in Sussex. My grandfather had also been in the Army, firstly in the Leicestershire Regiment during the Great War, and then the Education Corps after the armistice. He had been serving in Cairo when my father was born, and afterwards the family came to live in England, as my grandfather was posted to the Military Academy at Sandhurst as an instructor. They lived in a house in the Terrace, and eventually my father was sent to Ampleforth in Yorkshire, a Benedictine monastery which also ran a boarding school.

I was born in December 1962, the seventh of eleven children, eight of whom were boys. We lived in part of a school my father ran, which was situated in a large white house outside Arundel, Sussex, on the edge of the South Downs. It was an idyllic place to grow up, as there was an enormous garden and a real jungle of bamboo beyond the vegetables. We had a nursery and a nanny, and until we were thirteen ate with her rather than with our parents. Nanny's mother was of French stock and lived in Calais, and her father came from Bishop's Waltham, a village in Hampshire. She smoked more cigarettes than anybody I was ever to meet, and she cemented my loyalty to her with frequent presents of Airfix model aeroplanes.

I first talked about the war with my father on a train outside Bognor Regis, when I asked him how many Germans he had killed. He told me not to ask questions like that. I read comics, like *Victor* and *Dandy*. In the *Victor* the Germans were always getting slaughtered by plucky chaps with square jaw-lines and purple stubble. Men who didn't do up their helmets and who held machine guns in one hand.

— 4 —

The stories always came out well in the end, and if one of the officers was a coward or incompetent, you could be sure that by the end of the story he would have done the decent thing and charged the machine gun nest singlehanded, getting killed in the process. I read lots of *War-Picture Libraries*, which came out every week, and detailed the exploits of soldiers, sailors and airmen in World War Two. The Germans were 'krauts' and 'squareheads' and were portrayed as being stupid and incompetent. The Japanese had slit eyes and very bad teeth, and fought the Australians, who never rolled their sleeves down.

I played Knights with my brothers and sisters, wearing a suit of plastic armour and a helmet with a visor. At age seven I decided that I wanted to be a soldier, after I had watched a TV programme about the D-Day landings. I attended my father's prep school where I was one of the worst-behaved pupils, constantly talking after lights-out and fooling around in class. I moved to a school in Herefordshire when my father closed down Avisford and moved to mid Wales. St Richards was fun and strict, with not enough to eat and high academic standards; I developed a crush on the assistant matron who had a phenomenally large chest; I liked her because she used to sit on the ends of our beds and talk to us before we went to sleep.

I excelled at no sports at all, preferring instead to be one of the boys who was allowed to use the lawn mowers and keep the garden in trim – my one attempt at cricket was a disaster, and I was sent off the field for not paying attention. As far as I was concerned, cricket was, and certainly still is, the most tedious and unengaging sporting activity a man could possibly indulge in. Team games always put me off. Football meant standing on a muddy pitch hoping the ball wouldn't come anywhere near me, so that I wouldn't be forced to tackle some vicious little boy who really cared who won the game. The people who took sports seriously aroused deep loathing in me. Rugby was even worse, as it involved a large amount of physical contact, and there was nowhere on the field you could hide and no playing position which kept you out of harm's way. I had nightmares about scrums and tackles from a very early age and refused to play as a linesman, in case I got involved in violence. Rugby nightmares replaced nightmares about witches, which had been the basis of my bad dreams for several years.

I loathed sport well into my teens; a distinct disadvantage, as I had decided I wanted to be an Officer in the Parachute Regiment or the Royal Marines, a vocation which demanded exceptional physical fitness and courage, qualities I didn't possess. My first real contact with the military was when I went on a familiarisation course to the Parachute Regiment depot at Aldershot when I was fourteen, and spent two days living in the mess, where I looked around the regiment, met serving officers and had some basic interviews with retired Colonels, who were in charge of selecting the future leaders of the toughest regiment in the Army outside of the Special Air Service.

I tried boxing when I was fifteen and won a bout against an opponent who was smaller than me and who normally wore thick glasses; I went on to the second round of the competition and was beaten flat in thirty seconds by a demon midget who hammered me onto the ropes and kept hitting me until the referee stopped the bout before I suffered permanent damage. The referee was also the Quartermaster in the school's Combined Cadet Force, who paraded on Wednesday afternoons and ran around in the woods with Lee Enfield .303s practising ambushes in the rhododendrons.

With the advent of punk music in 1977 I transferred my energies and enthusiasm from the military and spent a lot of time dressing up and putting Vaseline in my hair, much to the annoyance of my house master, a quiet Benedictine who wrote on my term report, 'Christian seems to have developed a nihilistic attraction for punk rock, which is strange for somebody who avoids violence even on the rugby field. So what about some real punk rock with courage in the boxing ring?' I thought Father Ambrose had missed the point of modern music. I was sixteen and thought I was in love. I had lost my virginity to a Belgian au pair who was a friend of my eldest sister. The girl had told me that she was a virgin and that she was in love with me. I believed her on both counts, especially when she visited me for a weekend and gave me a bottle of 'Denim' aftershave which she had shoplifted from a Chemist in mid Wales. Bored, I ran away from Downside when I was sixteen and spent two days in Paris, sleeping rough, before hitch-hiking home. I was taken away from the school by my father and tutored in a caravan by an eccentric ex-priest.

I was turned down by all the universities on my UCCA application form, because I had received a bad report from my headmaster at Downside School who said I took drugs, which was true, but was also an admission made to him in confidence. London University had interviewed me for both of the courses for which I had applied: Arabic and Economics, and Swahili and Commercial Law. I had chosen these subjects specifically because I knew nothing about any of the four disciplines and because, having studied foreign languages at A Level, it seemed natural to develop my linguistic skills. Hitch-hiking home from London to Wales after attending my interviews, I was given a lift on a roundabout outside Monmouth in South Wales. It was a cold day and I had been standing in that particular spot for half an hour, so I was glad to get into the car, which was driven by a smart-looking man in a tweed cap. We had gone two or three miles when he asked me what I did and how I came to be hitch-hiking. I told him that I was a student and studying at London University, my course being Swahili and Economics. I was tired of all the conversations I had had that day and wanted to glamorise my life. I told him I was in my first year and that my curriculum to date had been based around mastering the basics of Swahili, its grammar, basic vocabulary and syntax. I enthused about my imaginary prowess in the language, telling him that I hoped to visit Africa that summer. He was silent for a while as we drove through the late afternoon towards Abergavenny and Brecon. I had told him that I was going to Builth Wells, near where my parents lived, and he had agreed to drop me there. It meant that I had another thirty miles in his car.

Turning to me suddenly, he pointed through the windscreen and said something in a tongue I didn't understand. I kept silent, thinking that he might have an embarrassing speech impediment. Two miles further on, he pointed out of the window again at a field of cows, saying something in his unintelligible language. I looked at him non-plussed. He still kept silent. Finally, he turned to me and asked a question, repeating it twice, in the same jumble of words and sounds which I couldn't understand. He was speaking Swahili. Brought up on a farm in Kenya, he had lived there until he was seventeen. He had been pointing out of the window and asking me if I liked the weather or the colour of the cows. I got out silently at the next roundabout.

Doing a lot of hitch-hiking, as I did from my parents' house in Wales to London, I met many different people. A middle-aged man picked me up on the M4 near Swindon and offered me a lift to London, which was very convenient. Asked where I lived, I replied that I was staying in my parents' flat in Knightsbridge.

'Oh,' he said, 'I live in Knightsbridge as well. Which part are you from?'

'Egerton Crescent.'

'Good Lord, how interesting; have your parents lived there long?'

I thought quickly. We had another seventy miles till London and at least another fifteen until the next junction where I could get out. I shouldn't get this wrong.

'Yes, since just after the war. My grandmother bought it so that she could be close to Harrods for the shopping.'

'What number is it you live at?'

'Forty-seven, in the basement flat.'

He was silent for a while.

I turned to him and asked, 'Is something the matter?'

'No, it's just funny, that's all. I had drinks there on Thursday with Paul and Angela.'

In May 1978 the Foreign Legion first came to my notice, through the pages of *Paris Match*. I was in a French class at school when I picked up a copy of the magazine, which had been lying on one of the tables. On the centre pages I found a huge black and white photograph of a Hercules aircraft disgorging paratroopers over a large expanse of grassland somewhere in Africa. The caption said, '*Enfin dans le ciel, ceux de la Légion.*' (At last, in the sky, the boys from the Legion.)

This was the *2ème Régiment Étranger de Parachutistes* jumping over Kolwezi in southern Zaire to save 2,000 European hostages from Katangese rebels who had attacked the small mining town some days previously. I cut out the caption and stuck it on the cover of my French notebook. It was the most powerful affirmation of strength and military prowess that I had ever seen, and I found it completely fascinating.

I was slightly built, and although I hated team sports and games, I spent much time in the school gym doing circuit training and fitness programmes. I was nicknamed Pune, an inverted pun on puny, a physical status I retained, no matter how many press-ups I did. To escape this branding of myself as a bodily failure, I longed to be able to attach myself to an organisation stronger than myself, an association through which I could derive a feeling of physical achievement and personal status I would not otherwise possess.

On holiday at my parents' house in Wales, I locked myself into the ground floor bathroom and swore that one day I would be a paratrooper in the French Foreign Legion.

After being turned down by university, I moved to London and joined the Territorial Army, attending evening training sessions in preparation for the physical selection tests. I had chosen to join the 10th Battalion of the Parachute Regiment, and the preliminary training evenings were geared towards physical exercise, getting us ready for 'P Company', the tests which every aspiring paratrooper, territorial or regular, had to pass before being able to wear his coveted maroon beret. At the time I was living in a bedsit in Chelsea and was unemployed; through a mixture of odd jobs and the DHSS I managed to keep myself in beer and cigarettes. Being unemployed in the TA was a positive advantage as it meant that I could devote all my time to training. I did a lot of my socialising at the barracks and at least twice a week would stagger down the King's Road towards my bedsit.

This was the autumn of 1982, immediately after the Falklands war, and the public image of the Parachute Regiment was in high profile after its members' achievements in the South Atlantic; they had won two Victoria Crosses and had fought at Mount Longdon, Goose Green and Wireless Ridge. As such, many people wanted to be part-time paras. Out of the eighty-two people who started the selection process from our drill hall, nine of us made it. I was one and felt that I could conquer the world. I rushed off to tell my girlfriend at her Catholic convent in Berkshire. She wasn't too pleased, as she thought I had been coarsened by the whole experience, which was true. She didn't like me wearing T-shirts with 'Death From Above' emblazoned on them at her friends' parties in Wimbledon.

Most of my new friends were paras, and we used to sit around listening to our Sergeant-Major, who had been seconded to us from the 3rd Battalion after an exemplary performance in the Falklands. He had been in the Parachute Regiment for twenty years and had served in Borneo, the Oman, Northern Ireland and the South Atlantic. I would go drinking with him at lunchtimes during the week, listening to his stories of combat and debauchery in distant corners of the world. After hours, we went to a bar in Knightsbridge, where one afternoon I met a fifty-five-year-old Italian woman who was wearing white leather flared trousers. I undressed her in her South Kensington hotel room and fucked her, only retreating to the safety of the street outside when she asked me to stay the night so that she could pretend to be my mother.

Having been awarded my red beret, I went on to RAF Brize Norton where I completed seven parachute jumps and was awarded my 'wings'. I attended every weekend exercise and had drill evenings twice a week. Most of the weekend exercises started off with a para drop on to a drop zone somewhere in the British Isles, after which we would spend two days marching with large packs, practising attacks and fieldcraft. On Sunday evenings we would return to barracks in London and head home. The other soldiers had wives and families to go to, but I felt slightly at a loss away from the TA. I was still unemployed, and happy as such, for it gave me more time for the TA. I perfected the technique of entering my bedsit without anyone hearing me or noticing me, but eventually it became impossible to stay there *ad infinitum* without paying my rent, so I took all my military kit and some clothes and set myself up in the changing room at the barracks. Friends were surprised at how often I would stay on their floors after an evening out, and I would alternate between trips to my parents' house in Wales and visits to friends from pre-army days, who I would surprise by telephoning to say I was on leave from the regular army. I received my mail at the barracks and showered there in the mornings.

Each summer and Christmas, there was a party held for every member of the TA unit and their girlfriends and wives; the price of the ticket included food and as much as you could drink. The year after I joined, I attended the party and drank several pints of a mixture of lager and gin, after which I lost consciousness in the changing rooms; I woke up to find myself being hit, kicked and pushed down the stairs. An unhappy gatecrasher, who had been asked to leave, had decided to vent his aggression on a defenceless paratrooper before he left. I passed out, but an hour later lurched downstairs into the hall. The evening was drawing to a close and everybody was dancing with new-found friends. In the middle of 'Nights in White Satin' I appeared on the dance floor, my face, head and shirt covered in blood, and with two teeth missing. I was bleeding from a laceration on my scalp and was so drunk that I had no recollection of what had happened; a Sergeant quizzed me closely and seeing that I was incapable of speech, took me downstairs and put me into an ambulance. I was allowed no anaesthetic because I was so drunk, but felt nothing of the emergency dental surgery or stitches.

The army continued with its exercises and I continued with my life; friends from the TA would join the regular army, returning months later with stories of how much tougher things were there. I couldn't join the regular army because of my criminal record.

In a moment of stupidity I had forged an entry into my building society account book with a pencil, attempting to draw out several hundred pounds. Not surprisingly, I was discovered, and when I presented myself at Wandsworth police station I was arrested. The magistrate did not consider a barrack changing-room to be a proper address, and so I was ordered to be confined in a bail hostel in Camden Town while social reports were completed. We were kept in on a strict curfew and given meagre amounts of pocket money each week, which was just enough to buy food and travel to the DHSS office. The other people were a mixture of juvenile delinquents and retarded middle aged criminals. I went to court a month later and was fined £175.

In the year which ended with my twenty-first birthday, I had made twenty-nine parachute jumps, been arrested, spent a month on bail, been in hospital twice, stabbed in the face once, and spent over two thirds of my days with the Territorials. Part-time soldiering essentially took second place to a full-time job, and it was impossible to make the TA work as anything apart from a weekend occupation. I saw that I was going to have to find a job before I did something rash which landed me in prison.

Two friends from the paras – one an ex-member of the Irish Rangers, the other a deserter from the French Foreign Legion – were saving up for a trip to South Africa where they intended to join the South African Army. I went to see the former legionnaire at the pub in Paddington where he was working. The Legion sounded like a good idea: the pay was good, the uniforms smart, the bullshit no worse than the British Army, and there were varied postings abroad. The idea of going to France and turning into reality something which for so long had seemed a dream was now a concrete possibility. I knew nothing about the realities of proper soldiering, and to counterbalance the tedium and boredom of my small-time life, I surrounded the idea of the French Foreign Legion with a cocoon of glamour that it didn't possess. Nothing could be worse than the life I was leading at present, I thought, where the pressures from being homeless and unemployed were likely to force me into a series of criminal acts which would result in prison, or vagrancy at the least. (I had taken to climbing over the railings of the barracks each night, as the watchmen on the gate had been forbidden to let me in as I was known to be sleeping there. Each morning started off with me trying to find enough small change to get something to eat, and gradually, I sold off all my army kit at government surplus stores to finance my drinking.

In late August I was finishing my day at the heart clinic, where I had been working for several months, when I decided that it was time to go. I had just received a telephone call from the barracks which informed me that officials from Horseferry Road magistrates court had phoned demanding to see me about nonpayment of fines. I hung up on them; I had had enough. It seemed as good a time as any to go, so I went down to the squat in the King's Road where I was living and picked up my passport. I went to see a friend in Regent's Park that evening but she wasn't there, so I climbed the railings into the park, crossed the grass, and settled under an oak tree . . .

— 2 —

'HAVE YOU EVER HAD SEX WITH AN ANIMAL?'

As I walked back into the Gendarmerie the following afternoon, I saw my first legionnaire. A small, tubby figure in olive fatigues and high-lacing combat boots was leaning on the counter drinking a cup of coffee; on his head was a white *képi*, the distinguishing box-like hat worn by all legionnaires. He looked at me as I walked through the door and looked to the Gendarme as if to say, Is this him? The Gendarme nodded and told me to wait outside. He gave my passport to the Corporal who put it into his pocket, then we got into the car and drove off in the direction of Lille. I wanted a cigarette; I had finished my packet and desperately wanted one to dull my hangover, but felt reluctant to cadge from the Corporal. He made little attempt at conversation and showed no surprise that he should be asked to drive to Boulogne in the middle of the afternoon to pick up a well-dressed but grubby Englishman. It was late afternoon as we drove across north eastern France through the Pas de Calais, past the fields and along the poplar-lined avenues where twice in one century the German Army had invaded. Eventually the Corporal gave me a cigarette, and in due course we pulled over at a roadside café to have a cup of coffee and to stretch our legs. As we walked into the café, a couple of the local farmers in denim overalls and caps looked up and welcomed us.

'*Ah, c'est La Légion!*'

From their smiles it appeared that the Corporal was a regular there, as he obviously travelled the road to Boulogne often. I felt nervous, out of my depth and completely at odds with the friendliness of the locals around me. I had sobered up by now and felt terrible. Looking at the menu on the wall I realised how hungry I was, yet I had no means of buying anything to eat; I had no money and so had no idea of where my next meal would be coming from.

We arrived in Lille as dusk was falling and drove through the centre of the modern sprawling town until we reached the citadel which was surrounded by a moat and an ancient drawbridge. We drove across it and through an arch where a conscript in a shabby uniform saluted the car as it passed. I asked the Corporal why he had saluted and he explained that it was because the Legion was the senior arm of the French Armed Forces.

We drew up outside a building which was surrounded by a walled courtyard. There was a sign above the gate which said '*Legio Patria Nostra*' (the Legion is our Country). I walked inside and sat down in a hall, whitewashed and cool with a red-tiled floor. On the walls hung faded photos of legionnaires drilling on parade grounds, jumping out of aeroplanes and marching across deserts. I wondered how long it would be before I was doing the things portrayed in the photos. It certainly wasn't too late to tell somebody that in fact I had made a terrible mistake and that I wanted to go home. But knowing, as I did, that there was little to return to in England, and buoyed up by the sense of adventure and risk brought on by the thought of joining the Legion, I knew I would be staying. I felt I was poised on the edge of something bigger and more unknown than anything I had encountered in life, and the mystery of what was about to happen added to the attraction. If I could have foreseen the progress of events over the next two years I would probably have stood up and run directly back to Boulogne.

After fifteen minutes, there came a shout of '*Entrez!*' from inside an office. I walked in and faced the desk. In front of me sat the smartest and most alert looking person I had ever seen in my life. His head was shaved almost bald and he was tanned. A scar ran from the corner of his eye to under his jawbone, and his tattooed arms rested on the desk in front of him, which was covered with mementoes of his Legion career. His tan shirt was ironed with the regulation creases; above one pocket was a set of silver parachute wings, above the other, three rows of coloured medal ribbons. His sleeves were rolled almost to the shoulder and the right one bore the three gold chevrons denoting his rank. He already had my passport in front of him, and he opened it and asked me my name, age, parents' names and a lot of other routine questions. He then asked me about my sexual habits, to which I replied that I was heterosexual. I wondered what would have happened if I had told him that I was bisexual or that I liked little girls. He appeared satisfied when I told him that I didn't have a criminal record and shouted for somebody to come and show me upstairs.

A Corporal appeared and beckoned me through to the kitchen; he was taller and thinner than the other one and his arms were covered with rough tattoos executed in Indian ink; on his right forearm were the words, '*Mon courage pour mon père, Mon coeur pour ma mère, Ma bitte pour une pute*' (My courage for my father, my heart for my mother, my prick for a whore).

I followed him through a washroom and into a barrack room with a tiled floor. The air was full of cigarette smoke and chatter in several different languages. Everybody stood up as the Corporal walked in. All the recruits were dressed in blue tracksuits and the Corporal told one of them to show me a bed and explain what was going on. The room was full of three-tier metal bunks made up with grey blankets and hung with clothes and towels. The walls were painted dirty cream and there was a poster advertising Air France stuck next to the door. It showed a bright-faced man running on a beach with two girls, both of whom were wearing fifties' bikinis. The colours had faded to blues and yellows and the caption said, To travel is to have fun. Standing there in my civilian clothes I felt completely out of place and wished that I could be wearing a blue tracksuit like the rest of them.

One of the recruits on a top bunk leant over and shouted, 'Here, mate, are you English?'

I told him that I was and suddenly the ice was broken. He jumped down, shook my hand and pulled a packet of Peter Stuyvesant cigarettes out of his pocket which he gave to me. I lit up and stood there trying to answer all the questions coming at me in French and English. Alex, who had given me the cigarettes, was Scottish and had been at Lille for three days; he had deserted from the Military Police in Germany, and thought that French food was nowhere as good as Glaswegian. I said that I had been in the British Army which prompted another Englishman called Chris to ask if I had known anybody in the Royal Signals in Aldershot or Catterick. Chris had a typical English soldier's moustache, thick and well-controlled, and on his bare arms were tattooed a combination of daggers, roses, skulls and messages to his mother. They showed me a bedspace and Alex went off to find me a tracksuit. I jumped up on to my bunk and looked at the others sitting around playing cards, arguing with each other or lying on their beds staring at the ceiling. Almost everybody was smoking. There were two Frenchmen in the corner with shifty eyes and scarred faces who looked away when I stared at them, and a friendly Scandinavian with a tan and fine blond hair who shook my hand and said, 'France fucking shit, yes?'

I smiled in answer to this, and started talking in French to a small, balding man who turned out to be Swiss and who was on the run from the customs in Geneva. There were Belgians and Dutchmen, a Spaniard and a silent Italian smoking through nicotine-stained fingers who, Alex told me, was suffering withdrawal from drugs. I changed into my tracksuit and took my civilian clothes downstairs to the Corporal.

The atmosphere in the barrack room was like the first day back at school, with everybody trying to outdo each other with stories of how exciting their holidays had been. Meeting a group of complete strangers from backgrounds very different to my own, in such an alien environment, was disconcerting. I had no idea how long we were going to be at Lille, or whether I stood any chance of being accepted by the Legion at all. I wanted to be accepted by those around me, and so joined in with their stories of soldiering, sex and drinking prowess. Immediately I felt worried lest I be seen as different from the others. As soon as you were noticed you became the butt for other peoples jokes and worries. But it was all right. The others were too bothered worrying about themselves and their chances to spend time thinking about the new arrival from England. I talked to Alex and Chris about the British Army and tried to look anonymous.

The English stuck together against those Alex called the 'fucking frogs', and Marius, the Scandinavian, attached himself to us. Life at Lille was easy and completely noneventful; it was only a recruiting post used for clearing volunteers before they were despatched on to Paris. There was a staff of three Corporals, one Sergeant and the scarred Sergeant-Major who had interviewed me, all of whom were veterans of some twenty years' service in the Legion, filling in their last years before retirement. Everyone gathered together in the room next to our barrack room for meals, which were brought over from the main kitchens somewhere else in the citadel. The Legion's recruiting post was only a small part of a large camp, which also housed French teenagers doing their military service; it formed an enclave of tidiness and order among the sloppiness of the conscripts' barracks. In front of our building was a patch of raked gravel with flowerbeds full of geraniums and palm plants. In one corner next to a store house was a rusting metal cage which housed a pet crow with broken wings and tatty feathers. That evening I had my first meal since leaving England eighteen hours before; by the time the pizza, chicken stew and gar-licked beans arrived from the kitchen they were cold, but I was so hungry that I had seconds, which amazed Alex. He was in the grip of severe constipation and was only eating fruit in an effort to clear himself out.

At 10.00 pm the Corporal came round to check that we were all present and in bed before turning the lights out and leaving us to sleep. I lay there with absolutely no idea what I would be doing the following day or if I stood any chance of being selected by the Legion. I was no closer to knowing the selection procedure, as my conversations about this with the other recruits had been based on mere speculation and gossip. The whole Legion surrounded itself with mystery in multiple layers, and the further one penetrated it the more complex the mystery became. There was little noise from outside the windows and we appeared cut off from the city and from civilian life in general. I lay in bed and pulled the sheets up over my nose. The bedding smelt of vomit and old sweat but the sheets were clean; I smoked a Stuyvesant and thought how nice it was to have no control at all over my future. Presently, I fell asleep.

We were woken up at 5.30 am, and Alex and I were told to go over to the kitchens to fetch the breakfast. I shaved in cold water and walked out of the gate and across the parade ground to where a queue of people were waiting to be served at the kitchen. The parade ground was surrounded by trees and it had rained in the night; the cobbles under our feet were wet and puddled. We walked straight to the head of the queue and helped ourselves from a huge cauldron which was steaming on top of an oven. Two cooks in white jackets and blue and white check trousers sat on the edge of a table having a conversation about their night out in Lille. Both were smoking and the pungent smell of Gauloise tobacco so early in the morning made me feel sick. When we got back to our building everybody else was up and busy cleaning the rooms. The Corporal who had fetched me from Lille was shaving in the washroom, wearing only tracksuit bottoms and flipflops; his back and stomach were covered with a mixture of hair, scars and tattoos.

We had another interview with the Sergeant-Major that afternoon. As I sat in front of him, I looked at a poster-sized photo which was on the wall behind him. It showed a group of legionnaires sitting on a wall in a wrecked and burning tropical town; the soldiers were filthy, looked exhausted and were draped with hand grenades and belts of machine gun ammunition. A couple had sun goggles around their necks and one a blood-stained bandage on his face. Their weapons were varied: Belgian FNs, Russian AK-47s (Kalashnikovs) and French MAT-49 submachine guns. At the centre of the group was the Sergeant-Major looking younger, with the whole front of his uniform covered with a vast brown blood-stain. He saw me looking at the picture and said, 'Kolwezi, Southern Zaire, 1978.'

I wanted to sit there and ask him all about it, but he finished questioning me and told me to leave. I really wanted to identify with him and wished that I could have said that I had been in the Falklands or in Northern Ireland, thereby establishing some sort of link.

That evening one of the Corporals made me clean out the crow's cage; I lifted the large black bird out and parked it on the gravel beside a flowerbed. Terrified that it would try to escape or fly away, and not wanting to risk the Corporal's anger, I pinned it to the ground by leaning a large stone against it. Peeling the shit-stained newspaper from the bottom of the cage, I emptied out the accumulated guano and went off to look for some fresh newspaper. Alex and Chris were playing poker as I walked in, and after explaining my predicament one of the Frenchmen handed over an old copy of the local paper which he had brought with him when he had joined. I didn't know what crows ate, so picked up some cabbage leaves and a lump of congealed moussaka from a dish in the Corporal's kitchen. I was relieved to find my protégé still motionless underneath his breeze block, so I picked him up, showed him the food and then laid him back on a fresh bed made from the local evening paper.

Unable to play poker, I looked at a poster on the wall of the room which described the different regiments of the Legion, their roles, and where they were based. Alex and I both favoured the *2ème Régiment Étranger de Parachutistes*, based at Calvi on the north coast of Corsica. According to the poster, the unit was made up of a number of different combat companies, each fulfilling a specialist role, ranging from amphibious and mountain warfare to sabotage. As I disliked swimming and Alex had already done some climbing in the British Army, we favoured the mountain warfare unit.

According to the poster, there were nine other regiments, divided between mainland France and the ex-colonies: units in Tahiti, French Guyana, Djibouti and Madagascar, and five regiments in France. The Parachute Regiment seemed to have the best time, for it was based in Europe yet each company spent four months of each year abroad on training attachments. I wanted to carry on as an airborne soldier, a paratrooper, enjoying the prestige which came from being part of an élite, and also the better pay and training opportunities that were the lot of such units. So when the Sergeant-Major asked me where I hoped to be posted eventually, I told him the *2ème Régiment Étranger de Parachutistes*; this didn't surprise him as most British recruits said the same thing.

We had an argument that evening in the barrack room between the English speakers and the French and Spanish; the recent Falklands conflict the bone of contention. We reckoned that the British Army was the most professional in the world and that it had been influential in training the South African and Israeli armies who we thought took second and third place. The Spaniards and Frenchmen claimed that the British victory in the South Atlantic had been a propaganda triumph over vastly inferior conscript forces, further demonstrating our need to re-establish our reputation overseas, which had been tarnished by the loss of Empire. Chris explained with rapidly diminishing patience that some of the Argentinian officers had received their training at Sandhurst; his brother had served in the Scots Guards on Mount Tumbledown and had said that the Argentinians they had confronted there had been good, professional soldiers. Some time after supper Alex finished the discussion by kicking one of the Spaniards in the face.

The whole of the following morning was spent gardening and weeding in the area in front of the building; there was the gravel to be raked and the flowerbeds to be kept tidy. I got the crow's cage again and afterwards was sent inside to do the washing up in the Corporals' eating area. The three Corporals had a dull time in Lille and would often invite prostitutes in from the town to cheer up their afternoons. Later on that day I was sent into the Corporals' quarters with a mop and bucket and as I went in a Corporal came out buttoning his flies. I went on into the room where a middle-aged Moroccan woman lay sprawled on his bed, open-legged and completely naked. Pointing between her legs, she looked at me and asked, '*Tu veux?*' I shook my head rapidly and mopped the floor as she lay there humming quietly.

Later the same afternoon, seven of us were ordered over to the medical centre for a check up by the doctor, who turned out to be a medical student doing his military service. One by one we went into the office for a number of basic tests: we read a letter board at ten paces, ran on the spot and had our pulses taken before providing a urine sample and having a hearing test. The doctor was friendly and shook my hand when he had finished, wishing me luck. I took this medical test to be a sign that things were happening and that we could hope to go on to Paris, which Alex said was the next staging post.

At no point had any of us been told the procedure that would lead to us being selected to start our basic training. What I knew about the Legion was based on a series of rumours and pieces of misinformation passed down from recruit to recruit. If we were selected at Lille, apparently we proceeded to Paris and then on to Marseilles after a number of further tests. The crucial time was the period spent at Aubagne, fifteen kilometres outside Marseilles, which was the depot of the whole Foreign Legion. Only if you satisfied the selection board there were you allowed to carry on and start basic training, which itself lasted four months. My posting to the *2ème Régiment Étranger de Parachutistes* seemed a long way away.

That evening there was another line-up, when, as a result of the medical tests, four more people were turned away, including the Spaniard Alex had kicked, who had been found to be suffering from bronchitis. This was a relief as his coughing at night had irritated us, and it meant that Alex could stop hitting him with a broom handle when he woke us up.

Although people would turn up every day to join, there was now a group of us who seemed likely to progress to Paris: Alex, Chris, myself, Marius the Scandinavian, the balding Swiss man, two Belgians and one of the Spaniards (who now kept a low profile). The latest addition to our English-speaking group was a Rhodesian who had served in the Rhodesian Light Infantry in the war of Independence and who told endless stories of shooting black terrorists, or 'floppies', in cross border raids into Zambia. He called them by this name because, he said, they went 'floppy' when you shot them.

The next day, all nine of us were lined up and given our civilian clothes; we were to take a train to Paris that evening. It was interesting to see everybody in their own clothes. My brogues and blazer were in marked contrast to Alex's jeans and Union Jack T-shirt, which he wore, he said, to avoid any confusion about his nationality. This was an unlikely eventuality since he also had a tattoo on his forearm showing the Union Jack with the caption, 'These colours don't run.' Roy, the gunman from Rhodesia, had a suede jacket with tassels on the back and sleeves, and a pair of boots which he swore had been taken from a dead terrorist. The quiet Swiss man had actually turned up in a three-piece suit and tie, with a large amount of baggage; one of the Belgians had two suitcases and a hand grip.

We drove off to another barracks in Lille where we were taken individually into an office occupied by a portly Major; he handed each of us a pile of papers and we were told to sign each one at the bottom. I tried to read them but he stopped me, so I signed my name nine times. It was a five-year preliminary contract. That evening we sat on the train bound for Paris. The fat Corporal had accompanied us to Lille station, bought us all a beer, and joined us on the train. I was sitting next to Alex chatting. After a period spent talking about the Legion and what we thought it was going to be like, he turned to me, shook my hand and wished me good luck. Then we both fell asleep. I woke as we were arriving in Paris. A lorry was waiting outside the station and we all got in, driving through the well-lit streets which were full of people. We left Paris behind and drove off on a series of flyovers and underpasses, before drawing up outside the gates of Fort St Nogent on the outskirts. The huge wooden gates were opened by a legionnaire in combat kit with a FA-MAS assault rifle slung across his chest, and his beret tilted over his right eye; we drew up in front of a five-storey building and got out. I felt terrified and utterly lost. It was the feeling that nobody around me gave a toss whether or not I got into the Legion; nobody cared what happened to me, or whether or not I succeeded. To them I was just another recruit, and if I did well, got myself through the first six months and became a legionnaire, then I would matter to them because I would be part of their system. As it stood then, I was a nothing and a nobody, with everything to prove and nothing to say. I didn't exactly want one of the Corporals to come up, put his arm around me and say 'Tell me all your problems', but I felt bloody intimidated by the impersonal approach. It was around midnight and the staff were lively and efficient. We went up to the top floor and were told to sleep in a room full of grey metal bunks and steel lockers, and to sleep fully clothed to avoid the lice. I took off my shoes and fell asleep immediately.

It was still dark the following morning when we were woken up by a screaming Corporal who came in, kicking the lockers and pushing us out of bed. I rushed off to have a shave and a wash, which I had hardly finished doing before we were ordered downstairs for breakfast in the darkness. We were allowed ten minutes to have our coffee and bread before being chased back to the barrack rooms for cleaning and tidying. The Legion used a word to describe any sort of menial duty to do with tidying, cleaning and arranging, '*corvée*'. As they were fanatically tidy this took on enormous importance. I was given '*corvée chiottes*' – the shithouse.

Later we assembled in a large room with the other recruits who had arrived from Cherbourg, Amiens and Rouen. One by one we had all our hair shaved off, in the regulation crop known as a '*boule à zéro*'. As people's heads were shaved, scars and cranial disfigurements came to light; most people had four or five different marks on their scalps, and there was a lot of story telling. I felt relieved that I had my scar from the fight at the summer party and so looked the same as everybody else – I was afraid of appearing different or clever which meant that I would be noticed by the Corporals and picked on by all the others. I couldn't wait to be issued with a uniform as I stood out in my civilian clothes, which were much nicer than anybody else's. The fact that everybody around me looked and sounded completely different from myself was worrying and disconcerting; I wanted to shed all semblances of my past civilian life and be assimilated totally into the system of the Legion. The haircut helped. At least I looked the same in one way.

We were paid 120 francs and interviewed again. The same questions. The same answers. No, I hadn't been in prison. No, I hadn't deserted from the British Army. I signed more pieces of paper and went downstairs to join the queue outside the clothing store. Passing one by one in front of a counter, a Corporal sized us up for height and girth before dumping a pile of cast-off clothes in front of each one of us. Trying mine on, I found that the trousers were several inches too short, the shirt was missing most of its buttons and the beret was like a sleeping bag. I picked up a pair of combat boots from a pile in the corner, found some laces, and looked at the other people wondering with whom I could swop my uniform. A small Portuguese man with ringworm scars on his scalp was holding up a huge pair of trousers in despair; I went over, took his trousers and shirt, told him that mine would fit him perfectly, and changed into his. When he realised that the trousers hovered round his calves and that the shirt didn't do up it was too late; I had put on my newer, better-fitting shirt, bloused my trousers on to the tops of my boots and was putting on his beret as he stood there looking like a circus tramp. I then went off for lunch which was soup and crayfish. I got picked for the washing up detail and with six others swept the kitchen and dining room, drank the dregs from the glasses and bottles and had a conversation with one of the cooks about Beirut. Then a French Polynesian with a rosary around his neck and scarred knuckles drew out his cards and we sat down to play. After a couple of hands, an officer walked into the dining room and we all stood up. This was the Padre attached to the unit. He wore full combat kit and a large silver crucifix on a chain, which matched his parachute wings. He asked us if we were all well and healthy; three of the Frenchmen started talking to him and the rest of us giggled and joked in English about this ridiculous figure who appeared to be out of touch with everything we were doing. A Spanish recruit I had been playing poker against started making faces and gesturing behind the Padre's back, when suddenly, without taking his eyes off the Frenchman to whom he had been talking, the priest jerked his elbow backwards into the Spaniard's face, slamming him against an oven.

We sat in a room all afternoon. Of the forty of us who had survived so far, another twelve were weeded out and the rest of us sat there until 6.00 pm looking at the posters on the walls and reading the few tattered paperbacks which sat on the shelves. I had a choice between a Western adventure in German, two American spy thrillers or a much-thumbed pornographic comic which had had all the lurid pages torn out as wanking aids. The posters on the walls were all the same old ones of 1950s legionnaires in tanks looking at the desert through binoculars, or cutting their way through the jungle with machetes. There was nothing explaining the makeup of the organisation which all of us were so desperately trying to join. None of the Corporals were forthcoming, explaining with a shrug of their shoulders or a smile that everything would happen at Marseilles. Each stage of the selection process so far had been a complete surprise: the waiting tended to heighten the anticipation and sense of cowed nervousness we all felt. Apart from the facts about the different regiments gleaned from the poster on the wall at Lille, I knew no more now than I had as I stood watching England disappear from the back of the ferry. In hindsight, if I had been aware of the exact nature of the Foreign Legion, how it operated, and how its members lived, I would have been much more hesitant about joining. But in retreating so hastily from my life in England, the decision to leave had been facilitated by the sheer lack of knowledge about what lay in store for me. I was nervous and frightened about the future, yet excited because of being so. I had a fixed image in my head of what I wanted to become, culled from history books and magazine articles in *Paris Match*. It involved parachuting, shaved heads, sunglasses and Africa. I thought that it would be possible to adopt the exterior trappings of the system without succumbing personally; yet because I was frightened of appearing different or cockier than the others, I fell in with their mannerisms, jokes and brutishness. They were being themselves, and it was I who was playing a game. Despite this, I felt it would be better to prove myself in basic training before allowing my real personality to resurface. I wondered whether, by the time it did resurface, it might not have changed already.

That evening we left Fort St Nogent on a coach for the Gare de Lyons where we embarked for the south of France on an overnight express. It was to be more than two years before I saw Paris again.

We were jammed eight to a compartment, smoking, playing cards and drinking beer; the lights were on and sleep was completely impossible. I went and stood in the corridor and watched the towns and villages flash past; we went through Chalon-sur-Saône, Dijon and on towards Lyons. In my compartment two Frenchmen and a Spaniard were losing their pay to a tiny Glaswegian who excelled at poker; he had already won most of the hands and was trying to explain in broad Scottish that he was open to credit arrangements. I fell asleep on the floor of the corridor somewhere near Lyons and woke up as we were drawing into St Charles station at Marseilles. We were met on the platform by an old man with a barrow selling coffee and sandwiches. I felt terrible and wanted some but only the Corporals were allowed it. Standing behind them looking at the steaming urn on the barrow, I felt worse than hungover; it was a mixture of too little sleep, being hot and unwashed, completely unaware of what was going on, and worst, I was hungry. A branch line train took us to Aubagne where a coach picked us up for the journey up to the camp.

I knew that Aubagne was the depot of the *1er Régiment Étranger* (the 1st Foreign Regiment) of the French Foreign Legion, through which everybody passed on their way to basic training, and where legionnaires spent time while on attachments from other regiments, and pending postings overseas. Until the sixties the headquarters of the Legion had been at Side Bel Abbès in Algeria, the country which for 150 years had been the Legion's home. Before 1965 none of the regiments had been based in France, and a man could expect to spend his entire five year contract without seeing Europe. After the end of World War Two the Japanese were expelled from Indo-China, and the French returned to their former colony. A war ensued between the French and the Indo-Chinese from the north, who were led by General Vo Nguyen Giap and backed by the Communist Chinese. The Legion, which was then largely composed of escapees from the German Wehrmacht and SS, had been thrown in its entirety into the war.

For nearly ten years a jungle war of incredible savagery had been fought over the same jungle tracks and expanses of savanna grassland where a decade later the Americans would lose to the Vietcong. The German soldiers – who had learned their fighting on the Russian Front, at Monte Cassino and through the hedgerows of Normandy – had proved a match for the guerrillas, and it was only the indifference and boredom of the French public to a war which proved astronomically expensive in financial and human terms which led the French government to seek a political settlement. The final showdown between the Viet-Minh and the cream of the French colonial Army had come in a deserted valley in the north of Vietnam, around a small village called Dien Biên Phu. For five months in 1954, the Legion and several regiments of colonial paratroopers were besieged by guerrillas before being forced into captivity with heavy losses. Those who made it back to Algeria after the débâcle were reformed into other regiments. The crack 1er and 2ème Régiments Étrangers de Parachutistes were staffed and run almost entirely by old hands from Indo-China who felt immensely bitter at the French government's handling of the war.

In Algeria, they found themselves in a similar situation, fighting a war against the regular Algerian Army and the guerrillas of the Front Libération Nationale. De Gaulle's new government, elected to the Élysée on promises of keeping Algeria French, were engaging in secret peace negotiations with Algeria's leaders, and in 1961, after peace talks at Evian, Algeria was declared independent. For the professional soldiers of the Legion, this was the final blow, and when Generals Challe and Salan led a revolt, the 1er and 2ème Régiments Étrangers de Parachutistes joined it almost to a man. The revolt was crushed, the 1er Régiment disbanded, and the Legion brought back to France, setting up its headquarters at Aubagne. The other regiments were sent off to guard France's ex-colonies in Africa and the Far East, and in 1967 the 2ème Régiment Étranger de Parachutistes was posted to Corsica.

*

Driving up to the gates of the camp, I saw my first legionnaire in parade uniform; he was wearing a white *képi*, a green tie and blue cummerbund. He saluted the coach and we drove through the gates and up a hill past the enormous parade ground at the far end of which I could see the *Monument aux Morts*, the memorial to every dead legionnaire. It took the form of a huge bronze globe supported by an enormous stone plinth. It had originally occupied a position at Sidi Bel Abbès, but when the Legion left Algeria it had been dismantled stone by stone and brought to its present resting place at Aubagne. Behind it was a stone wall on which was written in bronze letters the motto of the Legion, '*Legio Patria Nostra*'. It was only 7.30 am but already it was getting hot. The camp was full of pine trees and flowerbeds of bougainvillea and hibiscus. Square white buildings, three storeys high, sat at regular intervals on the slope, all looking down towards the parade ground. Uniformed legionnaires marched around, and there was a group of convicts from the regimental prison in filthy fatigues and greasy boots who were emptying the dustbins and sweeping the roads. A body of soldiers in sport's kit marched past at a slow, rhythmic pace, singing loudly. They were all in step and looked very smart. We drove on to the top of the road and drew up outside a compound surrounded by a wire fence; inside was a large white building surrounded by an expanse of gravel on which a huge group of people were drawn up in lines. This was the '*Section Engagés Volontaires*', the department which dealt with all prospective recruits. We got out of the coach and walked through the gates to the stares of those gathered on the gravel, and over to a low metal hut in the corner of the compound where we were ordered to go inside and sit down in silence. We stripped and sat on metal stools; we were told to take everything out of our pockets and wait until our names were called from the room next door. Some people, like myself, had very few possessions, while others had come with suitcases and rucksacks. Somebody even had a violin. Alex, Chris and I sat next to each other in our underpants, staring at the others: nudity revealed a lot of scarred, disfigured bodies, with missing fingers and toes, the marks of surgical operations, and huge tattoos. I sat with my head between my legs and looked at the dirt-encrusted toenails of the silent Yugoslavian on my left until 'Jennings' was called from the next room. I walked through to where a Chief-Corporal was standing behind a table. He took all my clothes, my underpants, my toothbrush and razor, in return for which I received a clean set of fatigues, underwear and a wash kit. After handling each recruit's clothes the Chief-Corporal swilled his hands over with surgical spirit, wiping them dry on a piece of grey towel. He had worked out that in his job he got to handle over 6,000 pairs of dirty underpants from sixty countries each year. Some of the others protested at being separated from their belongings, but a Brazilian Corporal in the corner hit two people in the stomach and things moved fast after that. I put on my clean uniform and adjusted my beret, blousing my trousers over the buckles of my combat boots. We were taken off for a shower – which was welcome as I hadn't washed properly since the night before I left London – and then shown our beds in the barrack rooms on the second and third floors. Going downstairs, I witnessed my first proper fight. A Spaniard and an Englishman were arguing over some duty, when the Englishman headbutted the Spaniard between the eyes; as the latter stepped backwards clutching his face, the Briton executed a curious hopping movement as he placed both his hands behind the Spaniard's head and wrenched it down to meet his upcoming knee. There was the squashing noise of bone meeting flesh as the Spaniard's upper lip and nose was split all over his face. A Sergeant-Major witnessed this from his ground floor office and leapt out to pull the two apart; he slapped the Englishman and pronounced the Spaniard ready for the infirmary. He was accompanied there by two recruits, his face pouring blood. The Sergeant-Major's attitude to violence was catholic so he kicked the Englishman once before letting the matter drop. I watched this before going to be interviewed by the Officer commanding the selection team. He asked the same questions as everybody else but noted the fact that I had served in the Territorial Army, and spoke French and Spanish. We then went off to a lecture room to watch a slide show on the history of the Legion, how and why it had been formed and where it was based. The lecture lasted two hours and I nearly fell asleep several times: the whole thing was conducted in French and delivered at high speed by a bored Corporal. It was hard enough for me to understand but almost impossible for the people who couldn't speak French. As a French speaker I was meant to explain it to the non-Francophones.

As we sat in the lecture room, the Legion numbered 10,000 men split up into ten different Regiments, based in mainland France and the ex-colonies. Each of the Regiments could trace its history back to one of the units which had fought in Indo-China or Algeria during the previous century. The only exception was the *2ème Régiment*

Étranger de Parachutistes which had been formed in 1948. There were infantry Regiments in Djibouti, French Guyana and Mayotte, an island off the coast of Madagascar. There was also a works Regiment building roads and sea defences on the Pacific atoll of Mururoa. Apart from the airborne unit in Corsica, the rest of the Regiments were in mainland France, forming part of her commitment to NATO.

The Legion was formed on 10 March 1831 by royal decree of Prince Louis-Philippe, who saw it as a good way of clearing Paris of undesirable elements and at the same time providing free labour to defend and build France's new colonial empire. The Legion had fought with distinction in the campaigns in Tonkin, Morocco, Algeria, Madagascar and Mexico. It was in 1863 at the farmhouse at Camerone in Mexico that they had fought their most spectacular action. Sixty-three legionnaires had held off a Mexican force of 2,000 soldiers for a whole day, at the end of which five legionnaires had been left alive; these five, thirsty, hungry and out of ammunition, had bayonet-charged the Mexicans. Two were killed immediately but the Mexican Commander had been so impressed by their bravery that he had spared the lives of the other three. The Commanding Officer, Capitaine Danjou, had been killed, but his artificial wooden hand, found afterwards in the wreckage of the farmhouse, became a symbol for the Legion's bravery and every year was paraded at Aubagne in the Camerone day celebrations. For the rest of the year, it was kept in the crypt of the museum behind the *Monuments aux Morts*. The Legion went on to distinguish itself in Africa and the Far East, in both World Wars and in Indo-China, where it was almost wiped out. Algeria was followed by small anti-guerrilla operations in Chad, Somalia, Beirut and Kolwezi.

Over the decades the Legion had developed its own style of soldiering. It was not soldiering where all hung on victory or defeat, as in other armies, but rather a stylish profession of arms, aimed at bringing greater glory to France and to the Legion. As at Camerone and Dien Biên Phu, the cost was high; but the Legion in its purest tradition saw only merit in dying for France. Painted on the walls of a barracks in the last century had been the words, 'Legionnaires, you are soldiers in order to die, and I am sending you where you can die.' This was the essence of its self glorification. It was an idea based on the lifestyle of the true legionnaire, who, before his time in the Legion, had been nothing, and therefore in the eyes of the Legion, anything he had done in his past life was immaterial. He only became whole in becoming a legionnaire.

The lines of a poem were written on a plaque at the end of our corridor, '*Lui qui est devenu fils de France, non par le sang reçu, mais par le sang versé.*' (He who has become a son of France, not through blood received, but by blood spilt.) In our history lecture I grasped only the most basic nature of this '*wunderkinder*' warrior creed, but it was something which I was to find permeating the Legion at every level.

Successors to this proud tradition, our group was now engaged in some cleaning duties. I had landed the shithouse. A Corporal had given me a coathanger and a broom and showed me the Foreign Legion's way of unblocking a difficult lavatory bowl; it involved unbending the coathanger, jamming it down the U-bend, and working it vigorously backwards and forwards. In particularly difficult cases he recommended using boiling water as well. There had been a tricky one in Paris, where an entire detachment of men had arrived back from French Guyana and left the ablutions in an appalling state. I didn't know what had been the last meal eaten before leaving South America but it took me twenty minutes to coathanger my way through it, and consequently I had missed breakfast.

The routine at Aubagne was the same every day; we got up at 4.30 am, washed, shaved and paraded outside before a breakfast of coffee and bread in the main cookhouse; then we cleaned the barrack rooms for an hour and paraded again at 7.30 am for the allocation of the day's duties. Each parade was preceded by a cleaning ritual known as '*corvée quartier*', which involved clearing up any litter surrounding the barracks. We would line up across the parade ground, shoulder to shoulder, and in a slow forward walk, eyes fixed on the ground, would pick up any cigarette ends or pieces of paper on the gravel. The resulting scene was bizarre, as ninety skinheads moved slowly over the stones, heads down like rooting chickens, with the occasional flurry of movement as somebody found a Marlboro butt. Whole areas were cleaned like this, and sometimes when there was a particularly fastidious Corporal in charge, there was a second reserve line which followed behind.

Every week a detachment of men who had completed all the selection processes, interviews and tests would go off to the *4ème Régiment Étranger* at Castelnaudary near Toulouse to start their basic training. Each week detachments would arrive from the main recruiting offices at Paris, Marseilles and Strasbourg. In between arriving and leaving for Castelnaudary, most people would be weeded out by the tests or fall short of the required standards.

After morning parade, those not required for any tests or interviews would go off on working parties around the camp. Our nucleus of myself, Chris and Alex, along with Marius, had been augmented by an Australian martial arts expert who had fled Australia after half-killing a nineteen-stone truck driver in a fight. He was six foot seven and had developed his own style of street fighting which he called Zen-Do-Kai. He felt attached to it so had tattooed the name in his right armpit where it matched the oriental dragon rampaging over the inside of his bicep. We all found him interesting, so when we lay in the sun after lunch, the white gravel covering our backs with powdery marks, his fighting demonstrations were keenly attended. His techniques varied from the basic side kicks and elbow jabs to more advanced methods. He had an impressive set of movements which he said were excellent for dealing with charging horsemen. I wondered if any of the desert peoples in France's colonies still rode horses.

I attended the medical centre for my test and stood in my underpants for an hour in a shiny-clean waiting room with yellow walls and a kitten sitting in the corner. Then I went in to face an English Corporal of ten years' service, who had a bad reputation. I pissed in a test-tube, had four injections and did twenty press-ups to get my heart going. The Corporal fired questions at me, all the time trying to catch me out. I denied homosexual inclinations but he still made me bend down so that he could inspect my behind with a wooden spatula.

In between the various tests there was a delay of two or three days when we would be left on tenterhooks in case we had failed; every afternoon people would be told to pack their bags and would be deposited at Aubagne station to take a train back to where they had come from. If you had joined at Paris, then you received a ticket back there; if, however, you had joined at Marseilles, then you only got fifteen francs to get you down the line from Aubagne. The Legion would return you to the place at which they had taken charge of you. I was terrified that I wouldn't be accepted. For all the assurances from those around me that I was perfect Legion material, I could not accept that the prestigious French Foreign Legion would have any need of the services of somebody whose military prowess was earned more at the bar than in the field. Compared to an Israeli paratrooper or a former member of the Black Watch, my pathetic charade at soldiering in London was risible. So I could jump out of an aeroplane and fire a machine gun. I was fit and could run well. I spoke three languages. This was all a glossy shell over an insubstantial interior. I used to get frightened at my parents' house in Wales when the boys from the village asked me to play with them. I had been thrown off the cricket team at school for making daisy chains on the boundary. There was no history of violence or physical hardship in my upbringing at all. Had I been born in the Middle Ages, I knew that I would have been one of those retainers who stayed inside the castle and embroidered whilst the knights went off to slaughter the French. The amenable supporter who changes his allegiance with each new king. So I wondered what chance I had of outstaying Lebanese men who had picked up their first Kalashnikov aged six, or the Vietnamese man who had seen his mother raped before going on to kill his first Cambodian at the age when I was doing my Common Entrance.

The Legion was being selective. Very selective. The percentage of people who were going on to start basic training stood at four per cent in September 1984. The myth that the Legion took anyone was being rapidly disproved and I didn't want to be a victim of it. There were very few people around who seemed to be telling the truth about their past lives, and what they told you was only meant to further their self image. A young Englishman, arms covered in tattoos, said that he had served in the Special Air Service, The Duke of Wellington's Regiment and with the Parachute Regiment in the Falkland Islands. As he was only nineteen and failed the medical test for being colour-blind this was impossible.

The most important interview was with the *2ème Bureau*, the Military branch of French Intelligence; it was their opinion which was ultimately decisive. Nobody knew how much they burrowed into one's past, and this ignorance coupled with a fear of being rejected by the Legion was enough to make most people tell the truth. I passed my medical check and after two days Alex, Chris, myself and a dozen others were ordered to report for our Intelligence tests which were held in a metal hut at the back of the compound. A multilingual Corporal explained to us as we sat at desks that the tests were aimed at determining our *'niveaux générales'* or basic IQs. The test papers were given out and we had an hour to complete all three sections, involving general commonsense, and basic Maths and language questions in our respective tongues.

'Which is the odd one out: cod, trout, sardine or lorry driver?'
'Divide 8.8 by 2.2.'
'What is the capital of South Africa?'
'What was Hitler's first name?'

I emerged after an hour confident on all but the maths. I was awarded seventeen points out of twenty but judging by the worried looks and furrowed brows there were some lower scores. Later on the results would affect our choice of regiment and our aptitude for specialist training.

Another Englishman called Harris had joined our group. His parents lived on the Isle of Skye where they spent a lot of time observing the habits of the puffins on the beach. Harris had wanted to get away from all that, and had tried to join the British Parachute Regiment, but they had turned him down. All of our group wanted to go to the *2ème Régiment Étranger de Parachutistes*, and I decided I wanted to be a high-altitude free-fall parachutist.

September finished and morning parade was colder each day. I passed my physical test which involved a lot of running and exercise, only being beaten by Marius. We had now spent three weeks at Aubagne and had seen detachments move off to Castelnaudary, and numerous people rejected. We had worked in the kitchens, in the Officers' mess and the clothing stores, and had spent afternoons and evenings discussing our futures together. One afternoon we had been taken for a walk up to the top of the mountain behind the camp, which had been good exercise; from the top I had been able to see the sea.

One morning I was called up in front of the *2ème Bureau* and walked into an office to be interviewed by three Sergeants who spoke perfect English. They were pleasant and quiet, asking me banal questions about my life in England. I was then told to go away and write down my entire life history on three sheets of blank paper. I sat in an adjoining room and started off, 'My father owned a Roman Catholic prep school in Sussex . . .'

I detailed my education, A Level results, the particulars of my brothers and sisters, everything that I had done while in the Territorial Army and my minimal brush with the law. When I had finished, I was made to wait two hours before being called back into the office for questioning. I stood at ease in front of them and the interrogation started.

'What did you say was your mother's maiden name?'

'How often do you take drugs?'

'What kind of parachutes did you use in the British Army?'

'What would you do if you were drunk and I ordered you to suck my cock?'

'Where did you move to when you were twelve?'

'Describe what it feels like to be in prison.'

'Where in Holland was your father wounded?'

'Have you ever had sex with an animal?'

All three Sergeants asked questions simultaneously, the interrogation wending back on itself, crisscrossing through my life in an arbitrary yet efficient way. When they had finished several hours later I felt confused and sat outside the room to smoke a cigarette while the Sergeants deliberated. I was called back in. I had passed, and the process of anonymity used by the Legion to protect itself and its members was now explained to me.

If I wanted to, I could change my name, regardless of the fact that I had not committed any crime. I would be issued with a completely new identity by the Legion, involving a different nationality, date of birth and name. This was done on a haphazard basis, so that a Peruvian Indian from the Andes could be issued with papers proving beyond legal doubt that he had in fact spent all his life in Godalming. This process completely protected the Legion against enquiries from Interpol. It seemed odd that a military organisation could have the power to change your entire identity. I assumed that somewhere in our contracts there was a clause in which we relinquished our rights to our own nationalities. It worked both ways, protecting us and protecting the Legion. If, for example, Interpol contacted the Legion and demanded to know whether Fritz Hemmeling who had killed a security guard during a bank raid in Munich two weeks before, was serving with them, the Legion could say no. Fritz Hemmeling from Munich was now Asseyake Dimpuna from Ghana. I wanted to change my name, because I thought it would be glamorous to be called Rudi Kesselreicher or Auberon de Hautevilliers. Unfortunately, the Legion chose your new name for you, so I remained Christian Michael Jennings.

In return for this anonymity and help with the setting up of a new life, the Legion demanded five years' service, wherever they chose to send you. After three years it was possible to revert to your own name or to have another false one, thereby preserving the anonymity. Most of our group changed their identities, as they all had something to hide. There were two Catholics from Northern Ireland who seemed to know a lot about the British Army. What a man had done before he joined up was the past, and the past was unconnected with the Legion, and therefore irrelevant. The present and future were all that mattered and everybody started afresh So men from the IRA mixed with British squaddies, and through necessity got on with each other. Traditionalist to the core, the Legion fully encouraged the romanticism of escape from 'real life' and forgetting, because in practical terms it gave them that much more control over their members. Everybody started equal, so that a uniformity of training and military technique was possible. Although it was difficult to pretend that a former member of the Rhodesian Special Air Service was on a par in purely military terms with a goat-herd from Bolivia, the fact that both were starting afresh made administration that much easier. The Legion knew that many of its recruits had learned their killing and soldiering elsewhere, in Beirut, Rhodesia, Vietnam or the Falklands, and was more than pleased to be able to recruit such proficient fighting men. It was evident that the skilled soldiers would naturally gravitate to the tougher units, like the *2ème Régiment Étranger de Parachutistes*, giving the Legion a regiment full of highly-trained soldiers who had received their instruction at somebody else's expense. Although it was called the 'Foreign Legion', many of its recruits were Frenchmen who had changed their nationalities. Thus it was possible for a Frenchman to hide from a crime committed in his own country by adopting another nationality.

A Section was made up of those who had passed the *2ème Bureau* interview, and we were given red strips of cloth to wear on our epaulettes to show that we had passed our selection. The others had nasty accounts of their interviews. An Irishman had denied belonging to an illegal terrorist organisation; one of the Sergeants had left the room and come back with a photocopy of a warrant for his arrest issued by the RUC in Dundalk. They had hit him several times for lying. Marius had confessed that he had crippled a Turkish immigrant in Stockholm and Alex was told the registration number of the Land Rover he had left behind at the German frontier when he had deserted.

We visited the Legion's museum the following day and wandered round looking at the different flags of the units which had fought all over the world for 150 years. There were displays of medals, weapons, uniforms and pictures. We went down into the crypt where the wooden hand of Capitaine Danjou lay in a glass case. It was the focal point of the room, and whenever visiting dignatories and military authorities came to visit Aubagne they would be taken down to the crypt where they would stand and salute the hand. There was a poem on the wall written by an American legionnaire called Alan Seeger during World War One:

> But I've a rendezvous with Death
> At midnight in some flaming town,
> When Spring trips north again this year,
> And I to my pledged word am true,
> I shall not fail that rendezvous.

> *I Have a Rendezvous with Death*

There were tattered flags from Dien Biên Phu and Algeria, and collections of medals belonging to famous Legion soldiers. I walked over and stood respectfully in front of Capitaine Danjou's false limb. It was made of dark wood and looked like a graceful gorilla's paw. I read another poem on the wall written by a God-fearing Captain who had been killed in Algeria, in which he implored God to look sparingly on humble soldiers performing their divine task as warriors of Christianity. It effectively conjured up the mixture of religion, fighting prowess and romanticism which the Legion held so dear.

As a military museum it was very interesting, but as an insight into the ways of thinking of the French Foreign Legion it was invaluable. It contained all the mementoes of an organisation for which pain and suffering (military and personal) became virtues, because they were experienced in the cause of the Legion and ultimately the cause of France. It was a cross between military masochism and romantic delusion, and was almost impossible to understand unless one could grasp the complete picture. It was warm inside the building as I looked at the uniforms from Algeria, Morocco and Tonkin. I used to get very sentimental during my period with the Territorial Army about the exploits of the British Parachute Regiment, despite the fact that my sole contribution to their reputation had been made in Aldershot discos. The romance of the French Foreign Legion struck me in the same way, and especially the exhibits from Kolwezi and Chad, where there were photographs of camouflaged paras with shaved heads and sunglasses helping starving babies. This was the visible humanitarian face of élite soldiering, and I fell for it. If I stuck with the basic training and did well I too could be one of them. I had yet to be disillusioned. Basic training and a posting to a Regiment lay ahead, all of it an unknown quantity, and my enthusiasm was so manifest because everything that lay in front of me was so foreign.

We were told that we would leave Aubagne to start our basic training on the following Monday. Although all the recruit instruction was normally carried out at Castelnaudary, we had been informed that we would be going to Orange, the base of the *1er Régiment Étranger de Cavalerie*, as Castelnaudary was overcrowded. We were given another haircut, issued with ID cards and complete uniforms. We signed our contracts, which we were not allowed to read, dispensing with, I suspected, every conceivable right as human beings. I thought nothing of it; it was all a part of the selection process and the more extreme it proved itself to be, the happier I felt, for I was enjoying the feeling of succeeding and managing while others failed. Of the twenty-eight who had arrived from Paris with me, only four were coming to Orange.

On the Saturday before our departure our group was sent off for a day's grape picking at Puyloubier, the rest home for injured and retired former legionnaires, in the foothills of Provence, about two hours' drive from Aubagne. Wrapped in old greatcoats, we left at sunrise in two trucks and drove across a plain covered in vines. At breakfast time we went through a forest of olive trees and arrived at Puyloubier. The building, white with red shutters, faced over the vineyards, which were tended by the residents of the home, most of whom had been wounded. They spent their days in the potteries, the ironworks or in the fields. Those in wheelchairs or too old to work outside helped in the kitchen or made elaborate Foreign Legion memorabilia for sale in the regimental shops wherever the Legion served.

Most of our group were sent to pick grapes under the supervision of an ex-legionnaire whose age and Germanic inflexion marked him as a former member of the Wehrmacht. Myself and another Englishman called Ronny were given rakes and told to clear the leaves off a huge area of gravel. We spent the morning raking gently, and he told me a long and obscene story about a girl called Tina Jelly from Aldershot. After lunch, where both of us drank too much red wine, we were taken to the wild boar pens and told to clean them out. Unsupervised, we succumbed to the effects of the wine and the sun and went to sleep, berets over our eyes, in the long grass underneath some olive trees. Driving back to Aubagne, Alex told me how the rest of them had spent the day throwing grapes at the old German and accusing him of being in the SS. Just before getting in the trucks, I had wandered down to the rooms where the crippled legionnaires lived. Looking in through the open door of one, I saw a fat, drunk skinhead in a wheelchair. The arms of his wheelchair were hung with all the accoutrements he needed; a lighter, two packets of cigarettes and a little leather bandolier which held his supply of Kronenbourg bottles. He was listening to old Legion marching songs and giving himself the Nazi salute in the mirror.

A Sergeant and four Corporals arrived from Orange to pick us up on the following Monday. There were forty-eight of us in the Section. Chris, Marius and the Swiss who had come from Lille were here; Alex had been turned down at the last moment on a medical detail. Three of the staff from Orange wore the silver parachute wings which denoted service in the *2ème Régiment Étranger de Parachutistes*, and all of them had the blue and white campaign ribbons denoting service in Chad or Lebanon. The Sergeant took us into the small canteen and told us quietly and forcefully that our holiday in Aubagne was over and that we were off to start four months of basic training designed to turn us into legionnaires. It was highly likely that only half of us would complete the training, he said, and that many of us would try to desert. I was surprised that I had made it this far. Many of the applicants who had looked suitable had been rejected and I deduced that I had been selected because I had not tried to glamorise my life history, and because I was medically and physically fit. I was bored with Aubagne and was looking forward to Orange. If I was to have any chance of being posted to Calvi, I would have to come in the top five in basic training. It sounded hard.

— 3 —

A MOUTHFUL OF ROCKS

Sergeant Moustaine punched me in the face, stuffed my shitty underpants in my mouth and ordered me to run around the parade ground
holding my kitbag above my head. Every time I ran past where he
was standing he hit me again or tripped me up, sprawling me in the
dirt. We had been at Orange for a week and were having a kit
inspection. Each member of the Section had dragged their entire kit
down to a patch of gravel behind the barracks and, standing in a
semicircle, we had lain all our uniforms and possessions at our feet. The
Sergeant walked past inspecting the kit, finding fault everywhere; my
mistake had been to try and conceal an unwashed pair of pants in my
bag. The Corporals followed behind him, throwing stuff everywhere
and beating anybody who did the slightest thing wrong. All our kit
was strictly numbered and counted, and anybody who was missing a
vest or who had an extra T-shirt got kicked or punched. While we
were outside, the duty Corporal was doing the rounds of the barrack
rooms, checking for cleanliness and tidiness; every two or three
minutes a pair of boots would sail out of the window, or there would
be the sound of a locker crashing to the floor.

We had arrived at Orange a week previously, and after disembarking
from the coach had been ordered into the barrack rooms by our
Corporals, who were waiting outside on the parade ground. The
barracks was a modern red-brick building set on the edge of the base
which housed the *1er Régiment Étranger de Cavalerie*. The Regiment
was made up of five squadrons, each comprising 200 men, and they
spent their time in tanks and armoured cars. Our training staff came
from the 3rd Squadron, which had returned from the war in Chad
three months before. Under the command of a Sergeant-Major, there
were a Top-Sergeant, four Sergeants, a Chief-Corporal and eight Corporals. They would spend the whole of the next four months with us
during the time it took to turn us into legionnaires.

Immediately after our arrival things had been quiet. We had been divided four to a room, with a Corporal in each and with the different nationalities split so that no nationalistic factions developed. Those who couldn't speak French were mixed in equal number with those who could. As the entire process of orders and commands was given in French, it was imperative to learn it and we were all forbidden from speaking anything else. In my room were Olivier, a Frenchman who regarded the Legion as a funny game; Macier, a '*pied-noir*' Algerian; and a Portuguese recruit called Da Silva. Our room Corporal was a tall Italian called Tambini who looked like an eagle with a head cold. He appeared reasonable at first, speaking to us slowly and explaining our daily routine. We unpacked our kit and laid it out on the floor, and then started the lengthy and tiresome process of folding it '*à carré*' so that it sat on our shelves in tidy, identical bricks. On the back of each barrack room door was a plan of how our lockers should look: trousers, shirts, socks, pants, vests and everything else had to be stacked in a certain order, and folded exactly thirty-five centimetres square. If done correctly, the end result was a pile of sharp, thin bricks exactly thirty-five centimetres across. It took a lot of trouble to get right. On our first night at Orange we were up until 10.00 pm when we were ordered to put on our brown nylon pyjamas with their maroon piping. Then we went to sleep. It all started the next day.

At 4.30 am the Corporal of the day, a squat pig-like Polynesian called Vigno, came round the rooms, turning on the lights, throwing open the windows and tipping people out of bed, at the same time screaming at us in French to get downstairs on to the parade ground for '*appel*' or roll call. I tumbled out of bed, threw on my tracksuit and joined the others shivering outside on the gravel; the Corporal kept us waiting about twenty minutes until the Sergeant arrived. This was Sergeant Moustaine, half French, half Moroccan. He lined us up, screamed at us, and decided that our turnout was unsatisfactory; we were ordered to return to our rooms to await his call, and then sprint downstairs while he timed us. We repeated this four times before he was satisfied. We went back upstairs to find that all the contents of our lockers had been thrown out over the floors, mixed up, trampled on, and that the lockers themselves had been hurled around the room, across the beds, which had been stripped, and out of the doors. We re-arranged the room, swept and mopped, cleaned the windows, dusted the lockers and changed into combat kit for the day. Breakfast was served from a room down the corridor, and consisted of an inch of coffee and a biscuit. Once it was finished we went outside and swept round the entire barrack block in an extended line, picking up litter from the damp grass. Halfway through, Corporal Vigno decided that we were slacking so we all had to do press-ups on the gravel, perched on our clenched fists. At 7.30 am we paraded outside for the Sergeant-Major, shivering at attention. We set off for a five mile run in the woods to the south of the camp. It was a nice morning and it was good to be able to get out of the barracks and just run; it became immediately apparent that there were some who were fitter than others, and the Corporals ran at the back encouraging the slow ones. At the front was the Sergeant-Major, who was an easy-going Italian with spectacles and fourteen years' Legion service. There was a simple logic to the run, which we discovered on our return to barracks. Those who kept up at the front got back to the barracks first, got into the showers first, got dressed first, and were ready downstairs in combat kit for our first singing lesson with Sergeant Moustaine. Those who were slower on the run missed the showers and were late downstairs, so they got kicked and hit by the Corporals. When everybody was present, we ran off to a classroom and copied the words of a song off the blackboard into our notebooks. The song was called *'Képi Blanc'* and its first two lines reflected our life well, *'Puisqu'il nous faut vivre/ Et lutter dans la souffrance.'* (Since we have to live and fight in suffering.)

We wrote it down and repeated it time and time again to Sergeant Moustaine, until he was satisfied that even the most stupid of us had understood it. We then went outside to practise singing it. The Sergeant stood fifty yards away from us and made us repeat those two lines again and again until our voices were hoarse; as our singing got worse, he became more and more frustrated and threw stones at us. After two hours we were dismissed upstairs, only to find our rooms wrecked again. Vigno had thrown our clothes on to the floor and poured a bottle of aftershave over them before stuffing them back into our lockers to ferment. All my different uniforms now smelt of 'Ziggi'.

We went off to parade for lunch; this meant ten minutes doing press-ups with the Corporal halting us in mid exercise so that we were poised between the ground and the arms-stretched position – as our limbs weakened so people started to slump and collapse, which resulted in kicks and blows. The cookhouse was only fifty yards away and was open from 12.30 pm to 1.30 pm; at 1.15 pm we were still hobbling round the block in an abdominal crouch with our hands behind our heads. We finally entered the building and lined up, eight to a table, behind the metal stools. Sergeant Moustaine shouted '*Bon appétit, tout le monde!*' to which we replied '*Merci, Sergeant, et bon appétit.*' Then we fell on the food set out on the table. It was a case of grabbing first and taking as much as you could before your neighbour pulled the dish away from you. We had six minutes to eat lunch, so I stuffed bread, yoghourt, fish stew and beans into my mouth, and chewed as fast as I could. Suddenly the Sergeant stood up which was a signal for us to go outside again. As Moustaine emerged from the cookhouse a small Scotsman called Haines was still chewing. Moustaine walked through the ranks, stuck his fingers into Haines's mouth and proceeded to pull out the half-chewed food, before hitting him hard in the solar plexus. Haines fell over and a Corporal kicked him in the stomach, shouting at him to stand up. Two of us dragged him to his feet and the Section marched back to the barrack block.

All of us had been hit several times already and there was a correct way of dealing with it. As soon as you saw that you were about to be struck, you stood at attention and waited for the blows. If knocked over, you stood upright again, at attention, and took the punishment until the staff tired of it. If you lay on the ground whining it incensed them and the subsequent kicks and punches were harder and aimed at the mouth and head rather than the stomach and back.

We had a lecture that afternoon in which the course and aim of our training was explained to us by Sergeant-Chef Gibeau, an angular Frenchman with a perfectly shaved head and a tendency to wear sunglasses in the rain. We would spend a month at Orange learning the basics of marching, singing, fitness, weapons drill and Legion history. Then we would move to a training ground in the foothills of the Alps at Canjuers, where we would spend a month away from the regiment and the barracks, and learning the basics of fieldcraft, tactics and shooting, and where we would spend a lot of time living outside as self sufficient soldiers. After Canjuers, we would return to Orange for six weeks, during which time we would celebrate Christmas and the New Year, before moving to a battle camp near Nîmes for a fortnight. After that, the final two weeks at Orange would be spent in taking tests and exams in everything that we had learnt. On the basis of this we would be allocated our postings with one of the Legion's Regiments.

So there were going to be four months of hard training and probably a lot of violence. There was absolutely nothing to look forward to except sleep and food, and these commodities had now become very important. I had a good friend in Marius, who had been in the Swedish Army before joining the Legion. We worked together and backed each other up on lessons and instruction periods. I was trying to teach him French, as he was finding it hard to keep up with the stream of orders and commands being issued by the staff. In return I was trying to grasp the basics of Swedish, whose inflexions and vocabulary I found hard to manage. It was like trying to whistle with a sardine in your mouth. Marius called me a '*mukis keeler*', which meant 'soft boy' or 'mother's boy' in his native tongue. He came from Kalmar and showed me photographs of his family and girlfriend. His girlfriend was very pretty with a flawless complexion and hair the colour of new parchment. His whole family was pretty. His mother looked about twenty-five and his brother looked like a hermaphrodite Greek deity. Both were photographed standing in the kitchen in Kalmar. The kitchen was made of very new-looking pine and the clothes of his mother and brother were very clean. Marius had been a skinhead and had assaulted a Turkish immigrant, fleeing the pending court case to join up in Lille. He told me that he had come to the Legion so that he could kill people without going to prison. This sounded a hollow threat while all we were doing was folding our clothes and learning how to be house-trained and use flushing lavatories.

The evening of our first day at Orange was spent folding our clothes and cleaning the rooms in preparation for '*appel*' at 10.00 pm. The routine was to be the same each evening: at 10.00 pm, the Sergeant on duty would go round all the rooms, counting the men present to make sure that none had deserted, and checking on the cleanliness. Lockers were immaculately arranged, rooms scrubbed, windows polished and shoes and boots lined up under the beds. Each man stood in total silence at the end of his bed in the at-ease position, his locker open behind him. When the Sergeant or Corporal entered, the man who saw them first would call out, '*Garde à vous*' (attention), to which the Sergeant would reply, '*Au repos*' (at ease).

As the Sergeant approached your bed, you stood to attention and presented yourself,
'*Engagé volontaire Jennings;*
Un mois de service;

Escadron Duransoy, Peloton Barlerin;
Premier Régiment Étranger de Cavalerie;
A vos ordres, Sergent.'

This demonstrated that I was not yet a legionnaire as I had not been awarded my white *képi*, and as such was still an '*engagé volontaire*' or recruit; it went on to say that I had one month's service in the Legion, and that I was part of the Squadron commanded by Capitaine Duransoy, in the section of Sergeant Major Barlerin of the 1st Foreign Cavalry Regiment. Even for somebody who spoke French it was a mouthful, and it was tedious because it had to be repeated each time one spoke to a Corporal or Sergeant.

Assuming that one's locker and bedspace was satisfactory, the Sergeant would salute and leave the room, meaning that you could get into bed and go to sleep. Unfortunately, on our first evening, things weren't in good order. Most of our clothes ended up on the floor, and Corporal Fleicher, a tall German, went round hitting people in the stomach to see how firm their abdominal muscles were. '*Appel*' was rescheduled for 11.00 pm and then 1.00 am; it was almost 2.00 am before I got to bed.

A week later I was running around with my underpants in my mouth feeling very stupid. We had spent most of the morning going through our kit, because a Rumanian and an Irishman hadn't been able to pronounce one of the lines of a song correctly. This had so infuriated Moustaine that he had decided to punish them, which meant the rest of us as well. Lining us up on the waste ground behind our barrack block, he had made the original offenders climb a pine tree until their bodies were jammed in the lower branches. He had then thrown stones at them for fifteen minutes before ordering a kit inspection for the rest of us. In this way everybody suffered for one person's mistakes; this was meant ultimately to draw the Section together. I had underestimated the importance placed on personal cleanliness and hygiene, and had been caught out on my underpants. It was very humiliating.

When Moustaine was finally satisfied, we replaced all our kit in our rooms; mine still smelt strongly of 'Ziggi' aftershave. Then we collected our rifles from the armoury for our first lesson in shooting drill. The weapons were FA-MAS 5.56mm assault rifles, recently issued to the French Armed Forces to replace the old FSA (*Fusil Semi-Automatique*) which had been in service since Algeria. The FA-MAS was a compact weapon which was no longer than a man's arm and only weighed eight pounds; it held a magazine of twenty-five rounds and could fire automatically, on single shots or in three-round bursts. Although smaller and lighter than the 7.62 Self Loading Rifles which we had used in the Territorial Army, its strength lay in its high velocity rounds and accuracy. At 200 metres you could be reasonably sure of a killing hit, or, if not, a wound which would cripple and which would therefore require the services of another man to look after the wounded soldier.

We picked up our weapons and went outside. It was still warm during the day, and the sun came in over the trees of the forest outside the camp. We lay on the hard, orange clay and went through the different procedures that we would use when we went off to fire on the shooting range. This involved repeating various commands given by Sergeant Moustaine, which was difficult as he spoke fast and only a third of our Section spoke French. As the class progressed, more of us started to make mistakes, and Moustaine lost his temper. We were lying on the ground in a row, pointing our rifles to our fronts, as he walked past each of us and made us repeat the different orders that we would be given, such as 'unload' or 'cock your weapon'. Of course he was dissatisfied, and he would kick your rifle back into your face. He also liked to make people do press-ups, but with their rifles stretched across the tops of their hands; he would then stand on the rifles so that his entire weight was pressing down on to their fists. Although he was only one of the four Sergeants in charge of us, he was Duty-Sergeant for the first week, so that all the complexities of dealing with a group of recruits at the start of their training fell to him. There was also a Corporal of the week – Vigno – and his duties included the more mundane tasks of getting us up in the mornings and making sure that the rooms were kept clean. He was in close proximity to us all day and was capable of making our lives hell. The Sergeants would take us for training sessions and escort us over to our meals, but it was the Corporals who governed our lives. All of them had served in Lebanon and Chad, and each of them had a minimum of three years' service, which meant that when they had done their basic training the violence they were employing with us had been the norm. Ours was a one-off Section in that we hadn't been sent to Castelnaudary where things were reputed to be much easier, and where there was a spirit of prevailing moderation which had pervaded the Legion since Mitterand had brought it into line with the rest of the French army.

The staff at Orange were faced with a hard task. Only eight of us had any sort of previous military experience: Marius, myself, Chris, a German from Oberammergau who had killed a tourist in the celebrations surrounding the Passion Play, a Frenchman, Mike the Rhodesian, and a Portuguese and a Rumanian who had both served with their countries' airborne regiments. Because everybody was treated equally at the start of their Legion service, Mike, who had learnt his killing in the bush war in Rhodesia, was treated the same as a South Vietnamese man who had never put on a uniform in his life. In other armies, the selection process assumed that people were of the same social balance. In the Legion, there was no guarantee that a man had even used a flushing loo before. However, toilet training took second place to skill with weapons or natural aggression. A man could be taught to handle, fire and dismantle a weapon, but an aggressive disposition was the result of upbringing and social conditioning. In my case, all my education and upbringing meant very little. I had learnt how to take orders and get up in the morning since I had gone to boarding school at age seven. But my education made things harder for me as a soldier, paradoxically, for I thought too much and questioned the wisdom of those in command.

At the other extreme was a Filipino who had been brought up in the slums of Manila, his father an alcoholic drug dealer and his mother a whore. He had watched his sisters slide into prostitution, through financial and practical necessity, and told me in his Spanish dialect that he had become used to sleeping on the floor at home while they fucked a random selection of Cuban, Puerto Rican and American sailors from the nearby US Naval base at Subic Bay in the Philippines. He had learned to look after himself, selling fake watches and drugs to anybody who would buy, and after killing a rival dealer had fled to Hawaii as a stowaway on a freighter. He had been discovered by a member of the crew and rather than be handed over to US Immigration officials had allowed himself to be buggered by three of the sailors, including the Captain. He had wound up in Marseilles, sore and desperate, and signed on at Fort St Nicholas. Then there were Mike and Marius. Both came from Western backgrounds, and both had received proper military training. More importantly, both were natural fighters. If we four were representatives of our platoon, it was understandable that the staff were having a tough time of it, pretending that we were all the same – physically, socially and morally.

A lot of the recruits found the orders process hard to take and didn't understand why they should do as they were told. When there was a confrontation between the casually civilian and the uncompromisingly military, the results could be frightening. An Italian, Gionesca, was absent from parade one morning as we lined up for inspection by the Sergeant-Major; Corporal Herve, a scarred Frenchman who had taken over from Vigno as duty NCO, went upstairs to find him. None of us saw what happened but we heard about it secondhand from an Irish Corporal called Ryan. Gionesca had been in the lavatory when parade was called, and had hidden in his room thinking his absence would not be noticed. When Herve charged through the door the Italian was lying on his bed reading a porn comic. Herve kicked him onto the floor, walked over, dragged him to his feet and broke his jaw with a side kick.

The disciplinary process required to keep people of low intelligence in order was simple. In the British Army, discipline was centred around self-discipline, and it was assumed that each man had enough self-discipline to carry out an order without being told twice. You appealed to his initiative, intelligence and commonsense. However, in dealing with people of whom there was no guarantee of social, professional or military competence, the system became more basic. A Corporal would tell a recruit not to spit on the floor because it was disgusting and because if he continued to do so he would be hit. They did not enter into lengthy explanations about the sanitary and social implications of such behaviour, because the recruit had more than likely spent his entire life spitting on the floor at home; the recruit responded to an order backed up with the threat of violence.

We carried on with our training, going for runs every morning, doing the assault course, learning about weapons, marching, singing and having very little sleep. The training was hard because we were hungry all the time and extremely tired.

Mike the Rhodesian and I were on 'corvée' duties one afternoon and were carrying the dustbins out to the shed behind the cookhouse where all the rubbish was deposited, which was home to a lot of stray cats and some aggressive rats. We both had large appetites and although we tried to get on the same table at mealtimes so that we could monopolise the food, we were permanently hungry. As we emptied our dustbins out we noticed another bin full of cold ravioli and bread left over from lunch; the bread was mixed in with the garbage and was soggy from being in a dustbin of cold ravioli for two hours. Several cats were feeding on it so Mike cleared them away with a kick from his combat boot and we started eating, dipping the wet crusts in the ravioli. I was full for the first time in two weeks.

Two days later Webb and Davies deserted.

We found out about this when an impromptu '*appel*' was called at 7.00 pm. The two Britons had climbed over the wall outside our block and fled into the woods. To the accompaniment of shouts and screams from the Corporals, we lined up in the corridor and were counted and recounted by them. They were panicking as it was their lack of observation which had led to the two getting away unseen. The situation was only just controllable, but it seemed that we might get to bed before midnight without being beaten up. Then Corporal Auriega, a fat Spaniard who sweated all the time, arrived back from town where he had been drinking all evening with his friends. As he was one of our Corporals, the Military Police had sought him out and made him return to barracks. He was drunk. He bellowed at us, yelling that he was fucked if he was going to let a group of dead-ass wankers spoil his time off. However, he added, since his evening was spoiled, then so was ours. He said in a deceptively reasonable tone that in the Legion everybody took the blame for everybody else's mistakes. He lined us up in the corridor and told the other Corporals that he would deal with us. They stood smoking at the end of the passage and watched Auriega. I was very frightened. I looked at Marius standing next to me. He nodded and shrugged. Being hit in the face hurt. It was also the anticipation of being hit that was worrying; would it be a punch in the guts, or the scarred knuckles of a Spaniard's fist in the eye? My nose was bigger than most people's, and being punched on it made me cry with pain. My stomach muscles were up to it, but I didn't want to lose any more teeth.

Auriega advanced the length of the corridor, stopping in front of each man, screaming at him and hitting him. He drew level with Marius and myself and started shouting about the English and how they were always the first to desert; how he, Corporal Auriega, with four years' Legion service, who had endured shelling in Beirut and the heat and flies of Chad, had finally had enough. He turned away and I thought that I was clear. Then he swung on his heel and brought his palm in an open-handed slap which crashed into my right ear with an explosive bang; as I reeled away from it, he drove his fist into my eye. It felt as though a grenade had gone off in my head. I couldn't hear and was crying from the pain, but I saw him put his foot sideways into Marius's midriff. Then we were confined to our rooms as the Corporals organised some sort of excuse for the Sergeants and Sergeant-Major. My eye swelled up in a matter of minutes, and I was unable to hear anything. Marius was trying to pretend that his kick didn't hurt, and the two Frenchmen, Macier and Olivier, were groaning and swearing loudly. Macier was spitting his front teeth into the palm of his hand.

Webb and Davies were caught two days later in the forests. They were kicked senseless and then handed over to the Military Police who locked them up in the roofless regimental prison before they were handed over to the Colonel of the Regiment for interrogation and questioning. The Legion considered desertion as the penultimate serious crime, the most heinous being stealing. It was understood that everybody became so frustrated occasionally that they tried to escape, but to desert and to fail was considered despicable in their eyes. The two Englishmen missed their family and their lives in England, and had thought that even with no money and no civilian clothes they would be able to make it back across France to one of the Channel ports. Few of us felt any sympathy for them, because apart from the beatings which we had received on their accounts, we all knew the rules by now, and being caught and failing in any way was wrong. Marius was dismissive about both of them and thought that if they couldn't manage two weeks of bedmaking and personal organisation then they should have stayed at home. I wasn't so sure. It was frightening how hunger and lack of sleep could make you behave and think like a real bastard. I knew that I shouldn't have felt sorry for them. Outwardly, I criticised them as much as anybody, feeling more than pissed off that we had been hit on their account. I couldn't hear anything with my right ear and my eye looked like a burst, over-ripe plum. Yet Auriega, I was sure, had wanted to hit us around a bit anyway, and the disappearance of Webb and Davies had provided an excuse. Inwardly I had a sneaking admiration for them because they had been sure that they didn't like the Legion and so had acted directly and left. Because we had all come from such different backgrounds, and were individuals bound together only by circumstance, I felt it was impossible to criticise their actions as I didn't fully understand their motivations.

But there was a huge discrepancy between my thoughts and my actions. Any rational person would disapprove of Moustaine, Auriega and the way in which we were being treated. Anybody with any sensitivity would have sympathised with Webb and Davies. We would all have liked to be able to eat normally at meals and not to have to hit each other to be first in the breakfast queue. (I had resorted to kneeing a Frenchman in the face over a biscuit the day before.) It was evident that those who were going to do well were those who ran faster, acted more efficiently and were more 'switched on'. I had set my sights on getting a good position in training so that I would be sent to the *2ème Régiment Étranger de Parachutistes*. The further we got into basic training the more obsessive I got about it. There were five or six who were in the running for the top places, and there was a fierce sense of competition between us. We treated each other within our little group humanely and normally, and passed over thinking about the others. It was the first time in my life I had acted like a complete sod to other people, and I felt that my behaviour was worse because I had loads of advantages the lesser recruits didn't: I could speak French; I was basically healthier and therefore found fitness much easier; I was a north European Caucasian which endeared me to some of the more racist instructors. Knowing full well that I was a wimp at heart, it was refreshing to be treated as something else.

There was one recruit for whom we all felt sorry. The Portuguese Da Silva had a permanent affliction in that he was very slightly hunchbacked. How he had passed his medical tests was a mystery to everybody; he was completely incapable of marching in time and swung his arms like a chimpanzee, unsynchronised and out of time. On a Saturday afternoon, Corporal Tambini tried to cure him of this structural malformation. He tied two broomsticks to Da Silva's arms and stuck one down his back, making him march up and down the corridor again and again, repeating 'I am a cripple'. This went on for three hours while the rest of us were preparing for the move to Canjuers. Of course, by the time he was finished, he was behind with his kit, so Tambini started hitting him.

Our four weeks at Orange had been made up of marching, singing, being hit and not having enough sleep. One afternoon we had made a forced march around the local countryside with our rucksacks on. Our military training had otherwise been minimal. We had been shooting once with our FA-MASs which had been tantalising, and most of us wanted to do something more dynamic than learn to fold clothes. As we loaded up the trucks with everything we would need for our month away at Canjuers I felt that we might be about to learn some soldiering.

Two days later, we had packed up our rucksacks, weapons, ammunition, heavy machine guns, camp beds, field stoves and stores and were ready to depart. We drove out of the barracks huddled in our combat jackets, and turned north towards the Alps.

We had been at Canjuers for a month when Auriega and Herve, who were both drunk, buried Vadgama. They made him dig a grave in the rocky ground at 1.00 am and then forced him to lie in it while they shovelled earth over him. When his entire body was covered apart from his head, Herve picked up a folding entrenching tool which he swung into Vadgama's face, splitting his nose and smearing it over his face. Both of them then took turns to kick him in the mouth and eyes.

Canjuers was tough. We had driven for five hours in open lorries through a rainstorm, climbing into the foothills of the Alps and then across a wilderness of a training area, with sharp mountains and expanses of harsh, windblown moorland. There were no houses or villages, only the occasional ruined farmhouse surrounded by pine trees and sandy, boggy ground. We had driven up a muddy track for ten miles and had arrived at a completely ruined farmhouse with no windows or doors, set into the slope of a mountain, looking over a marshy plain. Clumps of pine trees sat in hollows, and an icy wind blew around the bottom slopes of the mountain, whose top was covered in snow. It was the beginning of October and winter was coming. It was raining as we drew up in front of the building and started unpacking our kit. Corporal Tambini immediately made us lie down in the mud and do press-ups. As it got dark there was a nightmare of organisation and shouting; there were meals to be cooked for the Sergeants, marquees and tents to be erected in a rainstorm, personal kit to be unpacked and weapons to be put into a makeshift armoury. The Corporals ran around screaming and kicking us, as we climbed and scrambled up the muddy path to the house. It was an old farm building with numerous rooms with empty window sockets and a leaking roof; the floors were stone and the plaster was peeling off the walls everywhere. Next to it were two old barns and in the confusion, myself and an Italian recruit, Gionesca, were ordered to go and find wood for a fire. The wood in the barn was soaked and we stood there in our dripping combat jackets close to despair; we had been made to wear our helmets for the duration, and the oversized tin hats kept slipping over our faces, as we scrambled in the mud taking the wood to where the petulant staff were demanding hot coffee. Later we went through the routine of '*appel*' with our clothes laid out next to our sleeping bags, and at midnight were allowed to climb into them, sodden, muddy and cold. We were a long way from Orange, isolated in the farmhouse, and we knew how unpleasant the next month was going to be depended entirely on the whims of the staff.

We got up at 5.30 am and it was grim. The only source of water was a horse trough a hundred yards from the building, there was no electric light anywhere, and we dressed in the dark. I stumbled along to the trough to shave in the icy water, and without a mirror managed to remove what little stubble there was on my cheeks. I was glad that I wasn't one of those Portuguese or Italians who only had to go three hours without shaving for there to be a blue carpet on their chin. At school, aged fourteen, I was only just starting to trim the fur off my jaw while some of the Spanish or Arab boys would be tucking in with razor and foam. On parade that morning, Moustaine inspected our chins very closely and punished De Winter for not shaving by burning the stubble off one side of his face with a lighter.

At Canjuers we followed the same routine as at Orange. There was morning sport, meals, singing, '*appel*' and marching. Everything was much harder work because there was no light, no hot water (except what could be heated on a stove), no washing facilities and nowhere that was warm. It got colder each day, and rained nonstop. The roof of the farmhouse leaked and often you would return at the end of the day to find a puddle of water on top of your sleeping bag. There was mud everywhere, especially around the house itself where we all walked and where the lorries, jeeps and wagons drove. But it was preferable to Orange. We spent a lot of time outside on exercises, we had runs every morning in full combat kit which were longer and harder than the ones at Orange, we dug trenches, learnt how to camouflage ourselves and how to move across country at night. We were taught about hand grenades and explosives, and how to set ambushes and lay mines in the most effective pattern. We did a lot of shooting on the ranges, practising unarmed combat in the middle of a boggy field and singing all night.

The Legion attached incredible importance to singing. We would march along in step, doing eighty-eight paces to the minute, singing our hearts out. Singing was intended to enhance the bond between us, for by reciting verses and lines about the Legion, past and present, we were reinforcing our beliefs in the traditions we stood for. When it went well, it sounded magnificent, but if one person was out of step, it was a shambles. Each line and each verse of a song started as the left foot hit the ground, and with each particular song a different number of steps were left in between verses. The presence of one person like Da Silva could ruin the whole harmony of the section. We would be marching along in perfect time, waiting for the cue to start a new verse, when suddenly Da Silva, or Gionesca the Italian, who were both incapable of marching correctly, would pipe up by themselves. The Corporal or Sergeant leading would stop us, we would have to start again and try to sing the whole song faultlessly. None of it was made any easier by the fact that all the songs were in complicated French and to be able to sing them it helped to understand them. The songs were concerned with the same themes of love, death, deprivation, hardship, romantic yearnings and self-denial. All were new ideas to me. The themes centred around the lone legionnaire who has given up his past for the Legion, yet still longs for his former life and forgotten loves, his home and his happiness. All this is denied to him because he has made the irreversible decision to join up and his life will never be the same again. There is only hardship, pain and the possibility of dying for France:

> Loin dans l'infini s'étendent
> Deux grands prés marécageux.
> Pas un seul oiseau ne chante
> Dans les arbres secs et creux.
> Oh, terre de tristesse,
> Où nous devons sans cesse
> Souffrir, souffrir.
> Bruit des chaines et bruit des armes
> Sentinelle jour et nuit.
> Terre sombre, terre de larmes
> La mort pour celui qui fuit.
> Mais un jour dans notre vie
> Le printemps refleurira.
> Liberté, liberté, chérie,
> Je dirais tu es à moi.

Far into the distance stretch two large marshy plains.
Not a single bird sings in the dry, hollow trees.

Oh, land of sadness, where we must suffer endlessly.
Sounds of chains and sounds of arms,
A sentry guards us day and night.
Oh unhappy land, land of tears,
Death awaits he who flees.
But one day in our lifetime,
Spring will flower again.
Liberty, sweet liberty, I would say you were mine.

The legionnaire sees himself caught in a never-ending cycle of darkness and despair, until the day when he will be liberated through atonement of his past crimes.

Some songs were more romantic:

En Afrique, malgré le vent, la pluie,
Guette le sentinel sur le piton.
Mais son coeur reste au pays chéri,
Quitté pour voir les horizons lointains.
Ses yeux ont aperçu les ennemis qui s'approchent, qui
    s'approchent,
L'alerte est donné, les souvenirs s'envolent,
Maintenant au combat.
Dans le ciel brille
L'étoile qui lui rappelle son enfance.
Adieu mon pays, je ne t'oublierai.

In Africa, despite the wind and rain,
The sentry looks out from the crag.
But his heart has stayed in his beloved homeland
Which he left to see distant horizons.
He has noticed the enemy approaching. The alarm goes up.
His memories vanish. It's time for combat.
In the sky shines the star which reminds him of his childhood.
Goodbye, my country, I'll never forget you.

This was my favourite song as it was quite easy to sing and it had a stirring, catching rhythm. We sang a lot of SS and Werhmacht songs, including the Horst Wessel song and other Teuton airs which were meant to remind us of our Runic backgrounds. I think some of this was lost on the non-Aryan members of our section, such as the

Polynesians who could in no way pretend that their ancestry stretched back to the Vikings. Obsessed as the Legion was with tradition, many of the songs harked back to Indo-China and Algeria, to when a man could expect to serve his entire contract without seeing Europe. In 'Adieu vieille Europe' the legionnaire is on a boat off to Algeria:

> Adieu vieille Europe, que le diable t'importe.
> Adieu vieux pays, pour le ciel, si brûlant, d'Algérie.
> Nous les blessés de toutes les guerres,
> Nous les damnés de la terre entière,
> Il nous faut du soleil, de l'espace,
> Pour redorer nos carcasses.

> Goodbye, old Europe, may the Devil take you.
> Goodbye, old country, for the burning sun of Algeria.
> We are the wounded from every war, the world's damned ones.
> We need sunlight and space, to regild our bodies.

France and civilian life has done nothing for him, and so he is off to Algeria to get tanned and fight. He is saying goodbye to what is past and irretrievably lost.

The Sergeant-Major had said that like all other legionnaires we would learn to sing in perfect time, so sing we would. We sang marching across the muddy fields in front of the farmhouse, we sang in the cookhouse tent before we were allowed to eat, we sang at parade before we went off to exercise, and at any point that the staff thought we had nothing to do, it was out with the songbooks. Before each meal we ran halfway up a mountain and fetched rocks which we piled in the field in front of the farmhouse, to leave some sign of our presence there. We sang as we ran up the mountain.

After two weeks it started snowing and the ground froze. The mountain behind the farmhouse was lost in a mist of snow and sleet and we had to smash the ice on the horse trough in the mornings. I took to sleeping in all my clothes in my sleeping bag, and managed to get away with not undressing for ten days. Running and sport took on a new emphasis as it was the only way to keep warm.

> Contre les Viets, contre l'ennemi.
> Partout où le devoir fait signe.

Soldats de France, soldats de pays,
Nous remonterons vers les lignes.
Oh, légionnaire, le combat qui commence,
Met dans nos ames, enthusiasme et vaillance.

This was a difficult one to sing.

Against the Vietcong and the enemy, wherever duty calls.
Soldiers for France, soldiers for the homeland
We will attack the positions again.
Oh, legionnaire, the ensuing combat will fire your heart with
    bravery and enthusiasm.

We had been getting it wrong, so were face down in a foot of water
in the field doing press-ups. My uniform was soaked and each time
we dipped down at arm's bend our faces went into the muddy ice and
water. The Chief-Corporal in charge shouted out that if any of us had
any sisters, we were to stand up. I had three. In return for their
addresses he would allow me to stop doing press-ups in the mud. I
agreed. He took out his notebook and noted three addresses, one at
St Hugh's College in Oxford, another in south London, and another
at a Berkshire convent. He put his pen away. I went back to the farm
building, smoked a cigarette and got changed.
    Although our life was cold and miserable, I felt enthusiastic because
I was fit and because we were doing a lot of military training. The
urge to succeed and be competitive was stronger in some of us than
in others, and although the section was theoretically united there was
a faction which stood apart from the rest. The members of this group
changed regularly, and were composed of those who had done well
on this or that physical test. You only retained membership as long
as you succeeded on the runs, and in the classroom periods, which
were held in a sodden marquee on the hillside. Being in with the gang
didn't stop you getting hit but it meant that the Corporals might
think for one second before lifting their fists. Along with Mike the
Rhodesian, Marius, Robert from Oberammergau and Chris, there
was myself and a Frenchman called Tignet. Corporal Herve had
christened us '*Les Aigles Noirs*', The Black Eagles, after a comic strip
story about superhuman warriors. I felt less than superhuman. I had
boils and chilblains all over my hands, had had two days food
poisoning (when I had vomited over the Sergeant-Major's jeep), and

was tired all the time. But for all our fitness we were treated no differently from the rest of the Section.

We had a hard physical test one morning, which comprised part of our '*Certificat Technique Élémentaire*', the exam we had to pass on completion of basic training. With full combat kit, helmet, rifle and webbing, and weighed down by a thirty-five pound rucksack, we set off on a run. The course was only eight kilometres, but it was cross country and had to be completed in less than one hour. Vigno, who had served with the *2ème Régiment Étranger de Parachutistes*, intimated that if we ever got to Corsica we would be expected to do it in under forty minutes. It was a freezing morning and the Section had run for five miles over muddy paths and swampy fields. Gasping for breath, legs and backs aching and chafing, we stood at the finish, bent double, dripping sweat, while the Corporals read out the times. The Sergeant-Major walked alongside approvingly, waving his clenched fist saying, '*Eh, alors, les fuckings, ça va?*' '*Les fuckings*' was a generic term used for all English speakers as it was the word the staff heard us use the most.

Not all the Section had finished the run in the time allowed and so Sergeant-Chef Gibeau decided that we should all be punished. We were told to climb to the top of the mountain behind the farmhouse. Sergeant Moustaine gave one of the Frenchmen a walkie talkie and told him that on reaching the summit the entire section should sing all three verses of the '*Képi Blanc*' into the radio. I looked up at the mountain. It was over 1,000 feet high. The top of it was shrouded in mist and wind, and in this weather it would be an icy, treacherous climb. We set off, with our rucksacks, and halfway up the farmhouse had disappeared into the mist. Clambering over slippery, wet rocks we halted at a rowan tree just below the top. We gathered round, and before Moustaine was satisfied we had shouted the song three times into the mouthpiece of the small radio as the wind howled around us.

Two days later, we all suffered again for one person's misdemeanour. At '*appel*', the Rumanian Corporal Asioz asked if anybody felt ill, because on emerging from the back door of the farmhouse that morning he had noticed a spray of liquid excrement beneath one of the ledges where somebody had shat out of the window. Nobody owned up so he ordered us all to fetch our kit downstairs and to spread it out in a line on the wet grass, while he went along inspecting our underpants and spare trousers. When he got to Gionesca, he screamed in disgust. All his underclothes, his sports socks, his trousers and vests were smeared with shit. He had had violent diarrhoea and had wiped his arse in the night with his own clothes. The rest of the section were standing in the rain with all their clothes spread out on the wet grass because he had not wanted to admit that he was ill. On instructions from the Corporals, we stripped him naked and made him run across to the horse trough where he was thrown in. While three men scrubbed him with a stiff yard broom, the rest of us stood to attention in front of the trough and sang '*Képi Blanc*'. Marius and one or two others in the Section decided that possible pneumonia and deep humiliation were not enough of a punishment for Gionesca. We had been eight weeks in basic training and even in the most placid of us the qualities of self preservation and selfishness were coming to the surface. Apart from Marius, Mike and Robert, I didn't give a shit about the rest of the section. I hated Gionesca because he complained all the time, and I knew that I could get away with hating him because I was stronger and fitter than him. Marius and I were chosen by the rest of the group to finish off punishing him. Our chance came the following afternoon.

Meanwhile, Da Silva, the quiet, arch-backed Portuguese man, who had suffered such ill treatment, wandered off when nobody was looking. It was an hour before he was discovered missing and we spent the rest of the afternoon searching for him in the woods and plains surrounding the house. We never found him. He just disappeared. It froze again that night and everybody guessed that by morning his twisted icy body with its pathetic malformation was lying at the bottom of some gulley, where he would have taken cover from the snow and the wind. We were due to leave Canjuers four days afterwards and there was much to think about so nothing was done. We did get Gionesca, though.

While looking for Da Silva in an oak wood behind the farmhouse, Marius and I cornered Gionesca behind a lichen-covered rock. The Sergeant and Corporal leading our bit of the search party were out of earshot. Marius smashed the Italian in the face with his gloved fist and stood on his chest. I hesitated. Then I drove my combat boot onto his temple as Marius hit him again in the mouth. We got up, walked through the trees and left him. Sergeant Moustaine, however, noticed blood coming out of his mouth later that afternoon. He paraded the section and asked who had attacked Gionesca. Marius and I stepped forward. Moustaine explained in a low, controlled voice that any violence which was going to be dished out would come from him and the Corporals. He would not tolerate bullying, especially by two of the stronger members of the section towards one who was weaker and actually ill. He had punished Gionesca by putting him in the horse trough and that was it. He walked over, grabbed me by both lapels and screamed, '*Tu comprends, toi, ou quoi?*' He threw me over his shoulder in a judo hold on to the rocks and gravel we were standing on. He then picked me up and drove his knee straight into my balls. I wanted to throw up, pass out, scream and cry at the same time. It felt like an elephant had hit me in the guts. Moustaine made me stand up and slapped me across the eyes with his leather gloves. I stumbled off to be sick behind an armoured personnel carrier as he started on Marius.

There was one weekend left to go of our time at Canjuers. We had all come out of ourselves and were more self confident. We were fit, thinner than any of us had ever been, good at singing, proficient with a variety of weapons, and we could survive on three hours sleep a night. We were learning what it was like to be legionnaires. Sergeant-Major Barlerin left the following day for Orange, leaving us in the charge of Sergeant-Chef Gibeau for the weekend. Gibeau felt that we had had too easy a time of it at Canjuers and for the last three days introduced a new punishment.

Any petty misdemeanour resulted in the offender having to report to the Corporal of the day with his entrenching tool after evening '*appel*'. He was then taken outside and made to dig a grave in the rocky, frozen ground, which took about three hours, before sleeping in it for the night. The Corporals took it in turns to watch those digging from the shelter of the farmhouse, wrapped up and drinking hot coffee. By the time the graves were dug, it would be 2.00 am and far too cold to sleep in the sub-zero winds that blew around the bottom of the mountain. On the Saturday night, Gibeau devised one last piece of theatre. Being a fanatic nonsmoker and health freak, he made us enact the ritual funeral of a cigarette end. We dressed up in a combination of combat and sports kit, wearing gas masks and carrying makeshift torches made of sticks and rags dipped in tar. Gionesca wore a bedsheet and a necklace of rabbit-bones, and led four pall-bearers carrying a plastic carton containing a Marlboro butt. A small hole was dug, the cigarette buried, songs sung over the grave and then the whole procession wended its way round the field four times singing the funeral march from *Aida*, which we had been practising for a week. A bonfire had been lit and wine heated in a cauldron with sugar. Each recruit had to stand up and sing a song in his own language. I sang an obscene ditty I had learnt in the TA, Mike an African song in Matabele, and the Germans some carols. When the wine was finished, we went to bed, apart from those who had graves to dig. The Corporals pulled out some more wine and two cases of beer and carried on drinking while supervising the digging party. Around 4.00 am Vadgama was buried and had his face smashed in with a shovel.

We left Canjuers on the Monday morning and arrived later on that day at a small village, from where we would march back on foot to Orange. This was our '*Marche Képi Blanc*', on completion of which we would have passed the tests to become legionnaires. The presentation ceremony would take place in Orange and only those completing the march would be entitled to wear their white *képis*. We pitched our tents in a wood of olive trees and wellingtonias and went to sleep. Forbidden to speak any language but French, Marius and I had been punished by the Corporals for speaking English while dismantling the tents at Canjuers. Vigno had taken two lumps of granite from the side of the hill and made us keep them in our mouths for three hours. We folded wet canvas and icy guy ropes, sucking back streams of saliva which collected in our teeth, unable to smoke, talk or move our jaws because of a mouthful of rocks.

— 4 —

BLOWING UP RENAULT 4S

It was eighty-five miles to Orange, a distance we hoped to cover in three days' marching. Our section was split up into four groups, each under the command of a Sergeant and two Corporals. Sergeant Ninez, who commanded our group, had just joined us, and along with him there were Corporals Vigno and Herve. Ninez had recently been transferred to the Cavalry Regiment from the Paras in Corsica. He marched extremely quickly. As far as myself, Mike and Marius were concerned, this was a good thing, as it meant that the march was going to be tough and that those of us who finished would deserve their white *képis*. Of the forty-eight of us who had left Aubagne two months before only thirty-six were in a fit state to attempt the tests. Webb and Davies had finished their time in prison, had deserted again, been recaptured and imprisoned for a month. Da Silva had vanished at Canjuers; a Scotsman had been thrown out for being underaged; Gionesca was in hospital in Orange with dysentery and pneumonia after his bath; Gazil, the Rumanian paratrooper, had developed a massive infection on his back caused by the friction of his rucksack during marching; and the other six were ill or disabled after our stay at Canjuers. Vadgama was in hospital in Marseilles.

We marched fast and by noon had covered twelve miles. We stopped at the side of the road outside a small town for our lunch. One of us made a fire and we brewed coffee and lay in the autumn sun. Down from the mountains the weather was warmer, without the snow and wind of Canjuers. All of us had sores and infections on our hands and arms from the cold and the dirt. My knuckles and hands were a mass of windblown cuts and boils which meant that whenever I clenched my fists the gashes opened. Our faces were red and raw and most of us had blisters. So it was nice to lie in the sun and undo my shirt as, head propped against my rucksack, I dozed off. Occasionally a car would pass by on the road, but otherwise it was quiet. We lay under the trees and slept. Sergeant Ninez was playing with his compass and map, measuring distances and calculating the best route back to

Orange; Mike and Marius were playing cards in the dust, Macier was pricking his blisters and the others were asleep.

We moved off two hours later, through a town with white buildings with red shutters and dogs asleep in the road. The locals sat in the cafés and stared at us as we passed. We moved through the town and up a hilly field covered with vines before we entered a forest where the branches grew close above the path. We had to fight to make our way through as rifles, packs and radio aerials snagged on bushes and branches. The air in the wood was damp and smelt of peat, the path was muddy and wet, and it was exhausting constantly pushing brambles and twigs out of the way. It was a relief to reach the edge of the wood and come out into bright sunlight again. We walked along a narrow road with elm and oak trees on either side, moving slowly because Macier's feet were hurting him. As we could go no faster than the pace of the slowest man, Marius and I took his rucksack and FA-MAS to lighten his load. We walked at the end of the group, idling along, looking at the scenery and day dreaming. Marching long distances with rifle and rucksack was tiring and boring; you cradled your rifle in your arms, settled your pack in a comfortable position and let your thoughts drift away.

We stayed that night in an empty holiday home we discovered on the edge of a village. All ten of us crammed onto the porch to keep out of the wet grass and we slept in a tangle of sleeping bags, packs and machine guns. We woke abnormally late at 8.00 am and sat in the garden of the house for an hour drinking coffee and eating the bread one of the Corporals had bought in the village that morning. Away from the main body of the section it was very easy. Ninez saw no reason to complain or criticise so long as we marched fast enough. As we drank our coffee, a lorry arrived from the main group to pick up Macier whose blisters had burst, preventing him from walking. We carried on. Through the morning and the sun of the afternoon we marched, thirty-five miles across the *départements* of Savoie and Vaucluse, through woods and towns, up hills and across vineyards. We were all filthy, our uniforms, hands and faces covered with a mixture of mud, woodsmoke, sweat and dust. We stopped at a shop and bought apples and beer, which we guzzled on the march, assault rifles and ammunition belts swinging round our necks as we used our hands to prise the tops off the beer bottles. We spent that night in a field of asparagus seedlings. We crossed the wide River Rhône the following morning on a huge suspension bridge, then moved up a main road, poplars and plane trees to either side of us. We reached Orange before any of the other groups and went into the barracks. They were hot and dusty. I had a shower, scrubbing off the dirt of a month in the open. My hands stayed brown and cracked, the knuckles swollen up and bleeding.

When the trucks arrived we unloaded them, watching those who had fallen out on the march as they disembarked. Nineteen of us had made it to the end.

The following day we learnt that the Colonel of the *1er Régiment Étranger de Cavalerie* had ordered an inquiry into the incident with Vadgama at Canjuers. What concerned him was not the brutality but the fact that it had taken place while the Corporals were drunk. Vadgama emerged from hospital in Marseilles after a complicated facial operation; he had a bone transplant in his nose and cheek and his brown skin was marked with the fresh scars.

The Colonel decided that Herve, Vigno, Auriega and Tambini should return to their respective Squadrons, and that Sergeant Moustaine should leave the Section. We saw them rarely after that. Corporal Ryan, the Irish Corporal, went off for a week's leave in Marseilles and, for an unknown reason, killed himself with a hunting rifle in a hotel in the Old Port.

We were now legionnaires. It was only eight weeks since we had left Aubagne yet there was a difference in the way in which we behaved and in which we saw ourselves. For the nineteen of us who were to be awarded our white *képis*, there was the certainty of a place with one of the Foreign Legion's *Régiments*, and the satisfaction of having made it this far through basic training. No longer were we '*engagé volontaires*', who could be treated as nothings – we had proved ourselves to the instructors on our course, and henceforth they would treat us as legionnaires and expect us to behave as such. Each generation of legionnaires was expected to carry forward the traditions and ethics of the Legion, handing them down from one man to the next. These traditions were encapsulated in everything which we did and which we were taught. The most prominent and, as we had experienced, most problematic symbol of the Legion's past was the singing. We had been taught the history of the organisation, and each day were learning more about its curious codes of morality and behaviour. Within the space of three weeks we were to experience two of the most important ceremonies of any legionnaire's contract: the moment when he was presented with his white *képi*, and the celebrations surrounding Christmas.

At a torch-lit ceremony held on the regimental parade ground two nights later, we were given our *képis*. We ironed our best uniforms, sharing two electric irons, until Corporal Vigno, on a parting note, decided that irons were too much of a luxury. He made us fill up our regulation cups with hot water and press our uniforms using the flat base of the cup as an iron. We paraded the following night as it was getting dark, the parade ground lit up by flaming torches with four tanks lined up as a backdrop to our ceremony. In green ties, red epaulettes and blue cummerbunds we lined up; Marius, who had been chosen as the star recruit, would lead the parade and stand out in front of us as we received our *képis*. There were speeches by the Commander of the 3rd Squadron, by the Colonel of the Regiment, and by the President of the Association of Former Legionnaires of Orange. The talking finished, we stood to attention, sung the '*Képi Blanc*', and then put on our *képis*. I was now Legionnaire Jennings.

There was a party afterwards during which we were able to talk to some of the officers who seemed faintly bored by the whole process. I consoled myself by drinking a lot of warm red Martini.

Our training now got easier. There was less violence, the '*appels*' were not so severe, and we spent much more time in the classroom doing theoretical work for our exams. But we still did a lot of sport and work on the assault course, which was a set of twenty-four gut-wrenching obstacles set on the edge of the camp. We were even allowed to write home. Those who were sheltering behind assumed identities were discouraged from getting in touch with their friends and families, so it was a small group of us who sat down in a classroom. I didn't know how to begin, so began by assuming that my parents knew where I was and then proceeded to tell them all the details of the food, living conditions, pay and training. I left out any reference to brutality in our lives and assured them that I was well and healthy, which I was. I described our time at Canjuers, the singing and the landscapes. I filled four pages which I sent with a footnote requesting that they send me some books. I had had nothing to read for three months, and now that we had some time to ourselves reading was a good way of distracting myself from the immediacies of life around me. I asked for Hammond Innes, Frederick Forsyth, Iris Murdoch and Evelyn Waugh. It was nearly the same as writing a letter home from school.

It was important that they should feel that I was healthy and happy. They were so far away from me, and there was nothing that they could do to alleviate the hardship of Legion life, so it appeared unnecessary to burden them with minor worries about bullying and violence. I had always felt, partly as a result of my upbringing, that I should be able to fend for myself, especially in a situation which was one of my own making. At age eleven I had gone away from my parents' school to a boarding school in Herefordshire, and remembered crying miserably as my mother and father drove off down the drive, leaving me to be looked after by one of the older boys. Every weekend that they came to visit me would end in tears, and I was fourteen before I could manage without them, and before I stopped kissing my father goodnight. The years of dishonesty and drunkenness which preceded my trip to Boulogne had erased any feeling of homesickness, and by November 1984, I could write them a composed, controlled letter from a Legion barrack room without any problem.

As some of the other legionnaires couldn't write very well, they asked me to help them with their letters. We all read what each other had written, anyway. A New Zealander, Wilkins, who had joined the section halfway through basic training from Castelnaudary, asked me to write one for him. He wrote to his sister, who he hadn't seen for a year, as he had been travelling round Europe before joining the Legion. He told her that he was well and that he missed her a lot. His feelings for her as his sister were still the same, because although he was across the world he still thought about her every day. He had been travelling and had seen some pretty strange things. As she would notice from the heading on the notepaper he was in the French Foreign Legion and it was fucking tough work, but there were some good mates around him. He hoped the shearing had been successful so that the family could pay for their father's operation in Auckland. He promised to send more money home as soon as he got paid, and he wanted her to look after his puppy, which he guessed by now would be a full-grown collie. She should look after herself, as well, and he would see her in five years' time.

Mike wrote his own letter but showed it to me all the same. It was to his girlfriend in Harare and he told her straight away that he was showing the French a thing or two, but it still wasn't like the old days with the Rhodesian Light Infantry. He missed her very much, and thought often about their baby. But they all knew he was doing the right thing in joining the Legion, for her sake as well as his. She knew how important it was for him to be in a good army, and if the war had ended in Rhodesia, then perhaps another might start in one of France's old colonies so that the Legion could get involved. She shouldn't run off with any of his old mates or she would get a good hiding when he came home. She should give his hello to any of the boys who were still around and in the meantime could think of the home they were going to build in South Africa. He wanted her to make enquiries with some of his friends about his chances of getting into the South African Army after leaving France. But he was OK and he sent her a big kiss.

Chris had written a letter to Tina Jelly in Aldershot saying that he still loved her and missed her a lot, but was sure that until he came home she would be able to go out with his mates from the Royal Signals. He asked her to drop in on his Mum and Dad and say hello, and to make sure that his father wasn't drinking too much. He finished his letter by saying that she was still close to him and that he wanked about her a lot. I liked the sound of Tina Jelly. She didn't get many letters, he thought, so I should write her one. I gave him my butter ration at breakfast one morning in return for her address.

Marius had written a long one to his mother and sister, at home in Kalmar. At my urging, he asked for some more photographs as I was keen on the idea of this spotlessly clean, ruthlessly attractive family in their Nordic pine kitchen.

We posted our letters, and immediately started calculating how long it would take for replies to reach us. When my parents did eventually reply, their letter was full of the most ordinary details of life in England and seemed far removed from my experiences in the Legion. At the end of the writing session in the classroom, we filed out, back across the gravel to our barrack rooms. It felt as though our contact with the outside world had closed away from us again.

We took our tests on the shooting ranges the morning after. These tests were part of our 'Certificat Technique Élémentaire' and were important. From 200 metres we fired single shots at the targets depicting charging men holding machine guns. We then moved close and fired from the hip and shoulder in reflex action shooting. Despite its low calibre, the weapon was hard to control firing on full automatic, as it threw out 1,500 rounds per minute. It needed a lot of experience to be able to hold it correctly so that all the twenty-five shots in the magazine riddled the target. Mike was an excellent shot at short and long distances and taught me how to control my weapon, how to change magazines with a simple wrist flick operation, and where it was best to hit a person if you wanted to be sure of incapacitating him. He taught me to aim for the knees since any weapon firing on automatic would climb high and right, and thus the fall of shot could be evenly distributed across the stomach and torso, ending in the head. He was two years older than me and was only eighteen when he had first killed somebody. A ZANLA terrorist had risen out of the bushes with a Kalashnikov while Mike had been involved in an ambush on the Limpopo river which had been set up by the Selous Scouts, the counter-insurgency tracking teams of the Rhodesian army. The man had seen Mike first but had fumbled with his safety catch as Mike killed him. The war in Rhodesia had been a continuous sequence of search and destroy missions and cross border raids into Mozambique and Zambia. After the Lancaster House agreement, Mike had found himself in a similar position to the rest of the Rhodesian Army – over-qualified, over-trained, and unemployed. Many of his friends had travelled to South Africa, signing on with the South African Army. Mike, however, had travelled north, leaving his pregnant girlfriend with relatives in the safety of a Harare suburb as he went looking for another war. He had been playing the piano in a waterfront bar in Dar Es Salaam when he had heard one of the customers talking about the Legion. He had picked up his money, and caught a plane out to Marseilles. After stopping in Kinshasa, the flight had landed in France and Mike had walked into the recruiting post at Fort St Nicholas and joined up. He was better trained than anybody in our section, and the Corporals admired his physical prowess. He was the archetypal Legion recruit.

Ex-soldiers such as Mike would travel from one army to the other, hoping to be in the right army at the right time. The right time was when it went to war. For members of the *2ème Régiment Étranger de Parachutistes*, this moment had undoubtedly been when the Regiment jumped over Kolwezi in 1978. For the British Army, it had been Operation Corporate, the reclaiming of the Falkland Islands in 1982. Other armies, like the Israeli and South African ones, had been in a state of armed conflict for some considerable time. The mercenary wars of the 1960s in the Congo and Near East were over. Military combat in the 1980s survived within established armies where a man had to be a contracted, organised member of a unit. For those such as Mike, it was like a surfer trying to catch his wave. The ability to predict where hostilities were likely to occur, in what countries, under whose jurisdiction, was paramount to a man whose professional abilities lay in being a practising soldier. I supposed that I was trying to catch my wave as well. When, and if, I got to the *2ème Régiment Étranger de Parachutistes* I hoped that my efforts during basic training would pay off, and that I could get involved, if not in a war, then in something physically and militarily more adventurous than anything I had done so far. We had all heard rumours about the Legion's paras, and I was holding myself to my vow made in the bathroom in Wales nearly ten years before.

Meanwhile, in Orange, it was time for Christmas, and the section started to organise itself for the festivities. In keeping with the Legion's view of itself as a family, Christmas was an important event. The main celebrations were the midnight mass, the Christmas eve supper and the crib building competition. Each Section of thirty men would construct an elaborate 'crèche' or crib, and at midnight the results would be judged by the Colonel of the regiment as he made his rounds. The cribs were not the usual constructions of shoe boxes and straw, with small religious figures and matching sets of the Magi; they were a challenge for the ingenuity and imagination of each section and would often involve large amounts of gravel, stones, concrete and other building materials. Some would fill half a room, and the themes were normally an interpretation of the nativity in military terms. The mountain troop of the 4th Squadron were devising a crib which involved a lifesize figure of the baby Jesus abseiling down a mockup of a cliff face towards a rock grotto containing an edelweiss, the symbolic flower of the German Wehrmacht mountain troops.

Seven of our Section were detached for a fortnight to make our crèche, so each day after parade they would go off with a Corporal to hump sand, fill wheelbarrows with moss and look for things to add to the project. None of us were allowed to see the unfinished article, which was being built in one of the lecture rooms in our barrack block; the rest of us were involved in practising for the midnight mass carol concert where our section would be providing the choir. Each day we would assemble in a room under the supervision of a young Lieutenant and sing carols. Each nationality had contributed a song which we all had to learn. 'Silent Night' sung in German was the best. Christmas day itself was for sobering up and clearing up the debris from the wild night before, and after lunch the entire regiment was allowed '*quartier libre*', or free time in town. As every man would be drunk from the night before, this would be a continuation of the celebrations. Christmas ended officially with '*appel*' at 6.00 am on boxing day.

By Christmas eve our singing was practically perfect and we had a repertoire of ten carols in French, German, Spanish and English. The crèche was finished, and depicted two lifesize figures of legionnaires in the desert, one cradling the other in his arms as he lay dying. This was set against a background of rocks, sand, barbed wire and empty ammunition boxes, with large amounts of fake snow sprayed over everything. There was a cassette which provided a background commentary, a monologue about the glory of dying in the arms of a comrade at Christmas as the stars above sung out the glory of the Lord.

As we were still undergoing our basic training, we were not allowed to have a bar and nor would we be allowed to make a tour of the rest of the bars in the regiment, a ruling which Mike, Marius and myself were determined to do something about. It would involve crawling out of a window while nobody was looking and trusting in the spirit of Christmas goodwill should we be discovered.

Christmas eve arrived and at 5.00 pm we changed into our walking out uniforms which we had spent most of the morning ironing. We walked down to a tank hangar on the far side of the camp where the mass was due to be held, and filed in to take our seats. Normally the building was the repair shop and garage for thirty AMX-10 battle tanks, but for this evening it had been converted into a temporary church with the aid of some camouflage nets, 300 chairs and a platform where a nativity play would be staged, and from which the Priest would read out the lesson. The Officers arrived with their wives and girlfriends, the children following behind. As in the British Army, the cavalry was considered to be the aristocratic élite of soldiering and the Legion's Cavalry Regiment was one of the superior regiments in the French Army. The girlfriends and wives of the young officers were pretty, well-bred girls who leant over to each other and laughed a lot as they waited for the ceremony to start. The Colonel was there with his wife and children, and although it was not compulsory for the men to attend mass, there were a large number of legionnaires present, mostly Latin or East European.

The service started with our opening carol, 'Away in a Manger' and continued with all the normal Christmas readings; after the gospel we sat down for the nativity play, which was performed by a section from the armoured car squadron. Joseph was played by a Yugoslavian Sergeant, Mary by a slim Gambian Corporal and the three wise men by a trio of Tahitians with tribal tattoos and scarred faces. There was clapping when they had finished, and mass progressed with us singing well. Most people took communion. Then we went to the cookhouse to have dinner.

The tables were laid with white cloths and there were floral spreads of flowers and holly; plates of cold meats, salads and fruits were laid out, there were bottles of rosé and white wine in front of every man, and Christmas decorations hung from the ceiling. As the Captain commanding the 3rd Squadron came into the dining hall, we stood to attention to sing a slow lament called 'Souvenir qui Passe', before sitting down to eat. It was the first wine any of us had had to drink for nearly five months and we got very drunk, extremely fast. The main courses arrived, with more wine, there was singing, then pudding in the form of gateaux and fruit salads, and liqueurs and cigars. The decorations shone on the walls and I loosened the buttons of my tunic and slipped my tie down a few inches. Sergeant-Chef Gibeau leant over, tapped me on the forefinger with a table knife and told me to do them up again. I sat smoking my cigar and looked at the people around me.

At a table behind ours was the English contingent, laughing and drinking; they were the nucleus of the *Mafia Anglais* of the regiment. In every Legion Regiment, the English-speaking people stuck together in tight groups, drinking together, socialising together and looking after each other; Australians, South Africans and Canadians joined in with the club, which evolved its own codes of conduct and unspoken rules of behaviour. When an English-speaker went into the foyer of the regiment, a NAAFI-style canteen where you could buy beer, cigarettes, sweets and memorabilia, he would head over to the table where the *Mafia* was sitting. If he had no money, he could sit down and take a bottle of beer from the crate on the table, and carry on drinking until it had run out. If he had money, he would buy a case of beer from the bar which would gain him entry to the table. Taking a bottle, he would then open it with the bottom edge of the Bic lighters that most people carried, prising the top off in one movement. Cigarettes were placed on the table in front of you which meant that they were for everybody. Cigarettes were normally Marlboro, the lighters Bic, and the beer always Kronenbourg. This system of drinking guaranteed people a drink every night of the month, even when they had no money. Everybody in the regiment was paid in cash on the same day, so there were no difficulties in reclaiming debts. Most people were not taxed on their earnings as they were not French citizens, and there was nothing to spend money on apart from cigarettes, beer, and trips into town. The *Mafia* system worked subconsciously and introspectively. An Englishman in the *3ème Régiment Étranger d'Infanterie* in French Guyana had refused to drink with the English, had spoken French, and considered the *Mafia* a waste of time. Several drunk Britons tried to hang him one night, and would have succeeded had not a French Corporal cut him down in time.

Our Christmas food had been consumed and most of the drink had been poured down our throats. There were sketches by members of the Squadron who thought themselves good at acting. There were spoofs on the Officers, insinuating that they were upper class twits, and there were jokes about the Squadron based on its experiences in Chad that summer. There were photographs of the unit in the Chadian desert on the walls of the dining hall. Men sitting in the turrets of their reconnaissance tanks, men riding camels, and men driving through the streets of the capital, N'Djamena. In one, a Corporal inspected the remains of a blown up Libyan tank. There were a lot of sunglasses and Arab headscarfs in evidence.

Corporal Vigno held an African baby in one photo, and I looked over to where he was talking with Corporal Auriega. There was only Sergeant-Chef Gibeau to make our lives miserable now. His veto on our drinking after the meal was annoying. Most of us had reached the point where we wanted to carry on drinking until we collapsed. We had received our Christmas presents from 'La Marraine', the godmother of the regiment. She was a dignified octogenarian aristocrat who had been made an honorary Chief-Corporal in the Regiment since she had served with it in World War Two. She paid for the Regiment's presents each Christmas and presented them to the legionnaires. She looked extremely elegant in the tailored tunic and skirt of her 'Chief-Corporal's' uniform. Down one arm ran gold chevrons, denoting her length of service with the Regiment. She had offered her immaculately powdered cheek to each man and had received a kiss from everyone. As a present I had received a large book of complex Legion history written in difficult French. We sang for twenty minutes, the songs loud and impressive in the high-roofed hall, each man's voice resounding with the alcohol and the nostalgia of Christmas. We filed back to our barracks and went to bed. The Corporals then disappeared to the different section bars which were doing business all over the camp.

Marius and I waited for twenty minutes and then walked into Mike's room, only to find him snoring loudly, unconscious. We left him, got dressed again and walked down the fire escape. We headed for the 4th Squadron where we had been officially invited by some of the English members. We walked through the front door and into the bar. In the corner Jesus abseiled down his cliff face and at the makeshift counter two barmen worked furiously. All around were Officers and men getting extremely drunk. A Scottish Corporal waved at Marius and handed over two tumblers of neat Malibu which we swigged quickly. Beer, brandy, Scotch and Malibu were being drunk out of plastic cups, everybody was in uniform and there were lots of medals and badges in evidence. Most men wore the blue and white campaign medal from Chad and Lebanon as well as the ubiquitous red and dark blue of the General Service medal. One or two of the Sergeants had the red and white stripes of the '*Valeur Militaire*', awarded for bravery in action, and a Lieutenant with a bald head and tattooed hands had the '*Légion d'Honneur.*' From his wrinkled face and sunburned skin he looked as though he had risen from the ranks rather than graduating from Saint Cyr or the École Militaire. Nobody seemed to mind the presence of Marius and myself, and we got into conversation with two Officers about the respective merits of the different Legion regiments. They both urged us to go to the *2ème Régiment Étranger de Parachutistes*. The Chief-Corporal to whom I had given my sisters' addresses at Canjuers was there, and he told me that he had sent my oldest sister a photograph of himself in a tank and one of his apartment in La Rochelle. He awaited a reply eagerly and was going to drop in to see her on his next leave.

Three cups of neat Malibu mixed well with the rosé wine and Armagnac I had drunk at supper and I felt garrulous and cheerful, confiding in strangers and telling the story of my life. Two Portuguese legionnaires dragged a Scotsman out of the door before he was sick. Loud French pop music howled out of a cassette recorder and everybody danced with each other to a song which was in the charts at the time, '*La laisses pas tomber, tu sais c'est si difficile, Être femme libérée, c'est pas si facile.*' I waltzed across the floor with the scarred Lieutenant and as soon as the song was finished it was put on again.

Everybody joined arms and a bottle of whisky was passed round; we finished it between twelve of us in two or three minutes. The windows were thrown open and people began howling and screaming into the night as the drink mingled in our stomachs and the music got louder. I was in a deep embrace with a Rumanian mortarman when the door opened and Gibeau walked in. He saw Marius and myself and told us quietly and firmly to go back to our rooms. He would talk to us in the morning. People clung to our arms as we walked out and an Officer emptied Pernod over Gibeau's tunic, telling him that it was Christmas and that we had a right to enjoy ourselves. We walked out and staggered back to our beds, pushing out the dummies we had left there as decoys, using rolled up overcoats and our pyjamas. We fell asleep almost immediately but as I dropped off I heard Marius pissing over Macier as a Christmas present.

The next day was hungover and quiet; everybody wanted to know what we had got up to, and Girod told us that we would not be accompanying the section in town that afternoon. Marius and I were too tired to care, so carried on ironing regardless. Everybody else went out at 2.00 pm and at 3.00 pm Gibeau appeared, saying that we were free to go. We put on our *képis*, straightened our ties, pulled our fingers into regulation gloves and set off for the guardhouse. The afternoon was clear but cold and there was ice on the ground and frost still in the flowerbeds by the main gate. We saluted the Guard-Sergeant, slapping our palms down against our sides in regulation salutes, looking him in the eye and showing our leave passes. Through the little side gate, across the road, and we turned left to walk into Orange.

We stopped at the first bar we came to and walked inside, to where Johnson and Fleming, two English legionnaires, were drinking. We had a quick beer with them and teamed up with them as they knew the town better than us. Beer followed pizza and we looked round the Roman amphitheatre which had been built by Roman legionnaires 1,800 years before. Orange was a typical Provençal town, with streets lined with plane trees and houses with red and green shutters; the bars and restaurants were empty save for the Legion, and there was very little to do except spend money. All through our time at Canjuers, through the days of rain and abscesses on our hands, mud and sleeping in sodden clothes, we had dreamed of the moment when we would be able to walk into a cakeshop or bar and be able to buy what we wanted, but now that the choice was available, we did nothing about it. We had an expensive meal and tried to get drunk, but the evening had a forced feel to it as though it had been written on Orders that we would, compulsorily, enjoy ourselves. We sat in a bar with walls covered in red plush-velvet and watched the Rumanian Asioz chatting to the two waitresses. They had lowcut dresses and thick black eyeshadow, and one wore no shoes, toes crossed over each other from having her feet crammed into tight footware all her life. Marius jerked his head at them in disapproval but I liked their Romany appeal. Asioz bought them champagne, and they filled his glass with sparkling wine and their own with apple juice from a carton. He was so pissed he didn't notice. We smoked some dope with the girls and went to have an omelette. We ended up in the bar opposite the gates of the camp. This bar was run by an old woman who for twenty years had run a Legion brothel in Algeria before retiring to Orange after the Legion moved to mainland France. The woman ran a number of girls who were not technically prostitutes but more hostesses. They would chat and flirt with the legionnaires, making them buy champagne and other expensive drinks, in return for which they would provide female company and, if they found the legionnaire attractive, they would sleep with them. They found a lot of legionnaires attractive. I fell through the door with Marius and immediately started talking to a former member of the British Parachute Regiment who had known some friends of mine.

I asked him about the girls and he told me to offer them drinks, talk to them, spend 1,000 francs on them, and I would be away. I looked over to the corner where a pretty girl with long brown hair and freckles was sitting. I walked over and sat down. She smiled. I grinned lopsidedly and asked her if she wanted a drink. She did. We had several until I decided that it was time for me to sit on her lap. I stood up, suddenly slipped, and crashed across the table onto the floor. Standing up, I assured her that I wasn't drunk but tired and that I thought it was time for me to walk her home. She stood up, kissed me on the forehead, said '*Comme tu es mignon*' (How sweet you are), and walked away. Marius dragged me back to camp and afterwards I told the other legionnaires how she had wanted to sleep with me, but I had turned her down.

The next day was grim and hungover. We tidied up our rooms and cleaned the kitchens, dragging out the mundane tasks so that we could stay in the warm. We could clean swiftly and efficiently by now, and knew the special little ways that made a lavatory really white, or a tiled floor that bit more gleaming. We had two weeks to go before we finished basic training, and among those of us who had survived there was the blasé attitude of the old hand. We smoked without taking our cigarettes from our mouths and we shrugged like Frenchmen. I could talk to anybody in fluent French, and Marius had managed a good grasp of the language. Both of us strolled around the camp in an exaggerated swagger, saluting with panache and wearing our berets just above our eyes. I kept a book by John Mortimer in my side trouser pocket so that when I saluted, slapping my palm against my leg, there was a good cracking ring. I felt on top of things, and Marius and I had agreed that we would accompany each other to our respective regiments. The winter sun came out over the signals aerials on the top of the regimental headquarters and I warmed my neck, rubbing it against the collar of my knitted undershirt. We walked back to our rooms and packed up for our move to Nîmes. This was the last stage of our training, and would be based around a farm called Garrigues. We loaded the trucks up again and at 5.00 am on 27 December 1984, we left. The trucks were open at the back and we shivered as we climbed into the hills, Sergeant Major Barlerin in the jeep up ahead with Sergeant-Chef Gibeau.

At midday we reached Garrigues and piled out of the trucks to set up all our equipment in the farm building; it was better appointed than the one at Canjuers, and there was running water, lavatories, sinks and beds. At one point it had been somebody's house; the gardens were laid out with palm trees, yucca plants and arranged flowerbeds. There was curling, ornate moulding around the tops of the windows and coats of arms had been set into the metal work of the huge wrought-iron gate. In summer the gardens would have looked colourful and pretty but somehow in the depths of the Provençal winter they appeared melancholy. Gibeau set the tone of our stay at Garrigues by making us run and crawl around the house, singing all the time. He wasn't satisfied so we went down on our stomachs and leopard crawled.

Nîmes was unbelievably cold. One morning I went out into the garden to fetch some clothes from the washing line and walked past Gibeau, who was shooting sparrows with his assault rifle, as they fed on grain he had laid out for them. All the clothes on the line were frozen solid, as the water in them had iced as soon as we had put them out. The water in the sinks and basins froze, as well as the shithouses. There was a sheet of ice out in the courtyard from a burst pipe which had carried all the garbage from the kitchen with it. This meant that to go for a crap you had to take a shovel and dig a hole which was hard work when the ground was solid. It was difficult to shit cleanly. Obsessed as they were with hygiene and cleanliness, the Corporals had been worried ever since we had arrived at Orange that some of us were not adept at emptying our bowels neatly. To combat this recurrent worry, they had long since introduced random underpant inspections which could be sprung on us at the most absurd moment. In this way they assured that those among us who were anally lax or maladroit in the use of the hard, crunchy loo paper we used, would take care not to dirty their underpants. Since my episode with Moustaine during the first week of training, I had taken due care with my backside; but others hadn't got the point. At Canjuers we had been on the shooting range one afternoon, zeroing our FA-MASs on targets 200 metres away. It had been a bitterly cold day, and the gravel underfoot was frozen into tight lumps. Our hands had gone numb on the triggers of our weapons, and most of the staff, huddled against the wind under a group of scraggy pine trees, had lost their tempers due to our poor shooting. Suddenly Tambini had run over to where most of us stood, awaiting our turn at the firing point. He had shouted in French for a moment or two, then had screamed, 'Drop your trousers! Underpant inspection!' We were dressed up in combat jackets, parkas and webbing, rifles slung over our shoulders, and helmets on. Struggling with flies and belts we had dropped our trousers, taken down our underpants, and stood to attention, upper bodies wrapped against the slicing wind, hairy legs and bollocks going purple with cold. I was clear. Marius was clear. Mike had been lax with the Bronco. Vermulen, the Swiss man, had obvious stomach trouble and Wilkins's underpants looked as though a wild boar had been sick in them. Those who had failed had been made to scrub them there and then, using water from their water bottles and stones instead of soap.

At Garrigues, most of us tried to hold out as long as possible, preferring constipation to the risks of having a crap. Our barrack room was warm and we had a stove in the middle which kept us warm in the night. I had moved on to selling friends' addresses to the Chief-Corporal, and in return for the names and numbers of two Sloane girlfriends I had got the bed nearest the stove.

We spent our time at Garrigues doing a lot of shooting, both with

FA-MASs and pistols, and learning about explosives and mines. There was an old shooting range behind the farmhouse and we went up there one morning to put into practice all that we had learnt about explosives. We had been taught how to set up a simple charge with detonator and fuse. We had developed this principle by joining lumps of plastic explosive together with some machine gun cartridges to make a simple anti-personnel charge. We had stalked around the woods practising booby traps and trip devices, using thin wire and nails, and were getting good at setting nasty ambushes. Mike was adept at all this, and Gibeau, recognising a fellow enthusiast, had made him show us some of the techniques he had learnt in Rhodesia. We smeared mud (to simulate human excrement, which would infect wounds) on sharpened wooden stakes which we buried in holes in the path covered up with leaves and brush, and Gibeau showed us how to make a mine out of a spring, some ball bearings and a walnut-sized lump of plastic explosive. The point of this device was to spring the metal balls to stomach height only, so that they would tear through any human bodies within thirty feet.

We ran up to the firing range one morning to try out our destructive techniques for real. We broke open all the boxes of plastic explosives, fuses and detonators, and walked around with Sergeant-Major Barlerin looking for something to attach our bombs to. An old car which had been driven across in front of the shooting targets was ideal, so we attached fifteen kilos of the explosive to it in different places, fixed up the detonators, trailed fuse wire back several yards and clipped on the incendiary devices which would activate the firing process. There was a thick concrete wall which we were all going to hide behind and we had our helmets on in case any car parts came raining down out of the sky. We had thrown grenades before and used the LRAC rocket launcher so we were accustomed to the noise and strength of high-impact explosion. Gathered round the car, we watched Gibeau activate the device. We had two minutes to get into cover and walked round to the other side of the wall and crouched down with our hands over our ears and our helmets firmly strapped on. Mike advised me to keep my mouth open to absorb the blast on my ear drums. We waited for two minutes before the combined strength of thirty-five pounds of EP-12 plastic explosive tore the car apart. There was an air-displacing percussive whump combined with an ear-thudding explosive crack as the old Renault 4 was blasted thirty feet into the sky. The shock waves travelled through the wall and slammed into our heads and then there was silence as the dismembered vehicle fell through the air. Suddenly a hail of earth, stones, metal fragments, pieces of exhaust pipe and car door came down on us in a dust-covered mass. We all stood up and walked around the wall to where the car had been. There was a brown, ripped hole in the ground and a buckled, disgustingly distorted chassis torn and knotted on the side of the crater. The rocks and stones for thirty yards around had been flung outwards by the blast and an unlucky gorse-bush had been reduced and stripped to blackened twigs. We marched back to the farmhouse and had lunch.

The mail was waiting for us. Among it was a parcel for Mike from Harare. It contained a letter and some food. There were biscuits, sweets, chocolate and cigarettes. The Corporal who was with us at the time, a new one detached from Orange, immediately awarded Mike 2,000 press-ups. This was the usual practice when mail was given out: a recipient of a letter would normally get 150, two letters 300, and the penalties for a parcel were 500 and above depending on its contents. The parcel which Mike had received was a perfect target. In an organisation where a lot of people, through necessity or personal choice, were cut off from their families or friends at home, mail and letters took on a special importance. Most people would share their letters, reading them out to everybody else. We were all conversant with the problems of each other's friends and relatives. The Corporal had given Mike more press-ups than he could possibly hope to do, so the penalty had to be shared out among us all. We did 100 each and Mike shared out his parcel. We ate the biscuits and cake, and smoked his cigarettes, trying to swap things with him in return for the photo of his girlfriend. I read the letter. His girlfriend missed him and was miserable among the other whites in Harare. She wished he would leave the Legion altogether and come home. She didn't want to go and live in South Africa either. His daughter had never seen her father and had no idea of what he would be like. The girlfriend was miserable. Mike was silent and withdrawn that evening, and just after '*appel*' he beat the shit out of Macier who had put his feet on Mike's blankets.

We had finished everything we had come to do. The shooting was completed, and we had passed all our physical tests. We had completed our map reading and compass work and had tramped across the moors at night on a freezing combat endurance test where we map read our way from rendezvous to rendezvous. At each point we had been required to identify pictures of tanks, strip weapons in the dark, answer questions on mines and explosives, and demonstrate our radio technique. We were going to be interviewed by a selection team from Castelnaudary who would tell us our placings in the '*Certificat Technique Élémentaire*' exams.

We packed up all our kit again and set off back to Orange, across the frozen landscape of southern France, which was having one of the coldest winters in living memory. Snow was everywhere and there were television reports each night of blocked roads, stranded villagers and thick white fields of frozen cattle. Our trucks had open sides and Marius, Vermulen and I clung to each other, faces buried in our hoods, as we churned down the slushy autoroutes, the speed of the trucks sending icy, sawing winds through us at seventy kilometres per hour. We rested in a village at lunchtime where the phone lines lay across the side of the road and stretched into a field, and where the mayor welcomed us, his red face glowing underneath a huge fur hood. Flakes of snow settled on the muzzle of my rifle, and smoking a cigarette while wearing leather gloves left a gingery smell of burnt, nicotined hide in my gloved palm. We got back to Orange as dark fell.

I had come first in our exams and tests.

I could go to Corsica.

I stood in front of the selection team from Castelnaudary two days later. I told them that there was no doubt in my mind but that I wanted to be a paratrooper. I felt that although what we had done in Orange had been severe and shitty, in choosing to go to Calvi and the Airborne regiment, I was letting myself in for treatment and discipline I couldn't imagine. Having come this far, and having made the effort to come first, I reflected only briefly as the Commandant in front of me, with his four gold bars on his shoulders, signed a piece of paper and said, 'I'm posting you to the *2ème Régiment Étranger de Parachutistes*.'

— 5 —

LOVE WITH THE OVER-FIFTIES

The Lieutenant whirled his arm above his head and screamed, 'Get your parachutes on!'

We ran forward from the side of the runway where we had been standing smoking and stood behind our piles of parachutes and equipment. Sixty men grabbed their helmets and started to get kitted up for the parachute jump. It was 5.30 am at Calvi airport in Corsica and we were standing at the far end of the runway, just off the edge of the tarmac. At any moment the Transall C-160 aircraft would be arriving from its base at Orléans on the mainland. The runway lights had just been switched off and the sun was above the mountains behind the camp, 2,000 metres away on the edge of Calvi bay.

I shoved my beret into my inside pocket and strapped on my camouflage jump helmet, marked on the back with its black triangle containing a white figure 'one', which showed that I was from the 1st Section of the 3rd Company. These helmet markings simplified the process of rejoining your section on a crowded drop zone after a parachute jump. I bent forward, slipped my hands inside the straps of my main parachute and hoisted it on to my back, adjusting the pack so that it sat high up on my shoulders and so that the straps went through my legs and across my chest. Snapping shut the harness fastener, I attached my reserve parachute on to the chest straps, so that it sat across my front, just above my large equipment container which had my rucksack and FA-MAS in it.

Three officers, standing apart from the lines of men, turned and pointed over the bay to the north, where the landing lights of an aircraft could be seen in the sky. It landed before taxiing over to stop fifty yards away from where we stood for inspection by the Jump Masters, who checked our parachutes, the attachment of our containers and our helmets. When they got to the end of the line of men, they turned and signalled that we would be waiting five minutes before emplaning. I leant forward so that the combined weight of my parachutes and equipment would be taken off my shoulders. With my helmet, weapon, main and reserve parachutes as well as my rucksack in its harness on my legs, I was carrying almost the equivalent of my own body weight. All this was suspended from the harness of my main parachute so that I had seven stone in kit hanging off my shoulders.

The Air Load Master standing on the rear ramp of the Transall beckoned to us and we shuffled forwards in line on to the plane. We stepped up onto the ramp and into the fuselage which had four rows of webbing seats facing each other. The inside was cramped and smelt of aviation fuel; the sides of the aircraft were covered in panels, cables and instructions on emergency procedures. We flopped backwards on to the seats, lying half across each other in a tangle of legs and equipment while the Jump Masters clambered over our bodies, moving from one end of the plane to the other in their sequence of preflight checks. The rear ramp closed with a hydraulic whirr and the engines started, everything shuddering with the vibration of the two propeller motors. We taxied out straight on to the runway, and the aircraft pitched and swayed as the pilot awaited clearance for take off; the engines gathered power, the brakes came off and we accelerated down the airstrip, our bodies pushed sideways and backwards by the plane's momentum. Suddenly we were airborne, banking immediately over Calvi bay, climbing to reach our jump height of 1,000 feet.

The Jump Masters stood up and gestured to us to get up and attach our static lines to the cables, 'Stand up! Hook up!' Clambering to our feet, helping each other, we attached the clips on the ends of our static lines to one of the cables which ran the length of the aircraft. When we jumped out of the plane, the static line would pull taut and deploy the parachute out of its packing inside the bundles on our backs.

Stood up and hooked up, I checked my helmet for the dozenth time, pulling the chinstrap so tight that I couldn't open my mouth. The force of the slipstream of an aircraft travelling at 120 miles per hour could easily pull the helmet off if it wasn't firmly attached. Worse, the air turbulence could force the rim of it down over your eyes so that you were incapable of looking above you and checking your parachute.

The plane turned and straightened itself for the run in over the parachute drop zone of Fiume Secco, just outside Camp Raffalli. The Load Master opened the jump doors on either side of the aircraft and the tearing noise of the wind and slipstream filled the plane; the blue sea was visible on one side as the aircraft turned, and through the other door there was sky. Crammed against the side of the aircraft, we forced ourselves as close as possible to the man in front, so that on jumping out, we would be in a tight group. The plane would make two passes over the drop zone; two 'sticks' of fifteen men jumping out on each pass, one from either door, exiting the aircraft at half-second intervals. The 2ème Régiment Étranger de Parachutistes jumped faster, lower and more tightly grouped than any other airborne force in the world, and although the drop zone was only several hundred metres long, it was possible to get thirty-plus paratroopers on to it if the despatchers got the men out fast. They often didn't and the first one out would land in the sea, just before the start of the drop zone, and number fifteen ended up in the maquis, the dense Corsican undergrowth which covered half the island.

Pressed forward against the back of the man in front of me, one hand raised above my head holding my static line, the other gripping my equipment container, I was utterly scared at the thought of the jump ahead. We all had faith in our equipment and knew that parachute accidents were normally the result of human error, rather than equipment malfunctions. Men drifted too close to each other in the air and got entangled. Men jumped out of the aircraft badly, their parachute rigging lines twisted as they corkscrewed down the slipstream. Men didn't release their equipment containers in time, and landed with their packs on their legs, ruining their landings. Despite our faith in our equipment, the completely unnatural act of jumping out of a moving aircraft induced terror in most of us, especially in the moments immediately preceding the jump. Once the red light was on and you were on your way out, there was a sudden rush of exhilaration and adrenalin, coupled with the feeling that jumping out of aeroplanes was the one thing which differentiated us from other, non airborne units.

I was afraid of heights, but this wasn't why I was scared. My fear of heights was confined to climbing and swinging on ropes – in other words, situations where your body was in contact with the ground, either through a rope or on a cliff face. Jumping from an aircraft meant falling through 1,000 feet of airspace, where there was nothing to hold on to. The utterly foreign act of falling through 1,000 feet of sky, in however controlled or mechanically plausible a way, filled me with a terror so innate and subconscious that I knew that I hated it, without being able to understand why.

It was the stuff of nightmares. Falling fast through the air, then slower and slower and slower, till you touch down just so, and you are all right. But in between your breathing has gone haywire and your adrenalin levels have gone off the scale.

Every time I jumped, there would be a moment just before the jump lights went on when I cursed myself for not having stayed at home and chosen a safer profession. I knew how man must have felt when he crawled out of his cave in the morning to face a woolly mammoth, armed only with a spear. Pure terror. Primeval fear.

The first two men in each stick moved forward and crouched in the doors; the despatchers, Sergeants and Sergeant-Majors, held them steady, clearing their static lines with one hand, looking inward to the Jump Master who crouched with his hands over his headphones, listening to instructions from the pilot in the cockpit. He kept one eye on the red lights above the door. The two lines of men tensed, pushed forward and waited; suddenly the lights went on, the klaxon howled, and as the Transall screamed over the start of the drop zone at 120 mph, the despatchers yelled 'GO!' into the ears of the first two men and propelled them out into space.

Fifth back in the line, I stumbled and pushed forward towards the door, slammed my arm off the static line and over my reserve chute, saw the line whipped clear by the despatcher, heard him yelling 'Go! Go! Go!', took a half-step right into the doorway, closed my eyes and half-dived, half-fell out into the slipstream. The force of the aircraft's turbulence hurled me sideways horizontally, I felt my feet swing up in front of my face, my helmet slammed from behind, the thumping and tugging as my parachute was pulled clear from its pack, the feeling of falling at great speed totally out of control, sliding straight down the slipstream, then I was jerked upright, falling in a great swing as my canopy deployed and as I instinctively shouted, 'One thousand, two thousand, three thousand, check canopy!'

Bucking and twisting in my rigging lines, I threw my head back to look for any signs of malfunction, saw none, kicked myself out of a twist, took my hands off my reserve parachute, placed them on the parachute risers and looked down at the ground below me. The blue of Calvi bay stretched out in a curve, edged with pine forests, and over to the right was the town citadel set on its promontory of rock, with the shops and cafés on the front going down towards the beach. Swaying underneath the great khaki parachute, looking down at my feet, I saw the neat arrangements of the buildings of Camp Raffalli set around the parade ground. Around the camp was the drop zone, where an orange marker flare burned in the shape of a letter Alpha. The tangle of the *maquis*, green and inpenetrable spread out towards the base of the mountains, and I felt myself being blown gently inland, away from the pine forests around the sea. The harness constricted my movements, a tautness spreading out from my shoulders and groin whilst my container pressed against my legs. The other members of the stick were lowering their equipment on its suspension ropes, so I pulled the retaining pin loose on the top flap of my container and let it drop fifteen feet on its nylon rope, feeling the tugging jerk as it reached its full extension and swung below me. I was coming close to the ground and pulled my feet and knees tight together, tucked my chin into my chest and gauged the direction of my descent. I was drifting towards the middle of a track which ran across the landing area; two or three seconds before I hit the ground I felt my container land, then I rolled into my landing, taking the force of my impact across my shoulders, thighs and back, hitting the ground in a tangle of harness and suspension straps, the parachute inflating behind me.

I stood up, ran around to the apex of the canopy to deflate it, then unbuckled myself and rolled the chute up, repacking it in a haphazard manner before picking up my equipment container from where it lay on the track, extracting my FA-MAS, before setting off across the drop zone at a sloping run to the rallying point.

We had travelled from Orange to Aubagne, before catching the ferry to Bastia, on the opposite side of Corsica from Calvi. We had got drunk in Aubagne, and Mike and Marius had had a bitter fight over a triviality which had left Mike in hospital in Marseilles and Marius in the hands of the Military Police. He had been released from custody to travel with us, had been cautioned by the Colonel, and was now training with us.

On arrival at Calvi, we had been told that we would spend three weeks undergoing airborne training before being posted to our companies. The base, Camp Raffalli, was named after a former commander of the regiment who had distinguished himself in Indo-China, and was set 500 metres from the beach on the main road which linked Calvi to L'Île Rousse and Bastia. Set around an immaculate *Place d'Armes*, or parade ground, the camp was made up of cream-coloured buildings with red-tiled roofs. A network of tarmac roads led around and through the camp, with groves of pine trees growing in the sandy ground. The entire area was immaculately clean and most of the areas of sand and gravel in front of the buildings were raked into straight lines. At the top of the parade ground was the monument to every legionnaire paratrooper who had been killed in Indo-China, Algeria, Chad, Zaire or Lebanon. Each Company had a three-storey block with a gravel parade ground in front of it. Above the entrance to each unit's building was a shield or plaque displaying its insignia: the owl, signifying the specialisation of the 1st Company in nocturnal warfare; the edelweiss of the mountain Company; the trident of Neptune for the amphibious 3rd Company; and the lightening flash of the 4th, who specialised in sabotage and destruction. Around and behind, were the garages, kitchens and storerooms of the administrative company and the heavy weapons unit. On each of the buildings in the camp, a black metal rail ran along the edge of the roof at the level of the guttering; because of the proximity of the drop zone, this was to prevent any man unlucky enough to land on the roof from falling off.

Our group was billeted off to the edge of the camp; collectively we were called a '*promotion*', which meant that we had joined the Regiment but had not been awarded the para wings required before we could be posted to one of the Companies. We were put in the care of a Tunisian Sergeant who was also a parachute instructor. We spent three weeks being trained by him, getting up before it was light, running everywhere, learning the regimental songs, swimming in the sea and learning all there was to know about parachuting. We were looked on by the rest of the Regiment as beginners, and sometimes older members of the unit would drop by our building to regale us with tales of what it was like in the companies. There was one English Corporal who made a habit of telling each new '*promotion*' how proficient and excellent a soldier he was. He worked in the pay office. He was standing in our shower room one morning when another Englishman walked in. Nicholas, the Pay-Corporal, spun round on the ball of his foot in a single swift movement. 'I saw you in the mirror before you came in. Old habit of mine that. Saved my life in Belfast once.' Nicholas claimed to have served in the English Parachute Regiment and with the Intelligence Services in Northern Ireland. We all doubted the truth of his stories and thought him a complete prat.

As at Orange, time was in short supply and cleanliness was considered important. I managed to get the process of having a shower down to three minutes: undress, throw towel around waist, into shower, cover body with shower gel, rinse, wash hair with soap, dry and dress. We had different fragrances of shower gel. The regimental foyer sold a brand called 'Tahiti Douche' which came in four types: sea-mist, lavender, wild rose and essence of pine.

We spent hours on the training area learning about parachutes and how to pack them, fold them, carry them and put them on. We sat in a mock up of a Transall in the training area, swung on the wires and cables which simulated the feeling of being under a parachute, and we learnt the hundreds of technical details connected with jumping. We ran our eight kilometre battle run again, which I managed in thirty-six minutes, and we climbed ropes in the gym. I lost more weight than I had at Orange, and after three weeks was down to nine stone. We learned the history of the Regiment and its traditions, we practised unarmed combat and we sang everywhere we went.

After three weeks we made our first parachute jump. We kitted up early in the morning and jumped from 1,500 feet, in sticks of five. As we gained confidence, the size of the sticks increased and on our third jump we had equipment containers. We jumped at Borgo on the other side of the island and at Calvi; on our last jump, there was a strong wind blowing and we exited the aircraft directly over the camp. We were blown all over the drop zone, into fields at the other side of the road, into trees, and into the *maquis*. One of our section landed on top of a stationary car, and it took us most of the afternoon to retrieve our chutes from the eucalyptus groves and the sharp thorn bushes. Didier, a Frenchman who had come from Castelnaudary, was dragged along a muddy track on his face. He tore his uniform and ripped his parachute to pieces in the thorn bush which finally stopped his progress through the mud. His face was cut and bleeding as well, and when he had finally retrieved his parachute he had been escorted off to the sick wing, almost blinded by the gravel and earth which had been forced into his eyes.

Two days later we paraded in front of the regimental Colonel to be awarded our parachute wings and our red lanyards, which signified that we were fully fledged members of the *2ème Régiment Étranger de Parachutistes*. Our silver wings were pinned on our chests and our lanyards placed round our shoulders; the Colonel shook each of us by the hand and made a short speech about what it meant to be a '*Légionnaire Parachutiste*'. There was a celebration afterwards set around some tables in the sun on the edge of the drop zone. We had a barbecue and there was lots of beer and Pernod. The Colonel was present with the Regiment's senior Officers.

All of our '*promotion*' had been allocated to the 1st Company, apart from a small group who were going to the 3rd Company which specialised in underwater and amphibious warfare. This group consisted of Marius, myself, two Frenchmen and an ex Royal Marine called Slug. Slug came from Middlesborough and had a dry sense of humour and tattoos on both arms. He had served in the Royal Marines for nearly five years, had fought in the Falklands and completed two tours of Northern Ireland. Taller than me by four or five inches, he had a wild laugh and an ability to bring his sense of humour to bear on all the ridiculous and mundane situations which we found ourselves in from day to day. He had lived with a prostitute in Plymouth for six months which had suited him well as she earned a lot of money and as all he had to do was to vacate the bed by midday. She spent her time fucking Royal marines and sailors whom she met in pubs in Plymouth. Slug used to receive long love notes from her in which she declared her affection for him and swore that when he came home they would have children together. I knew very little of Slug's childhood or early life, as we generally talked about that which we had in common – the army. Myself, Marius and Slug got on well together and had all asked to be sent to the 3rd Company so that we could stick together. Having spent four months in Orange deliberately not getting to know people, because I knew that we would be split up at the end of training, it was good to have two people with me whom I could count as friends. My time in the Legion so far had been a transient period; being posted to the 3rd Company was the first time that any of us three would be with the same group of people for any length of time. Perhaps now I would be able to make some friends and get to know other people properly.

After the barbecue, we had packed up our kitbags and shouldered them over to our Company buildings to present ourselves to the Captain, the Company Sergeant-Major and our Section Commander. He was a Yugoslavian called Lodvic who had served all of his thirteen years in the Legion in the same section of the same company of the *2ème Régiment Étranger de Parachutistes*, starting as a legionnaire and working his way from Corporal and Sergeant to his present position as Section Commander. He would be directly in charge of us, and his decisions would ultimately decide whether or not our lives were bearable or utter hell. He dictated how the Section was run and how the new legionnaires were treated, made all the decisions regarding discipline and welfare, and was responsible for our training as professional soldiers. Adjutant Lodvic was six foot five, walked with a stooping gait, wore a large waterproof Rolex and had his head shaved into a cropped Mohican cut. He had served in Beirut, Chad and at Kolwezi, where he had earned himself the 'Médaille de La Valeur Militaire'. In his office there was a poster sized blowup of a photograph which had been taken by somebody else from the first section at Kolwezi. It showed the then Sergeant Lodvic in combat kit, beret tilted across his shaved scalp, dragging a rebel out of a hut in a village surrounding the town of Kolwezi. The terrorist's face was screwed up in terror as Lodvic propelled him forward by the scruff of the neck. Behind him another legionnaire crouched with his sub-machine gun at the ready; we heard that there was another photo, taken afterwards, showing Lodvic placing the barrel of his MAT-49 in the rebel's mouth and blowing his head off. As a Section Commander Lodvic had a reputation for being hard and fair, and some people called him 'Papa'.

The Section was composed of thirty-two people: eighteen legionnaires and fourteen Corporals and Sergeants. It was sub divided into four groups of eight men each, one group being the HQ element, and the other three being combat groups. Each of these was in turn made up of a marksman, armed with an FRF-1 sniper's rifle, a legionnaire who carried and fired the LRAC 89mm rocket launcher and another who humped the rockets and acted as loader. The other five members of the group were armed with FA-MAS assault rifles. The headquarters group comprised the Adjutant, the Sergeant-Chef who was second in command, a signals expert, the medic and four others, two of whom manned the FM heavy machine gun. We had a lot of firepower at our disposal.

Still feeling pissed after the Pernod we had drunk at our barbecue, we wheeled in to meet the Captain of the Company, a limp Frenchman called Trousseau who welcomed us and told us that we would have no problems fitting in if we pulled our weight. His uniform shirt bore few medal ribbons and his voice lacked authority. His forearms were almost hairless and his watch slipped over his slim wrist. I saluted and walked out. We then met the Company Sergeant-Major, an Arab called Benmoudi, who was a parachute instructor and who had a huge, wide chest. He spelt my name 'Djenigs' on the list and greeted us, slapping us in a friendly way across the shoulders with an arm like a lump of wood. He was pleased to hear that we had all had some previous military service, and cocked his head, interested, when Slug mentioned the Falklands and Northern Ireland. He told us that there were plenty of Englishmen in the company, and that morale was high since the unit's return from Chad the year before.

I liked the look of the 3rd Company, with its hard, professional Non Commissioned Officers. Marius, Slug and myself felt that we were moving closer to the heart and spirit of the French Foreign Legion, which we knew existed but whose whereabouts had been hidden and blurred through all the months of bog-cleaning and ironing which had made up our basic training. There was an air of purpose and élitism in the men moving around the camp. Hair was short, most men wearing it cut in the regulation mohican crop; legionnaires and Corporals saluted Officers and Sergeants as they walked around the barracks; lorries and jeeps drove hither and thither; Transalls roared overhead disgorging men on to the drop zone; and whole sections marched past at a go, singing their hearts out. Everything moved at the double, and there was no sense of slackness or lack of direction. The camp was impeccably tidy, the insides of the buildings spotlessly clean with everything in place, and underneath the differences of rank was the shared feeling of belonging to an élite regiment.

Hefting our kitbags again, we marched into the barracks of the 1st Section and presented ourselves to each Corporal in turn, before being allocated our beds in one of the eight-man rooms. These were sparse and bare, with faded wallpaper and grey metal lockers. The beds were iron and the mattresses stained, covered with red bedspreads, blankets stacked at the ends, sheets crossed over them. Lockers were open, clothes immaculately folded in the same thirty-five centimetre blocks we had learnt in Orange. Boots were polished and laid out in rows on wooden boards on the floor, next to regimental Adidas trainers. There were no slippers. Corporals and legionnaires walked in and out, green berets tilted over their eyes, ironed black tassels hanging down the backs of their shaved heads. Each man wore the emblem of the *2ème Régiment Étranger de Parachutistes* on his beret. This was in the form of a seven-winged fist holding a sword. Each room housed two Corporals and six legionnaires, the Corporals responsible for the cleanliness of the room and the general discipline within each group. The rooms, showers and toilets were swept, mopped and cleaned three times a day, and would be inspected by the Duty-Corporal after each cleaning. As the new boys, it was normal that we should be detailed all the shitty jobs; this was accepted practice, so the five of us would be doing a lot of cleaning until some new people arrived in the Section to supersede us. The Corporals in our room were Antonin, a Spaniard, and Carver, a thin muscular Englishman who had attended a public school in Hertfordshire. He had joined up with another Briton called Johns, from the same school, at the same time. Johns was the fittest man in the Section and was being groomed to join the Regiment's reconnaissance section, who specialised in high altitude freefall parachuting and advanced soldiering.

I was still drunk as I unpacked. I fumbled around folding my kit and preparing my locker. Next door, Marius, who was even drunker than myself, was being beaten up in the showers by three Corporals. He had told a Spanish corporal, Oliviera, that he was fucked if he was going to do as he was told by a spic.

Carver told me in detail about the Regiment. The 3rd Company was due to leave for Djibouti in East Africa in three weeks' time, and until then we would be occupied preparing our tropical kit, getting vaccinated, and having lectures on hygiene and first aid. He told me about the Sergeants in the Section and how to treat them, and about the discipline in the *2ème Régiment Étranger de Parachutistes*. It was equivalent to that we had experienced at Orange. There was '*appel*' and locker inspection twice a day, there was a veto on speaking anything but French, and violence was used as the normal method of enforcing discipline.

The Regiment had moved to Corsica in 1967 after the end of French colonial rule in Algeria. It was while they were in the doldrums awaiting disbandment after the unsuccessful coup in Algiers that their Commander had decided to form a unit consisting of specialised fighting companies, each one trained in a different form of warfare. Two kilometres behind the camp the mountains began, and there was snow on top of them until June; the mountain company was able to practise its skiing and kept a chalet at Vergio in the interior of the island where they held specialist mountain training courses. In front of the camp was the *maquis* leading down to the beach, where the 3rd Company had their amphibious warfare training centre, which was stocked with Zodiac rubber dinghies complete with outboard motors, and which contained a workshop and store with advanced scuba diving equipment. Behind the citadel in the town of Calvi were two old forts, one of which had housed the regimental prison until it had been closed when a prisoner had died in custody. This building, Fort Charley, was now the base of the regimental police and the site of an assault course built on and around its battlements and towers. Both the 1st and the 4th Companies trained extensively on this course, practising sabotage and commando techniques. The surrounding countryside in the region was used for training and exercises, and we would go for long runs in the surrounding hills and moorlands every morning, running fast through the heather and gorse which surrounded the vineyards owned by local farmers. The airport was two kilometres away from the camp, and Transalls would arrive from Orléans; it was possible to make parachute jumps quickly and efficiently due to the proximity of the drop zone and the airstrip. A Transall could land, pick up fifty paratroopers, take off and disgorge them over the drop zone within twenty-five minutes. Calvi was five kilometres away and provided a source of drink and fun for legionnaires on their evenings out.

There was little to do in camp when we were not involved in training. There were few books to read, but we did have pornographic French comics, most of which revolved around the activities of three main characters. There was the series about Zara, the nymphomaniac vampire, who rampaged through eighteenth century France in a frenzy of bloodsucking and sex with peasants, servant boys and well-endowed noblemen. She had an insatiable sexual appetite and you could guarantee that every third page there would be a sex scene. This was an advantage as legionnaires would often tear out the pages, so even if you came across one which had been half-destroyed, there could still be some fun left in it. I preferred the stories about Ophelia and Jeff. Ophelia was very beautiful, with long blonde hair and a plunging neckline. She got to be fucked by Jeff frequently, although Jeff was a revoltingly ugly dwarf who had been transformed from being a beautiful Prince by a wicked witch. Jeff would occasionally revert to his normal, handsome form just to remind Ophelia that underneath his bewitched dwarfishness lay something else.

Leaving behind the fantasy world of the '*bande dessinée*', Marius, myself and Slug went out in the evening after our arrival in the Company. Carver told us where best to go, and instructed us on the formalities of leaving camp. We had to iron our uniforms immaculately and scrub our *képis* until they were completely white, without a trace of windblown dust or dirt on them; parachute wings had to be polished and our hair cut almost bald. Most of the legionnaires had their scalps shaved every ten days, keeping it a fraction longer on the top than on the sides, in the style of a Cherokee Indian. Not only did very short hair look uniformly smart, but it was easier to keep clean which was hygienic and time saving. We picked up our leave passes at 6.00 pm, saluted the Sergeant on duty at the guard house, and went through the gate to catch a taxi. Each of us had 1,500 francs (about £150), which we were prepared to spend in one evening as Calvi was astronomically expensive. Standing underneath a clump of eucalyptus trees opposite the camp, we smoked and waited for a cab. In front of the barracks, a sentry in parade uniform stood at ease, FA-MAS slung across his chest, white *képi* on his head. The golden metal letters of 'CAMP RAFFALLI' and '2ÈME RÉGIMENT ÉTRANGER DE PARACHUTISTES' stretched out in gilded capitals along the wall to one side of him. Directly behind was the flagpole with its tricolour flag, which was taken down each evening before sunset.

The Bar Select had a jukebox in the corner and a bar running the length of the room; a girl with long brown hair and tattooed arms was serving drinks. Marius and myself toasted each other in Pernod and Crème de Menthe and I put a Bruce Springsteen record on the jukebox. There was little to do in Calvi in the evening except eat, drink, and look at the expensive shops. Most legionnaires followed a strict routine on their evenings off. Two or three hours' drinking followed by a meal at a restaurant which preceded the serious celebrations which normally went on till 3.00 am or 4.00 am. Then they would catch a taxi back to camp, stopping off at the Dolce Vita restaurant for twenty minutes drunken sex with one of the whores.

The three of us walked round Calvi looking at the shops. There were expensive boutiques and camping stores which had extensive selections of knives and other hardware for the legionnaires. Everything was expensive: the beer cost nearly £1 a bottle, and the meal we ate at a restaurant overlooking the yachts in the harbour came to 700 francs, because Marius had steak and lobsters as well as crabs. He started to eat the shells on the crabs until the waitress stopped him. None of us had had crab before and thought this was how you ate it. We discussed the contents of his letter from his girlfriend in Sweden. Her name was Carina and she had sent a photograph; she had ash-blonde hair and was sitting on the lawn at home in a white T-shirt and jeans. Marius said that she was coming to Calvi in the summer after we got back from Djibouti. I looked forward to it. Slug said he wanted to fuck her but Marius said she was a good girl and didn't chase after people like him. Slug laughed and said that once she had caught sight of the tattoo on his inner thigh she wouldn't be able to resist him.

We were bored and there was nothing to do except get more drunk. I suggested the Dolce Vita so we caught a taxi back towards the camp. Inside the restaurant was a huge bar with half a dozen legionnaires playing pool and chatting to the girls who were waiting to be bought drinks. We deposited our *képis* which one of the girls hung on the optics and were approached by a woman in a leopard-skin leotard and black stockings who looked a badly-preserved fifty. She asked if we were going to buy her a drink, so Marius slid a mineral water towards her. She took one sip, leant over and whispered: '*Si on fait l'amour?*'

Marius snorted into his Kronenbourg and I followed her downstairs to a room which contained a turquoise fur carpet, a double bed and deep brown walls. In the corner was a sink and a bidet and whilst she peeled off her leotard she told me to go and wash before getting into bed; I took off my tunic and tie and laid them out on a chair before soaping my hands and washing my face. She cursed in French, walked over, grabbed the soap and tore my trousers down. Naked, I walked over to the bed where she set her watch and started muttering endearments meant to excite me, 'Mm . . . do anything you want to me. Oh, *Mon Dieu*, you're so huge . . . I don't know if I can fit you all in. Come over here . . . we've got all the time in the world. I love soldiers when they make love to me . . . they're so in control . . . so fierce . . .'

I didn't know if she meant it, as my ardour had been savagely depleted by the effects of eleven hours of Crème de Menthe and wine. There was no way that I would be able to get it up. I told her that it would be better if we didn't do anything, so we sat and talked for the remaining twelve minutes. I told her about London, about my parents' house in Wales. I dressed, gave her 250 francs, kissed her sloppily and walked out. On my way upstairs I passed one of the other prostitutes' rooms where a huge Czechoslovakian Sergeant from the 2nd Company was lying in the arms of a black woman explaining that all he wanted was a hug.

Marius and I crawled into bed at 3.00 am, only to be woken two and a half hours later for '*appel*'. Everybody dragged outside in their tracksuits and stood there in the pre-dawn chill while the Duty-Sergeant counted us. In between 5.30 am and 7.30 am we had to clean the rooms, mop the floors, clean the showers and loos, wipe the windows and mop the corridors. Most of this fell to us five new boys. During our first weekend with the section, Marius and I got drunk with some of the others. Sitting at a table in the barrack room with Pete the Royal Marine and Josh from Dublin, we talked about the first section. The group was joined by Mick, who had a tattoo on his arm saying that he was an airborne warrior, and by Max, the illegitimate son of a legionnaire who had fought in Indo-China. It was after '*appel*' and the lights were out. A candle burned in a pool of wax on the plastic-topped table. Two empty crates of Kronenbourg were thrown on the floor and another one opened, the five of us prising off the tops with our lighters. I was having the piss taken out of me for having a middle class accent.

'I bet your sisters go to fucking gymkhanas,' said Pete, running the glowing end of his Marlboro round the rim of a bottle.

'And fuck blokes with stupid surnames.' This from Josh, slurping his beer and grinning, his ears stretching out from his head, looking over-large because he had no hair.

'They haven't met me yet, then, have they?' smiled Mick. 'I tell you exactly what I'd do. I'd take the youngest one, what's her name? Perpetua, that's it. I'd take her out . . . very nice, all quiet, like, start off with the prawns, couple of bottles of Blue Nun, all going OK . . . not touching her. She'd love it. Prawns all right, darling? Plenty of chat. I know all about those convents, I do. Just dying for it, they are. I've heard they have to have the door knobs out of harms way, just in case. Anyway, on to the steak, another bottle of Blue Nun. Lean over and whisper in her ear about how she'd like to come round and meet the blokes, nothing flash, just Terry, Ronnie . . . p'raps Ginge, too . . . yeah, bring Ginge . . . deserves it, he does, working all day on that market stall . . .'

I was enjoying this. After all, what can you say when you've sold your sisters to a dwarf Corporal on a rainy day in a field full of mud?

'She hasn't met the Royal Marines, yet . . .'

'Don't interrupt, you bootneck cunt. Let me finish. So there we are. Finish the main course, another bottle of the old Nun, ice cream, all the trimmings. Lean over, grab her hand, gentle, like . . . light her Sambucca for her . . . then lean in, nuzzle her ear lobe a bit . . . no biting, just getting started. She'll be dying to come round the house by this time. Pay up . . . flash the wedge a bit to impress her. Then it's a cab over to my house . . . Oooh, I can just see it. She wouldn't know what's hit her.'

'I bet she'd love it, Christian. Or perhaps you wouldn't know. You might be a virgin.'

'Piss off.'

Over in the corner, somebody groaned for silence. Mick threw an empty beer bottle, which smashed on the wall above the bed. Just out of candle's reach, there was a stirring underneath the blankets and a subdued, steamy hiss. Slasher Moulton had just pissed his bed again.

I was drunk and the scene around me seemed perfect. Here I was, being accepted by the gang, in with the boys, the 3rd Company, the real '3rd Reich' as they called themselves. Beers were passed round, Marlboros lit up, and we drank on. The windows were steamed and the curtains half-closed. The candlelight flashed off the silver parachute wings on a dress uniform hanging on a cupboard. The table was a mess of ash and bottletops and the third crate was nearly empty. Marius was displaying a prodigious thirst and was telling Josh how he regularly used to beat up immigrants.

'So what are we going to call him, then?' asked Pete, trying to come up with a nickname for me.

'No clue . . . got to get it right . . . what about Jenny?'

'Come on, Mick, all the other sections would think we were gay or something . . . We need something like Oswald, or Nigel.'

Josh ventured Rupert.

'Can't do that,' said Mick. 'The 3rd Section's already got one.'

'I think pratface would be fine,' said Mick, 'till he's proved himself.'

Mick grabbed two empty beer bottles, turned sideways on his chair, pulled his cock out of his sports shorts and filled them both with piss. He put them under my bed.

'Something for you to do in the morning.'

I wanted to go to bed, but couldn't leave the table until the others got up to go. It was nearly 2.00 am and we were up in three hours. It was Monday and we had amphibious training.

'I know,' howled Josh, 'you're a Wilfred!'

'Make it Wilf, sounds better.'

'Yeah, that's it.' They all smiled.

'You're Wilf.'

Pete leaned back and finished the last of his beer, the candlelight dancing off his acne.

A list of names was posted on the notice board that morning and those mentioned were told to report to the amphibious centre after afternoon parade. There were thirty of us who went to the magazine to draw weapons and I was given the LRAC 89mm rocket launcher for the afternoon. This was a fibreglass tube which was light but bulky, and a nuisance to carry; it came with a sophisticated telescopic sight which enabled you to hit tanks 500 metres away, but which needed careful looking after. The system for dealing with kit losses or breakages was simple: the offender was required to write out on a plain piece of paper a report to the Captain explaining what had been lost, where, when and how. This was simple enough, except for the method of laying out the report, which had to be done with a degree of graphical skill and precision that would have astounded a professional draughtsman. The lines had to be exactly half a centimetre apart, the name and rank of the offender positioned in a certain way at the top of the paper, and the whole article perfectly laid out. For somebody who could just write this presented massive problems, but even for the more intelligent among us it meant sitting up with a candle until 3.00 am. When the Captain received the report, he would make the loser pay for a new version of whatever he had lost. On the notice board outside the company office was a huge list of all the equipment we used, from compasses and maps to lorries and jeeps. They were all very expensive. If I lost my telescopic sight that afternoon it would mean that I wouldn't be getting any pay for twelve months.

We assembled at the amphibious centre. There were a small number of staff from our Company based there permanently, chosen for their amphibious excellence. It was considered a good attachment, as in the summer there were a lot of tourists to impress as you roared around in a Zodiac or emerged from the surf in a black wetsuit wielding a diving knife. One of the Corporals there told me how he had developed a series of chat-up lines based entirely around amphibious terms, such as asking Swedish tourists if they could help him take off his wetsuit, or emerging from the surf after a parachute jump and pretending to have nearly drowned.

We put on life jackets, cold, wet and salty. Mine had sand rimmed around the inside of its wet plastic collar which rubbed against the inside of my neck as I struggled with its flapping, soggy bulk. We climbed into Zodiac rubber dinghies and bounced across the waves out into the bay. Spray jumped up and soaked us and sea water ran down my neck. The life jacket rubbed. My hands were cold. A TV crew from *Antenne 2*, a major French station, had come to Calvi to film the regiment on exercise as part of a programme they were making called '*C'est La Vie*'. They were on the beach with their cameras waiting for us, and all we had to do was to line up our Zodiacs, speed at full throttle towards the beach, disembark and charge over the shingle in a display of controlled military aggression. Just before we did this, a small team would land ahead of us having 'wave jumped' from a Puma helicopter. This involved wearing a wetsuit, packing your FA-MAS in a waterproof sleeve and jumping straight out of the side door of the helicopter as it sped along fifteen feet above the sea. It was a risky process, wearing flippers, controlling your equipment with one hand and holding your diving mask with the other, as the impact of hitting the water at that speed was considerable.

From where we sat in our Zodiacs, 500 metres offshore, we could see the camera crew setting up on the beach; we had been told that one or two of us might be interviewed by a female journalist afterwards.

The camouflaged Puma went overhead. Pete, Hapipi, Andres and Carver fell in pairs, sideways out of the doors and into the sea. We could just see their heads bobbing above the waves as they swam ashore. They crawled out of the surf, dropped their flippers and took cover in the bushes beyond the edge of the shingle. The Sergeant-Major in charge of our group raised his hand and let it drop forward in a chopping motion. The legionnaires on the outboards opened up the engines, the Zodiacs lifted in the water and we moved towards the shore abreast, the waves frothing and foaming about us. On the beach the cameras pointed straight at us. I knelt up, grasped my rocket launcher and prepared my legionnaire's scowl. Sunglasses were forbidden but I saw a Corporal knotting a discreet headband in one of the other boats. We roared at the beach, felt the propellers touch bottom, then the Sergeants at the front of each Zodiac screamed '*Allons-y!*' and thirty camouflaged amphibious paratroopers rose as one out of the boats, leapt on to the beach and into film. Twenty-nine charged up the beach. I stood up to jump through the surf, caught my foot on a rope at the bottom of the boat, tripped, and executed a neat somersault backwards into six feet of water. I scrabbled on the sea bed for my rocket launcher, not looking forward to a year's penury, and waded onto the shingle, my clothes so heavy with water that I couldn't run. The camera caught me perfectly.

We squatted in the bushes for ten minutes while the reporter interviewed Thierry, before emerging to stand in a line as the film crew chatted to the Sergeants. The director, a coughing middle-aged man in cowboy boots and a sheepskin coat waved a clipboard at us while his assistants stumbled around dismantling the camera. The reporter was squat and plump. Thirty pairs of eyes mentally undressed her. She lurched across the shingle, unsuitable boots with heels sinking in the stones.

Three months later in Africa we saw a video of the programme. I shamed the whole company with my farce, and Corporal Thierry, who had never considered that his friends might watch the video, told the woman that he had joined the Legion because he enjoyed a life of violent action and because he saw the purity of combat as the only answer to a mediocre world. Then he asked for her address.

We were off to Africa a week later. We had been issued with our tropical kit, which included regulation issue sunglasses, a huge khaki headscarf called a '*cheche*', shorts, lightweight shirts and canvas boots. We had had lectures on tropical diseases, on how to avoid sunstroke and dehydration, and on how the African heat affected the European metabolism. Our lecture on the social life in Africa was given by Sergeant Loup, a Frenchman who had completed tours of duty in Chad, the Central African Republic and Djibouti. From his descriptions of life in Africa with the Legion, we got a picture of heat, disease, hard work, ill health and dust. Europeans found the temperatures and filth debilitating and were prone to infections, hepatitis, malaria and blood poisoning. We had been warned again and again that it was unwise to drink alcohol in tropical climates, as it lowered the body's resistance. We all drank too much. The mid morning snack break was accompanied by a couple of Kronenbourgs and at lunchtime in the cookhouse there was a selection of soft drinks, beer or wine. The foyer was open after lunch so you could guzzle three or four beers then, and in the evening all the English headed down for the session in the foyer, two or three tables pushed together, crates of beer piled up, ash swimming in spilt Kronenbourg. Going out in Calvi involved thirteen or fourteen hours of mixed alcohols. We were all very fit, so our tolerance to drink was increased. It seemed pointless to go out in town without getting totally plastered. It wasn't escapist drinking where we tried to obliterate the miseries of the day or the rigours of the Legion; it was alcohol consumption taken to its final conclusion: an empty Malibu bottle and an unconscious legionnaire.

A poster had been put up outside our section building showing the effects of the African sun on the unsuspecting soldier. Beneath a headline saying 'Watch out for sunstroke' there was a picture of a skeleton lying stretched out across an expanse of red sand, bones protruding from his boots. This had been taken in Chad the year before by one of the members of the 3rd Company. It was the corpse of a Chadian soldier caught in a rocket attack. Alongside the poster was a list of recommendations from Capitaine Trousseau on how to enjoy a healthy, happy, tour of Africa. He advised against drinking, sunbathing, eating local food or whoring.

He was being optimistic.

Take a legionnaire, coop him up in the middle of the desert for six weeks, fuck him around senselessly, make him perform mindless military rituals, keep him thirsty, and don't let him near any women. Make him drive around the scorched wilderness of East Africa in summer in an open truck, ration his water, make him eat vile food and beat him up occasionally. While he is in camp, inspect his locker twice a day, add on plenty of shithouse duties, throw in lots of ironing and don't let him speak his own language. Restrict his privacy so that he can't even wank in peace and don't give him enough sleep. Keep him up half the night once he comes back from the desert and make him clean his rifle till it gleams. Then, suddenly, give him £800 in local currency, dress him up in a ruthlessly smart uniform, with gleaming para wings and bright lanyard, and let him out in town. A town where every street has five or six bars and each bar has ten prostitutes. A town where every single female inhabitant costs 5,000 Djiboutian francs (about £25) to fuck. A town where money can buy anything. Get him drunk first, of course, and then, in swift succession make six fifteen-year-old black girls sit on his lap. And ask him to show self-control. Ask him to put his *képi* back on and say, 'No thanks, I'm fine.' Ask him to pretend that his hormones aren't going barmy and that he hasn't got a hard on that could poleaxe a rhino. Optimistic, our Captain.

Tell him that there is no stigma attached to venereal disease and that all he has to do is pay for the Tetracycline injections required to cure it. Create an atmosphere where he's one of the boys if he gets the clap. Tell him syphilis is just like NSU and don't tell him that most of the prostitutes have a deadly, unknown disease called Green Monkey Fever. Tell him that on his afternoons off he can fuck one of the whores in the Company brothel, one of the four shared between 130 men. Optimistic.

Give him a quick medical check when he gets back and so long as he's not pissing blood or discharging pints of pus then he's fine. He can go home on leave to the mainland and see his wife or girlfriend. Pick up a teenage tourist on the ferry, even. Or keep him in Corsica, send him down the Dolce Vita. Or let him loose in town. Optimistic and irresponsible.

But I didn't know. I didn't care. I was off to Africa.

On the day of our departure, we put on our summer walking out uniforms and paraded with all our kit to wait for the coaches which would take us to Bastia airport. From there we would fly to Djibouti City, capital of the Republic of Djibouti, which lay on the Red Sea, squeezed in between Somalia and Ethiopia. We took the coach, drove across the mountains and squeezed into the civilian passenger jet in our best uniforms. I was next to Slasher Moulton and I was very excited. I had never been this far from home before, and to me Africa was the continent of Wilbur Smith books, where the skies were plum-coloured velvet and every dawn an orgasm. I hadn't sweated it out in Chad with the rest of the boys, and was looking forward to the biggest adventure of my life. There was Slug across the aisle, telling a joke to Marius, there was Corporal Carver behind me, passing round a photo of a girl from England. There was Slasher next to me, talking about life in South Africa, and two rows back was Adjutant Lodvic to look after us. The Company Sergeant-Major told us to keep our uniforms clean while we were travelling, but to no avail. An airline meal was served halfway through the flight, and as the plane turned over Egypt heading for the Sudan and Djibouti, I spilt my chicken provençale down my shirt front.

I was off to Africa.

6

PAINTING WINDOWS AND SHOOTING PUPPIES

I opened a tin of pâté with my combat knife and spread it on the slice of hard bread. I took it over to Sergeant Loiseau who was leaning on the bonnet of the truck, looking at the map. The four lorries of the 1st Section were drawn up on the edge of a track overlooking the railway line to Addis Ababa. A train had just passed on its way to Ethiopia, people clinging to the outside of the carriages and sitting in tight groups on the roof. The old French locomotive had pulled past us round the side of a mountain and disappeared.

We were on patrol along the southern border of Djibouti, in the stretch of mountains and rocky desert near Somalia. We had been away from camp for four days, driving around in our open-topped lorries, showing our presence and getting used to the country. Adjutant Lodvic was on the bonnet of his truck, binoculars to his eyes, booted feet braced on the lorry as he panned round the surrounding wilderness. The other Sergeants studied their maps, planning the route we would be taking that day; ahead of us was the village of Ali Sabieh, which lay on the other side of the mountain. It was 10.00 am and the sun was already very hot. I had made a fire and brewed coffee for the group, who were standing around in their sunglasses and desert head-dresses, smoking and eating bread and pâté. Down from the track, dirty red rocks and volcanic debris covered the slope. The dust underneath my boots was yellow-grey, and spiky, dry scrub grew out of the cracks in the ground. The sky was dirty and I was sweating. The trucks were parked at intervals along the track, their yellow and brown camouflage blending in with the barren rocks of the hills around us. Each one was loaded down with enough food, water and equipment to keep a group of ten men alive in the East African interior in mid summer. It was nearly 115 degrees. We hung our rucksacks over the sides of the vehicles, along with bundles of firewood collected from the few dead trees we came across; one truck had a .50 calibre Browning machine gun on an anti aircraft mount, its dust cover pulled tight around it to stop dirt and sand getting into its working parts. A long whip aerial swayed above Lodvic's truck. This was our radio contact with the rest of the 3rd Company at the base at Arta, fifty miles away from the capital. The Adjutant had the command group in his vehicle, and each of the other three lorries contained a composite combat group. We had Sergeant Loiseau, the son of a woodman from the Jura, Corporals Thierry, Andres and Carver, Meunier driving, and Maujard, Josh, Slasher and myself making up the rest of the group. We got along well and Loiseau had a relaxed attitude to discipline which ensured that everything got done without shouting or bullshit.

Marius and Slug were standing some way away, being fucked around by Corporal Garcia. Sergeant Loup's group was hell, and already Slug and Marius thought they were in for a tough four months. Corporal Garcia was Spanish, yet had adopted France as his country. He didn't like the English and thought I was a troublemaker, because I spoke English too much and because I flashed my opinions around. Corporal Garcia wasn't interested in the opinions of an untried English legionnaire with only six months' service. Although he wasn't in our group, he conspired to make life difficult for the younger legionnaires and was constantly on the lookout for people speaking English or expressing anti Legion sentiments. It was in the nature of my sense of humour, and Slug's as well, to be facetious about everything that we did, and I had decided that the only way to keep a balanced perspective on our lives was to take everything lightly. Garcia didn't approve of this; because he took his job within the Legion very seriously, he expected others to do the same. Luckily for us, Corporal Thierry had been fucked around a lot as a legionnaire, and was tolerant of my mistakes and shortcomings; he didn't hit me and consequently I did as I was told and respected him. Corporal Andres, who I nicknamed Aunty, pretended to be an upperclass intellectual, always telling us stories about the chateau in the Loire valley which his parents supposedly owned, and about how he mixed with the cream of fashionable society on leave. We took his stories lightly as there was a rumour that his father was a poor farmer who had fled from Algeria.

The group functioned as a composite unit, each of us performing tasks which kept the daily routine in order. As the most junior legionnaire, it was my job to make the coffee, keep the truck tidy and act as batman to the Sergeant. I was holding his FA-MAS as well as my own as we stood there in the morning sun waiting for the Adjutant to finish his briefing. Despite the heat, we were all wearing long trousers as protection against the sun, and most of us had wound our scarves around our heads to keep the flies away and to avoid sunstroke and dehydration, both of which came quickly when the temperature was 120 degrees at midday. Sunglasses were obligatory to protect our eyes, and in a small pouch on my right shoulder I had a tube of Nivea and a tube of Roc protection factor ten suntan cream. Our faces and arms were covered with a film of sand and red dust which got everywhere, blown around by the wind and as we travelled along. Our uniforms were filthy; dust, grease and dirt smeared over the fronts of our trousers and combat jackets. We polished our boots every morning, but four or five steps in the sand covered them with dust and grit; the only part of us which was really clean were our weapons, velcroed into their sand covers and wiped and oiled each evening. We had the magazines for our assault rifles hanging from our web belts, along with water bottles, rifle cleaning kits, first aid dressings and combat knives. All thirty of us were identical in appearance, and the only items in which we were allowed any degree of personal choice were our sunglasses and our combat knives. The regulation sunglasses were American pilot-style with green, easily broken lenses. Being part of our tropical uniform, they were accountable if lost, so many of us had bought our own in Calvi. Thierry had a smart pair, with a cord to suspend them around his neck and small leather flaps on the corners which protected his eyes; Slug had spent 400 francs on a pair of deep, black wraparounds but had been told by Sergeant Loup that he wasn't on a film set. Marius had some from Gianni Versace which covered his face like a pilot's visor. All of us had our own knives which we used for a variety of tasks from opening tins to cutting up food; those of the section who had been on Operation Manta in Chad had lived off gazelles which they shot from the trucks, and they had used their knives for skinning and gutting the dead animals. My knife was a French copy of an American K-Bar; it had a seven inch blade, serrated on one side and sharpened on the other. There was a runnel down the centre of the blade which ended in a sharp point. I had stuck abrasive tape on the handle so that it wouldn't slip out of my grasp while I was using it, and there was a sheath with a small sharpening stone attached. So far, its victims included some small branches and four tins of pâté.

Adjutant Lodvic stood up, folded his map and replaced his sunglasses; the Sergeants walked over from his truck and told the groups what would be happening. We were going to continue our patrol through the village of Ali Sabieh before driving out towards the desert which lay on the other side of it; we would stop for our siesta and lunch break just before the desert began, lying up underneath the lorries to escape the heat of the midday sun which was so hot that any travelling or movement became impossible. We would cross part of the desert and then turn down towards the town of Dikhil which lay towards the Ethiopian frontier, camping up for the night in a dried up riverbed to the north of the town. The following day we would sweep round in a huge semicircle towards the north of Djibouti and the huge, dried up salt plains of Lac Assal, where there were lunar-style landscapes and where springs came hot from the ground, their clear waters riddled with cholera viruses.

We jumped up into the trucks and I sat down, my rifle across my knees, staring at the mountains and ravines around me. There was only one tarmac road in the whole Republic, which ran from Djibouti City to Addis Ababa; the rest of the country was made up of narrow rock tracks in a variety of stages of disrepair. On some of them it was possible to reach thirty miles per hour, and on others the trucks had to crawl metre by metre over the huge boulders which lay in their paths. We were driving quite fast at that moment, raising huge clouds of dust which settled on the men in the trucks behind. On the rocks and cliff faces at either side of the track were lumps of concrete and strands of barbed wire left behind by the Italians who had invaded Abyssinia in 1936, fighting a one-sided war against the Afar and Issar tribesmen. There were old pill boxes and lumps of rusty metal jammed into the hillsides, and Sergeant Loiseau, who had been to Djibouti before, explained the history of the country to us as we drove along.

When Africa was split up and colonised by the major European nations in the nineteenth century, one of the countries which the French had taken as their own was the arid, volcanic wilderness of French Somaliland. A dry and featureless country of extreme heat, it was made up of two small deserts and several ranges of mountains. It was just a barrier before the huge kingdom of Ethiopia. However, it had perfect facilities for a port, which was a tactical advantage as France could retain a maritime presence in the Gulf and in the Indian Ocean. The country was granted independence in 1976 and became the Republic of Djibouti. In return for financial support in maintaining the economic and commercial status quo in a country whose exports were non-existent, the Djiboutian government allowed the French to station several thousand troops in the country and to use the deep water port on the Red Sea. Most of the troops based in the country were from the French regular army; the Air Force maintained a base at Djibouti Airport, flying Mirages out of the dusty airstrip set south of the capital on the edge of the sea. There was a regiment of the Foreign Legion permanently based in Djibouti City at Camp Gabode. This unit, the *13ème Demi-Brigade de la Légion Étrangère*, guarded the ammunition dumps and carried out a lot of patrolling on the country's borders, while also taking care of the French governmental installations in the capital. Men were attached for two years to this regiment and I had heard that it was possible to go the whole time without seeing a white woman.

The *2ème Régiment Étranger de Parachutistes* provided a 'Compagnie Tournante' which did consecutive four-month tours in the province, based away from the rest of the units in a small village called Arta, overlooking the Red Sea. Our camp there, named Poste Lieutenant Colonel Amilakvari, after another famous Legion figure, was set outside the village, and consisted of barracks, a parade ground, cook house, offices, stores and a mini brothel. Out of the 130 men based there at any one time, there would normally be one Section on guard, one out on patrol and one Section involved in specialist training in the countryside and mountains surrounding the village. The unit ran in exactly the same way as in Europe, with all the attendant '*corvée*', '*appels*', singing, and bullshit which were the hallmarks of the Legion anywhere. The Section was mobile, each group having its own vehicle, and there was a helicopter landing point at the edge of the camp.

Our Section had driven out of the gates five days before, past the white-washed guard house at the entrance and down the road to the village of Oueah which lay at the bottom of the mountain. There we had branched off into the wilderness.

We drove off the track as the slope eased away, and sped along on the hard sand towards Ali Sabieh, which, although it was only a small village, was still the fifth largest town in the country. One truck behind the other, we drove slowly through the town along the main street. Children ran out from the buildings to scamper behind the trucks, shouting for money and food; some had stones in their hands to throw at us but none dared as they had thrown stones at a Legion patrol in the past who had stopped, caught them and beaten them senseless.

Corporal Thierry, sitting next to me, leant over and said that it was fun to spread jam from the ration packs on paraffin tablets for portable stoves and throw them to the children who would think they were sweets. It was only when the tablets were chewed or swallowed that they reacted with the gastric juices and made the children ill. As it was, Thierry contented himself with swinging his saw-edged steel garotte at the children, calling '*venez, venez.*' As we had driven into the village, I had waved at some of the kids but Andres and Thierry had shouted at me, saying that they were just '*boo boos*' and '*boucaks*' and if they saw me doing it again there would be trouble. I had nothing against these children, except if they threw stones at me, and was interested in them because they were different and because I had never been in an African village before. Two of the others in the truck laughed and said that it wouldn't be long before they got me round to thinking like a real legionnaire. Certainly, if any of them had thrown jam-covered paraffin tablets to the children, I wouldn't have tried to do anything to stop them.

The village was made up of white houses, shacks built from corrugated iron and more ramshackle constructions of goat skin and cardboard; there was one white building which had a Coca Cola sign attached over the door. This was the local shop. Halfway along the dirt street was a clump of willow trees which stood in front of a long, low building which housed the local Mayor. Meunier took the truck round in a sweeping curve and we stopped underneath the trees. We got out of the lorries. Slug came over and we lit up. He immediately started telling me a story about his time in the Royal Marines. His Commando had been in Crossmaglen and the supplies helicopter had been delayed. Because of the dangers of snipers and mortar fire from the IRA, all stores, ammunition and food had to come in by chopper. One of the few ways of distracting the boys off duty was with videos, and because the helicopter was delayed they had been stuck with *Dirty Harry*, which Slug had seen so many times he could recite it by heart. After one evening when he had watched it three times, they had gone out on foot patrol the following day and had cornered an old woman behind some houses. Wanting only to do her shopping and buy the paper, the poor old girl had been outraged to have a self-loading rifle thrust into her face while Slug said, 'Go on, punk, make my day.'

He stood next to me in the dust, pulling on his Marlboro, scratching his crotch. Both of us had our sunglasses on, FA-MASs swinging from our shoulders. I was wearing a huge canvas bush-hat, its strap swinging under my chin, sweat-stains seeping through the rim. My head felt prickly and hot, lines of perspiration flowing down the back of my neck and along the contours of my back; I was thirsty but didn't dare touch my water bottle as our drinking was rationed. Slug and I spoke quietly in English, in case Corporal Garcia heard us; it was hot and dirty, and I didn't feel like getting hit. Carver told Slug and myself to get cigarettes and sweets from the shop. The cool gloomy interior hung with the sweet smell of heat and filth, the floor was hardened earth and boxes of Coca Cola and Marlboro were stacked up to the ceiling, alongside cases of Tadjourah, the locally bottled mineral water. The proprietor, a fat Djiboutian in shorts and an Olivia Newton John T-shirt, stood behind the counter, which was made from Orangina boxes, and watched. There were no prices marked on any of the things as it was normal for him to charge the villagers one price, and then to quadruple it as white soldiers came in. Garcia came and stood outside the door, carving slivers off a stick with his combat knife. He watched and said nothing. Two children walked in and started clamouring for 'baksheesh'. Slug pushed them aside and I swung a kick at the smaller one, looking to Garcia for approval. He stared back, eyes almost invisible behind his sunglasses, and said, 'achtung, les fuckings'. We chose packets of Marlboro and tins of Fanta, paying from the rolls of Djiboutian banknotes in our breast pockets. We had been paid just before we left camp and had plenty of money.

In Calvi, a para-trained legionnaire with six months' Legion service earned 4,500 French francs per month which was paid in cash. We didn't have to pay any tax as we weren't French citizens, and the payments towards the 'Mutuelle Militaire', an equivalent of National Insurance which covered any hospital bills which required treatment outside the Legion, was deducted before the money reached us. The Section ran a 'caisse section', a kitty which provided funds for leaving parties for departing members, material for the barrack rooms and loans to those who spent all their money before pay day. To apply for a loan, you approached Adjutant Lodvic, saluted, presented yourself, explained your requirements, did some press-ups and were given the cash. In the event of a relative or a friend dying, there was enough money in the kitty to fund an emergency trip to the mainland if the person in question could be trusted not to desert in the process. As we were considered to be on active service in Djibouti, our pay was doubled. We were paid in Djiboutian francs, a currency only used in the Republic and unchangeable at any bank outside the country. The bank notes were made of worn and flimsy paper which tore easily and were stained by being passed from dirty hand to dirty hand. On the banknotes were pictures of camels, mountains and tribesmen with spears, giving a picture of Djibouti as a quaint, pre-colonial land. As Slug and I stood in the shop, we had nearly £2,000 between us in local francs.

We walked out into the sun, ignoring the children and old women who tugged at our clothes begging for money, and distributed what we had bought. It was good to be able to buy cigarettes. Some people miscalculated how many they would smoke on patrol, running out of fags miles from the nearest shop and being forced to scrounge off those with more foresight. I had run out the day before and Andres had helped me out. I was getting through twenty-five a day sitting in the back of the truck; every time that we stopped or made coffee it was an excuse to light up, and during the middle of the day as the sun lay overhead, it was too hot to do anything except smoke, sweat and lie motionless underneath the lorries.

I walked over behind one of the vehicles and pissed into the dust. An old woman, thin and shrivelled in her wrappings of blue and purple cloth, stared at me without saying anything. Her two children sat beside her, looking resigned. Their heads were out of proportion with the rest of their bodies and their arms and legs were wasted and almost without any muscular definition; their joints were lumpy and one of them had a huge sore around his eye, black flies crawling hungrily in and around it. An insect crawled out of the woman's nostril and meandered over her lip. Her breasts were like deflated balloons and hung in an irrelevant way over her chest; one of the little boys banged at her stomach whilst I stood watching her, absolutely fascinated. It was the first time that I had seen at such close quarters somebody so thin, so dirty and so hungry. I took my hands off my assault rifle and wiped the sweat from my face, tilting my hat back over my eyes. Garcia walked over, and I took a chocolate bar out of my pocket to share with him while we talked about Africa. Throwing the wrapper on the ground by the old woman, I took out my cigarettes, offered her one, which she turned down, and lit up, feeling companionable towards Garcia because he wasn't hitting me or shouting at me. Adjutant Lodvic walked around to his truck and we climbed aboard again, fixing our sunglasses and scarves as the villagers stared at us and a couple of children threw stones half-heartedly into our dust.

We saw two youths walking along holding hands in Muslim fashion. '*Dirty queers*,' muttered Thierry. He was no more racist or homophobic than the rest of us, only more vociferous in the expression of his preferences. Like most others he thought that anybody outside the Parachute Regiment of the French Foreign Legion was lacking, faulty or inferior in some way, probably because they were black, left wing, civilian or homosexual. There were many black legionnaires, and presumably some homosexuals, but they were legionnaires first, and anything else afterwards. It was like our nationalities: during basic training, when asked 'What is your nationality?', we had been ordered to reply, 'I am a legionnaire'. So it was with everything else. Thierry, for instance, thought Legionnaire Mauchard to be ideologically dubious because he was educated and articulate. So he was called an '*intellectuelle de gauche*'. One afternoon in Calvi, Mauchard had tried to reason with a Corporal who had ordered him to do press-ups for having left his beret on the radiator when it should have been in his pocket. He had been joking about it when Corporal Johns, who had been sitting on a bed nearby jumped up and kicked Mauchard in the stomach. His leg swung in an arc, connecting from foot to knee across the Frenchman's solar plexus with the sound of a carpet being hit by a cricket bat. Mauchard deflated and went down, bent double and twisted on the floor as Johns assured him that if he ever argued with a Corporal again he would disfigure him for life.

Marius had told me that he joined the Legion so that he could 'Kill people without going to prison', and his descriptions of beating up immigrants in Stockholm sounded true. There were so many black and coloured people in the regiment, and being surrounded by fifty-two different nationalities should have made racism impractical. I heard a black Corporal refer to a Pakistani as a 'nigger'. All the Frenchmen were outspoken in their preferences, and their opinions of the other nationalities were nationalist rather than personal. In return, more or less everybody despised the French, although the ones from Brittany, itself practically independent from the rest of France in idea and principle, mixed with the English and were granted the status of 'honorary Englishmen' by the *Mafia Anglais*. The idea of forgetting our nationalities meant little to most people. Chris, the man from the Royal Signals who had done basic training with Marius and myself, and who had stayed with the *1er Régiment Étranger de Cavalerie*, was adamant that he wasn't forsaking his nationality. Back in Orange, Sergeant-Chef Gibeau had been telling him to consider himself a son of France, a member of the family that was the Legion. This was impossible, Chris had explained, drawing back his sleeve to reveal his forearm. There, tattooed in a swirl of roses and snakes, were the words 'Hartlepool: forever faithful'.

In encouraging people to think of themselves as legionnaires rather than individuals, the process of discrimination was fostered. As elsewhere, the difficult, biased people remained difficult and biased, while those with character and personality intermeshed with the system and thrived on it, still retaining their integrity. There was no need for any of us to be pleasant to each other, as the organisation only required us to act as a cohesive body of disciplined men. There was little preference or favouritism, and as we had no personal possessions there was no charity. Again, in basic training, we had been forbidden to say please or thank you as such words implied the existence of gratitude, charity and benevolence. The bonds between people were formed by professional respect and a sense of humour. The British, South Africans, Rhodesians and other professional soldiers respected each other's skill and so took each other seriously. When each day could be filled with the most frustratingly boring tasks, it was vital to be able to make each other laugh.

One afternoon at Camp Amilakvari, Slug, a Dutchman also called Christian and myself had been late on parade before lunch. The Duty-Sergeant of the week, a slim efficient German called Hasser, had decided that instead of having our siesta as was the normal practice between lunch and 4.00 pm, we would do some weeding. He took us behind the company offices and pointed at a patch of ground which stretched down to the barbed wire fence 100 metres away. Beyond the wire, the rocky desert extended across to Somalia, Kenya and the Indian Ocean. Small tufts of wiry grass grew here and there. Hasser pointed at the ground, and in a sweeping gesture which encompassed the area in front of us and half of Africa beyond the wire, he said, 'Weed.' For three hours we stooped over the bare ground pulling out bits of greenery. Slug kept us amused with an endless round of stories about the Royal Marines, the Falklands, life in Plymouth and about girls. As we weeded our way towards Zaire, he told us how he had been necking with his sister in a Middlesborough disco while drunk on leave. It had been very erotic, he said, adding, 'I got her tits out but she sobered up.'

Unfortunately for me Slug wasn't in our group. I enjoyed having him around as his sense of humour was invaluable, as were his soldiering capabilities. Having been trained as a soldier by the Royal Marines, possibly the most professionally capable fighting corps in Western Europe, what he had to teach me as a result of his time in the Falklands and Northern Ireland was enormous. Typical of many of the English soldiers, he was more experienced than a lot of our instructors, whose only knowledge of soldiering was what they had learned in the Foreign Legion; unless they had been at Kolwezi, seven years before, the chance was that they had never been in combat and as such all they had to teach was theory. No amount of instructors' courses at Castelnaudary or specialist cadres could give them first hand experience of what it was like to be under fire. Apart from peace keeping in the Lebanon, the *2ème Régiment Étranger de Parachutistes* hadn't undertaken active service duties since they had jumped over Zaire in 1978. Whilst in Chad in 1984, there had been a near miss: the 3rd Company had kitted up for a combat parachute jump after a French Jaguar jet had been shot down by anti government rebels. The operation had been called off, however, at the last moment, but not before some of the legionnaires had made their 'fragging' lists.

'Fragging' had originated in Vietnam, where soldiers and Non Commissioned Officers, pissed off at the behaviour of their Officers and the treatment they received from them, would kill them in the middle of a fire fight, either by shooting them or disposing of them with a hand grenade. It became an acceptable practice, for if the men felt that their Officers were incapable of leading them or of making decisions correctly, they saw no reason why they should die themselves through somebody else's stupidity. In the Legion, it took on a more personal nature. A Sergeant or a Corporal could hit, kick and harass a particular legionnaire as much as he liked, certain in the knowledge that the legionnaire couldn't strike back. Personal grudges between men could stretch out for months, especially if both men remained in the same unit. A Corporal could make the life of a legionnaire absolute hell if he chose; being in close proximity to the legionnaires in the section, hour after hour, day after day, he could fuck people around senselessly. So at N'Djamena airport in Chad, waiting around on metal bunks, sweating in their combat uniforms, filling their magazines with live ammunition and preparing their kit for battle, some men's thoughts had turned to killing those in their own sections. Three people I had met had been completely prepared to kill various Sergeants or

Corporals because of the treatment they had received from them.

In the sand and dust of African combat, the possibilities were endless. The Section charging forward, possibly under incoming artillery fire, up a rock-covered slope, lungs bursting with the effort, all frightened, rounds coming in on them . . . Suddenly a smoke grenade goes off; it is bloody noisy, nobody can see, it's getting dark perhaps, there's sweat in your eyes when suddenly the Corporal you've hated since your basic training flits across your front, moving up the slope towards the enemy . . . It's the work of a moment; raise your weapon . . . tap tap . . . straight through the back of the skull, don't stop to look, nobody else has, he's dead all right. And who's to know? Didn't see, Sir. No, Sir, he was over to my left, and there was incoming shellfire . . . Oh, that's terrible, Sir . . . Straight through the head? Oh fucking dear. The weapons you have these days as well . . . high velocity bullet would take his face off and go on to kill somebody else. His fault – he shouldn't have treated me like that.

Luckily, then, for some, the 3rd Company hadn't jumped and so the various differences had remained unresolved. But I had heard that on that day in Chad, there had been one or two worried men who were being nice to legionnaires they normally brutalised.

One thousand miles north west of Chad, a year later, our patrol was off in the direction of the Grand Bara desert to the north of the town of Ali Sabieh.

We drove for another hour and stopped for our siesta in a dried up river bed. The sides of the wadi were composed of rocks and crumbling dirt and there were only three or four trees within 500 metres, so each truck chose one and stopped underneath it. The trees were umbrella thorns whose canopy of tightly interwoven branches spread out above us. It was 11.30 am and I built a small fire for the group while Josh and Slasher made lunch. In the truck were two iceboxes where we kept the supplies of fresh meat we had brought from camp. We had tinned food as well. We cooked lunch, ate it and scraped the mess of grease and uneaten food off the plates with a mixture of sand and water. I stuck my fingers in the green beans which annoyed Andres who tried to make each meal as civilised as possible. He took me behind the truck and threatened to hit me unless I started behaving myself. I added his name to my mental 'fragging' list – he joined Corporal Garcia. Slug and I had developed a mutual understanding about these two Corporals and amused ourselves by dreaming up ways of torturing them. Slug's methods were direct and to the point, involving basic crucifixion and skinning alive. I veered towards the anally baroque and wanted to pour boiling water up Garcia's arse through a metal funnel after sellotaping scorpions to his prick.

After lunch we settled down for the siesta. The sun was directly overhead and despite the shade afforded by the thorn trees, it was unbearably hot. The ground was covered with rocks and boulders, and there were only small spaces of clear sand on which one could lie down; nine of us were trying to occupy the space under the tree, stretched out on ponchos with our bush hats over our eyes. Lying flat was impossible as our limbs intertwined and crossed in a confusion of combat boots and legs; the only alternative was to go underneath the lorry itself, which meant lying on a pile of stones. In the trees above us, small insects flitted around in the branches. There were no leaves on the trees, just two inch long thorns jumbled together in a mass of spikes. Ants crawled on the ground among the tree roots, which spread out in a tangle above the surface of the ground. Leaving Thierry, Loiseau and Josh stretched under the tree, I joined the others underneath the lorry. Rocks pressing into my back, I sweated and stared up at the oil sump. The heat and discomfort stopped me from getting to sleep so I crawled out and pulled my book from my rucksack.

A friend at home had sent me a parcel of novels, and among them was *Brideshead Revisited*, the only reading matter I had brought out on patrol with me. Like most of the other legionnaires I read little apart from Wilbur Smith or Frederick Forsyth. Myself and John Williams, a Corporal from the 3rd Section, would have competitions where we would test each other's knowledge of extracts from Wilbur Smith and Frederick Forsyth. One of us would start a sentence which could be taken from any book by either author, and the other would have to complete it. I was very good on *The Day of the Jackal* and *The Dogs of War* whilst John thrived on the Zulu War novels by Wilbur Smith. Both of us were beaten by Phil, the martial arts expert from John's Section. He could quote, word for word, the long paragraph from *The Dogs of War* where the hero, in bed with the teenage daughter of a mining magnate, explains why he became a mercenary. The previous day we had stopped for our siesta and I had lent *Brideshead Revisited* to one of our Section who had nothing to read and who was bored by the heat and flies. He had sat down in the rocks and sand beside our lorry and started to read. Shortly afterwards, the book had sailed over the truck to his exclamation 'fucking students'. But he persevered into the book, finally demanding, 'Chris, when does Charles get to fuck Julia?'

We had had a major inspection of the rooms and lockers at the camp a week previously and the Company Sergeant-Major had been perplexed and annoyed to find that I had written 'Et in Arcadia ego; a quotation from Brideshead Revisited, on the inside of my locker door. Corporal Garcia had taken exception to my intellectual posturing and had hit me several times. He thought that I lacked respect and that my attitude towards the Legion was at fault. One afternoon, he had discovered me reading an English book; we were not allowed to read or speak in any language other than French. He had made me translate an entire page of the book into French as a punishment; I did this in the same way as I used to do French A Level proses, using correct grammatical constructions and subjunctive clauses. The result had annoyed him even more. I was dragged into his barrack room three days running during the siesta and made to stand to attention and sing every Legion marching song I had ever learnt. Slug, Marius, Christian the Dutchman and any other English speaker they could find were made to join me. If our voices faltered or cracked during the recitations either we would be made to do press-ups or we would be hit. I forgot the line 'Et pour notre France cherie' from one song and stood to attention as Garcia headbutted me four times.

Corporal Garcia and his wimpy sidekick, Dautremont, made my life hell whenever they could. The day to day mechanics of Legion routine were just bearable if one kept organised and 'switched on', but as soon as any extra fatigues or duties were handed out, I found it impossible to keep up with the demands on my time and energy. I got worried because Garcia was always criticising me about my uniform and turnout, and as a result my ironing standards slipped and got worse. The shirts which we wore for parades and ceremonies had to be ironed in a certain way with fifteen different creases, each one, whether on the sleeve or arm or back, spaced three and a half or five centimetres apart. There was nothing that was demanded of me that wasn't demanded of everybody else; I was not the only one to find ironing, cleaning, sweeping and coathangering the shithouses a pain. We all took turns performing the most mundane, boring tasks, and adjusted ourselves and our own routines to coincide with what we had to do. The older soldiers, and those who had served in the regular army before, were used to the particular ballbreaking process of military discipline and didn't complain. Slug had been fucked around too much in the Royal Marines not to be able to cope with the demands made on him by the Legion. He knew when to shut his mouth and carry on with things, and he knew when it was acceptable to moan. I was lazy and thought too much about everything we did, tending to over analyse and dramatise the smallest incidents. I was also a consistent complainer, whinging wildly about any extra task that came my way. So the Corporals reacted in the most predictable fashion and unloaded more fatigues on me. By now I was getting disenchanted with the Legion fast, and Corporal Garcia's mission to make my life a misery only served to increase my frustration. I hadn't the experience or age to realise that most soldiering, in a regular army anywhere, consists almost entirely of performing countless small, menial tasks. The logistics of organising and maintaining a group of men in a foreign country in a hostile environment meant that there were many occasions when the things we were ordered to do seemed absolutely pointless.

The worst offender, as far as I was concerned was Sergeant-Chef Malekovic, a Yugoslavian who ran the company stores and who had served in French Guyana for a period before coming to Calvi. He had left for Guyana after his first spell in the *2ème Régiment Étranger de Parachutistes* when he had distinguished himself at Kolwezi. He was a very good soldier and an agreeable man but the jungle had got to him and turned his brain a bit. In French Guyana, there were local Indians who lived in the forests and woods outside of the town of Kourou, where the Legion was based. Some of Malekovic's boys had been beaten up by the local Indians in town one night and Malekovic had taken revenge. He had discovered that the Indians in question lived in treehouses built high up in the forest branches. Leading forth a group of men armed with chainsaws, he had brought their houses down to earth.

One afternoon at Camp Amilakvari, Malekovic made myself and two others go round and paint the window frames on some of the barrack rooms. He didn't have enough white paint in his store, so he had decided to thin down the thick, white gloss with water. As the resulting solution refused to blend together into any sort of paintable product, he had stood over the bucket, screaming at the substance to do as it was told and fucking well mix. Off we went to paint the windows with a thin, divided gruel of white paint and dirty water. Slapping it on the frames, we did exactly as we were told, regardless of the result. All was going well and it looked as though we might get away with our decorating. Suddenly, Sergeant-Major Benmoudi appeared round the side of the building, jogging along and sweating. He was shooting puppies with a 9mm automatic pistol. A stray bitch which lived in the camp behind the kitchen had given birth to nine brown and white puppies, which tumbled and romped appealingly round the dustbins, and Benmoudi had decided that they were untidy and unhygienic, and so was spending the morning killing them. The puppies sensed their impending doom and chased off round the camp, tails flickering, eyes terrified. Benmoudi stalked them and whenever he blew one of their little bodies apart with his handgun he would throw the corpse over the cliff behind the foyer. He saw us painting and lowered his weapon to his side. He ran a broad forefinger down one of the window frames, looked at me in disgust and told us to clean it all off. So we wiped all the paint off with rags and told Malekovic what had happened. He was furious. The Captain had told him that the windows would be repainted, so repainted they would be. We started again. Benmoudi reappeared, his canine holocaust completed, and hit all of us. He was a hefty, muscular Arab and it hurt having his fist in your eye. Eventually our decorating was suspended while the authorities considered the problem of paint supply. In the meantime we had wasted a whole afternoon. It didn't bother me particularly, but I wondered what life would be like in war if they couldn't get ten window frames painted without major discussion and personal antagonism.

I was bemoaning their lack of organisation, unfortunately unaware that Garcia was within earshot. He challenged me to a wrestling match and I only got to have tea after being strangled and thrown on the floor three times. At tea, Dautremont was sitting on the same table as I was, chatting away. Suddenly, he looked up from his cous cous and announced that on our return to Calvi he was going to tear my head off. The meal finished in silence.

Out on patrol, away from ironing, puppies and gloss paint, I scrambled back under the lorry and smoked. The brightness of the overhead sun reflected off the grey stones of the river bed and hurt my eyes. Nothing moved out on the road or on the hillsides around us. There was no wind so there was silence, the only noise the occasional crackle from the radio in Adjutant Lodvic's truck where Denis Berchon, the Breton Radio Operator, kept a listening watch. Men lay under the thorn trees or the lorries, immobile, gently, relentlessly sweating. The outsides of the trucks heated up in the sun until they became too hot to touch; our skin went pasty and pulpy from excessive perspiration. There was nothing to do until the heat wore off later in the afternoon. The temperatures dropped as the sun went down but the nights were not cool. I had heard lots of stories about how cold it was meant to be in the desert at night, but had experienced nothing to back up these stories. I lay on top of my sleeping bag in my underclothes and still found it too hot to sleep; occasionally there would be a muttered exclamation from one of the others as a spider or scorpion on its night-time travels moved over a sleeping bag.

My first night in Africa was spent sleeping outside on a camp bed at Camp Amilakvari. I had read books where the African stars were described as 'blue velvet pincushions' or 'diamonds set in inky black-ness'. It was disappointing to discover that the skies and constellations of the southern hemisphere looked the same as those over Wiltshire.

At 4.00 pm we climbed back into the trucks, setting off along the river bed towards the road. We hit the desert twenty minutes later and fanned out into a line abreast formation, driving across the hard sand at top speed. Clouds of dust rose up behind us as we charged across the wilderness of the Grand Bara desert, and in his truck, Lodvic stood up waving his arms like General Patton. Those of us sitting in the rear of each lorry were covered in a fine coating of sand and dust, which filled our eyes, ears and noses. The driver of each vehicle accelerated until all four lorries were charging across the sand at maximum speed, the occupants laughing and shouting. Meunier swerved fast to avoid running over the corpse of a dead donkey which lay in our path, its stomach swollen and bloated by the gases inside it. We reached the road, slowed down and turned left towards Dikhil and the Ethiopian frontier. We were heading towards the salt lake at Lac Assal in the north of the republic. The Adjutant had plotted a route and we would spend the night in an oasis near a dormant volcano. The pace slowed to a crawl; each driver rolled his way over the rocks and boulders. The countryside had changed again. There was no vegetation. Only scorched, dry, volcanic rock undulating towards the horizon. The air was thick and clouded with dust. The lorries stopped regularly as we negotiated our way up a steep incline; Meunier, his tongue clenched between his lips, gripped the steering wheel tightly. Loiseau stood up and flicked his eyes from map to road as he checked the route. In the back, I clung on to my seat as the bumpy ride bounced us around; we smoked and waited for this tortuous journey to end so that we could make camp for the night.

The thirst, heat and dirt out on patrol were preferable to the bullshit which accompanied our life in camp. Out in the middle of nowhere I felt that what we were doing formed part of the image I had of what the Legion should be like. As we left Camp Amilakvari, Josh had said that out on exercise in Africa, the regiment came into its own. He had served on Operation Manta in Chad in 1984 and had visited the Central African Republic with the regiment before being posted to Biltine, a fort near the demarcation line which separated the Chadians and the Libyans. Officially designated as active service, Operation Manta had been different from anything else he had done. At Biltine, the company had been based in an old fort, much like Fort Zinderneuf in the novel *Beau Geste*. The trucks had gone out on patrol, looking for any rebels sympathetic to the Libyan government. They had taken prisoners and had kitted up for their abortive parachute jump at N'Djamena airport. There had been a lot of patrols in the north of the country, where Adjutant Lodvic had served as a legionnaire in the early seventies during another counter-insurgency operation with the *2ème Régiment Étranger de Parachutistes*. The fort at Biltine had been situated 2,000 metres from an African village, and every day the local inhabitants would come over to the camp to beg food, carry firewood and to help the legionnaires with the building work. Two members of the company had been digging a trench for a machine gun emplacement, a long, hot and tiring task in the midday heat, when a tribesman had approached with his wife and children in tow. The two children, both girls, were ten or eleven, and the father had asked the legionnaires if they wanted to swap any food, money or cigarettes for a bout of oral sex with his children. One of the legionnaires had handed over two tins of sardines and a bar of soap and beckoned at the children who stood in the sand looking nervous. The father egged them on, and the legionnaires handed over their shovels and made the two children dig the trench.

Things in Djibouti were more restrained than in Chad. The country was not at war with anybody and it was an independent republic dependent on French financial support. We had to behave in a way becoming to an army which was there on sufferance. This meant that we had to treat the inhabitants in a reasonable manner, not chop down the trees for firewood, behave ourselves in town, and not machine gun the wildlife. It had been normal practice in Chad to shoot gazelles to eat. The lorries would drive behind a herd of the animals; the Section snipers would start shooting first with their FRF-1 rifles, and as the trucks overtook the running gazelles, the rest of the group would join in with their assault rifles and shotguns. By the end of the tour of Chad, everybody had become sick of eating gazelle and tomato salad, which for many people was one of the lingering memories of Operation Manta.

Life in Djibouti for us was split between patrols and periods in camp. When a Section returned from a spell out in the wilderness, there was a session of weapon cleaning and reorganisation which took a day or two, after which there was weekend leave. This could be spent in one of three ways. There was Djibouti City, with its bars and prostitutes; a visit to the beach at Arta Plage, where it was possible to go swimming or skin diving in the Red Sea; or there was the rest centre in the village of Arta itself. The beach was two kilometres away from the camp at the base of the mountains. There was a commando training centre set on the cliffs leading down to the water, with climbing wires, aerial walkways and abseiling facilities. The *'Centre d'Estivage'* or rest centre, in Arta village was a compound of bungalows with verandas and balconies, which housed a bar, dining room and kitchen. There was a swimming pool and patio underneath the willow trees. White civilians and regular army soldiers from Djibouti City would leave the scorching heat of the coastal strip at weekends and drive up to Arta, where they could enjoy the fresher air and slightly cooler weather. We were allowed to go and swim in the pool on weekend afternoons, walking down in black T-shirts, regulation running shorts, white socks and Adidas trainers, with towels rolled and sunglasses on. The French families from Djibouti City sat around the pool and watched their children play. Suddenly twenty tattooed skinheads would arrive, rowdy and shouting after two weeks in the desert, staring longingly at the pubescent teenage girls in bikinis whose bodies made one bow-legged with lust. We fooled around in the pool doing fancy dives and showing off to anybody who was watching, but as soon as we arrived the area would clear rapidly. After a swim, we would go and drink beer at the outside tables, watching the huge, prehistoric shape of a pet turtle which lumbered around the sand of the bar area. It was big enough for children to ride on, and while the youngsters played with the animal, we stared at their mothers. The feeling of sexual frustration was cramping and intense. The white women wouldn't dream of fucking any of us, and their complete inaccessibility annoyed and frustrated us. I could understand why they preferred the subtler attractions and assets of civilians or regular army personnel, with their home clothes, cars and houses in Djibouti City. This was nicer than a brutal coupling with a tattooed mercenary who at some time had probably fallen prey to every sexual disease known to medical science. Had I been on my own, I might have been able to use my French to improve the situation, perhaps with one of the less discerning and more myopic of the housewives. There was always wanking. Unfortunately, the satisfaction, though intense, was extremely brief, and once the waves of fantasy had cleared you were left standing downcast and hormonally incapacitated in some stinking African khazi.

The basis of gratifying and effective self abuse was the ability to conjure up the correct images to spur yourself on. The row of shit-houses at Camp Amilakvari were cleaned twice daily, but the combined effects of heat and digested Legion food made them cabinets in which only a brave man lingered. To be able to overcome the smell and the dirty, smeared walls, the piss-stained footmarks in which you parked your combat boots while squatting, and the flies the size of small sparrows, meant that you had to be able to conjure up a potent fantasy. In Calvi, a Corporal had disappeared one morning with a fistful of porn comics and a pleasured look. Two other legionnaires noticed the locked door in the washroom and heard the noises of furious page-turning. One by one, silently, gesticulating to each other with signs, the entire Section gathered outside. Making no noise, they waited, ears straining, until the sound of flaying flesh reached a climax. The Corporal let rip. The entire Section burst into a fury of applause.

At the end of our first patrol in Djibouti, a detachment from our company had been assigned to a spell of guard duty at the General's residence in Djibouti City. The officer commanding all the French forces in the Republic was housed in an old colonial villa on the beach towards the outskirts of the city. A detachment of legionnaires or regular army soldiers took turns to provide the security at his home. This involved a week in parade uniform, and the group chosen was to be supervised by Corporals Garcia and Dautremont. With two hours of guard, followed by four of rest, consecutively for seven days, it was considered a nightmare posting. I had been chosen, along with Marius and five other legionnaires, and I was terrified. I had a huge backlog of kit to prepare at camp, the new tropical parade uniform issued to me didn't fit, and I was panicking the more I thought about it. Garcia had told me plainly that any laziness on my part would simply mean that he would make my life hell. Dautremont, as well, was looking for an excuse to get me, and the Sergeant in charge of the detachment was an incompetent Tahitian who changed his mind every five minutes and whose intelligence was stuck somewhere round his rectum. When each mistake in kit presentation, cleaning, ironing or behaviour resulted in violence, the cumulative effects were panicking and disorienting. I was pleased to be out on patrol, and was shutting out of my mind the moment when we would arrive back at camp.

Down in front of our truck, Lac Assal appeared, a huge grey-white expanse of dried salt stretching into the distance, surrounded by volcanic lava which had dried up and solidified into strange, wonderful formations, rising and falling in petrified waves of black rock. We drove down the salt beds and along the edge for an hour. After two miles of precipitous driving, we came round the edge of a rock wall and drove through a ravine whose steep, pitted sides reared up on either side of us before debouching on to a huge area of grey-brown sand with palm trees and clumps of thorn bushes. Lodvic waved his arms towards the trees and the trucks stopped in a line against a rock face. We piled our rucksacks on the ground, unloaded the food and water, and took out of the lorry everything that we would need for the night. Piling scrub branches and palm tree roots together in a crevice on the rock face, we set light to it and started to heat water for the coffee. The other members of the group were taking off their combat jackets and scarves and stripping down to their shorts. Thierry sat down on a rock with a piece of paper and a stub of pencil to draw up the rota list for the evening's guard; between the time we stopped the trucks and the moment when we set off the following morning, there would always be at least one legionnaire with his rifle patrolling around the perimeter of our camp area, keeping an eye out for any tribesmen who might try to approach the campsite in the middle of the night to steal food or equipment. Although Ethiopia and Somalia were in the middle of civil wars, there was very little danger of us being attacked in the middle of the night as we were twenty miles away from the nearest frontier. We opened a tin of pickled vegetables and poured them in their salt water into a saucepan to heat up; we had large, dry loaves of local bread, tinned beef stew and potatoes which we would put in the fire to bake. We had packed bottles of beer in our rucksacks and in the iceboxes in the lorries, so we could have some sort of a drink around the fire after we had eaten. That evening the Adjutant was talking to two English Corporals about soccer violence at the Heysel Stadium in Brussels where more than thirty Italian football fans had been killed in the crush after fighting had broken out with English supporters. Lodvic was annoyed because one of the English legionnaires had scrawled with his finger in the dust on the side of one of the lorries: 'England 1 Italy 32'

When the pickled vegetables had boiled and the potatoes had baked, we sat down to eat. We squashed down on our rucksacks and talked about the events of the day. I enjoyed these conversations as I was fluent enough in French to be able to join in. Mauchard questioned me closely about my background in England, as he was fascinated by my grasp of the language. He suspected that he had discovered another *'Intellectuelle de Gauche'*. We drank our beer, and I felt more relaxed than at any other time during the preceding months. In all the other regiments of the Legion, the bullshit and excessive discipline stopped at the end of basic training. This was not the case with the *2ème Régiment Étranger de Parachutistes*. Discipline was equivalent to that of basic training, and it was only after one was promoted to Corporal that the standard of living improved. Corporals could hit legionnaires, but a legionnaire was expressly forbidden to strike back; if he did the other Corporals would round on him, and then he would be dragged up in front of the Section Commander who would hit him as well. It was possible to ask a Corporal to take off his stripes and adjourn behind the building, but most Corporals, like Dautremont, who inspired hatred and dislike were too afraid to do this and hid behind their rank. Garcia, the Spaniard who terrified and traumatised me so much, would back up his braggadocio with physical achievement; he was only too ready to remove his stripes; he had worked as a bouncer in Paris for a long time and was an accomplished street fighter who enjoyed wrestling and brawling. Painful as it was, being hit by him was not as demeaning as being hit by Dautremont, who was a closet wimp.

The other Corporal who was difficult was a Chilean called Verdura. He had assimilated the ways of the Legion in an overwhelmingly totalitarian way. I did not know what he had done before coming to France, but his character appeared derived from his army experience, rather than from anything in his past life. It was as though he had been trained as a civilised human being by the Legion, adopting its habits, its codes of speech and behaviour, along with its warped sexual and professional mentality. But he had moments of personal recidivism. He was in Sergeant Loup's group and slept in the barrack room assigned to it. One night he had gone to bed drunk after too many bottles of Kronenbourg. In the morning, the other members of the group were surprised to see a pile of shit in the corner of the room at the bottom of a locker. The doors of the room had been shut during the night as had the shutters to prevent mosquitoes and wild insects flying in. Verdura's explanation that a baboon or wild dog had broken in while everybody slept was therefore implausible. He tried to blame the incident on one of the legionnaires in the group but nobody was convinced, especially when they saw the excrement-stained footprints leading from the shit to the edge of Verdura's bed.

That evening, I was allotted guard duty from 2.00 am to 3.30 am, and while the rest of the group slept fitfully in the night heat, I prowled round the edge of the camp area with my FA-MAS in my hands, smoking discreetly through my cupped palms, watching the nightjars flying through the air. It was quiet and a good time to dream. I was dreading returning to camp, so while I had the time I enjoyed the stillness and tranquillity of the warm desert night.

— 7 —

BABOONS AND PIGS

The five-foot thick mass of barbed wire surrounding the camp proved easier to negotiate than I had at first expected. I climbed into it rather than over it, slinging my small backpack through to the other side, and managed the whole obstacle with no more than a cut knee and a gashed sleeve. Below me the volcanic rocks that littered the mountain-side promised difficult going, especially in the darkness; some were the size of a man's head, others as large as small cars. Hurrying from rock to rock, stumbling and making far too much noise, I went down the steep slope towards the shadows some 1,000 feet below, well away from the arc lights and glow of the camp set on top of the mountain. Jumping down from one particularly large pumice stone boulder, I disturbed a family of baboons who barked at me before disappearing; I dropped my pack in surprise, smashing one of the precious plastic water bottles. I hastily wrapped it in my headscarf, before moving on in panic. Only when the ground levelled did I pause for breath, turning to look behind me at the buildings lit up on the summit. One way or another, I had made my move.

I had deserted Camp Amilakvari. Around me were the wadis, mountains and desert scrub of Djibouti. In front of me, 1,200 miles and 900 miles away respectively lay Nairobi and Addis Ababa. I had plenty of time to choose which one would be my ultimate destination for, after all, I was walking. The night-time temperature was 110 degrees.

Endless, tedious bullshit, persistent harassment from Corporals Garcia and Dautremont, combined with a stupendous impetuousness, had finally led me to desert. I had thrown everything up for a rashly-conceived plan which involved walking by night across some of the most inhospitable country in the world, and surviving daytime temperatures in the height of the East African summer of 130 degrees. Ahead lay the desert interior, very little water and hostile natives, who made a living collecting the bounty on captured French deserters. If I made it out of Djibouti, I would find myself in Somalia or Ethiopia, each engaged in civil war – neither would look favourably on a Legion deserter wandering around their countryside. However, I was prepared. In my rucksack, I had two litres of water, a commando knife, seven packets of Marlboros, a lighter, a tube of Roc protection factor ten suntan cream, my poncho, five inches of garlic sausage and a small bottle of aftershave. In a country where an average European soldier could drink twelve litres of water a day, my two litres of mineral water would be hard pressed to last the distance, but I had heard that there were wells along the main Djibouti City to Addis Ababa highway.

Djibouti is one of the hottest countries in the world, alongside Death Valley in California and the Kalahari desert. Outside the wet season, the land is parched, and the local tribesmen tend to lie motionless in goatskin and twig huts and let their itinerant flocks find what shade they can, as they make their way between waterholes and sparse grazing areas. The presence of a single, dusty soldier in shorts and Raybans would be quickly noticed. I decided that it was best to travel at night.

It was 9.00 pm. Evening '*appel*' at the camp would quickly reveal my absence. The list said that 132 men should be present at evening inspection. 131 would be there this evening, the missing kit and open locker clear indications of my intentions. As the obvious culprit was some way away, a scapegoat would be found to take the blame. Anticipating the search parties that would be sent out to find me before I got too far away, I decided to hide for the first night and the next day, to let the initial disturbance subside, and to collect my thoughts and prepare a plan for the coming week. For the first time since joining the Legion, I was by myself and dependent on my own intelligence, knowledge and initiative. If I was captured, I would be fed back into the Legion's prison system before rejoining my unit. But now, with grazed knees and sweat running across my shaven scalp, I was alone, and it was extremely comforting and reassuring.

Ahead of me lay a rock-strewn ridge. I made my way slowly upwards and looked behind me for any signs of pursuit. Around me baboons shouted. I had already seen a family group of these large primates scamper off into the darkness as I approached, and I wondered at what point they stopped being frightened and started thinking about going on the offensive. One of the companies based at Camp Amilakvari some months previously had seen how these animals could behave. A Sergeant had had the idea of buying a couple of sows which could be fed on scraps, kept in a little wire enclosure near the ammunition compound and slaughtered at the end of the four month tour to provide a barbecue. The idea had worked well, until the sentry watching the ammunition dump next to the pigs, reported seeing a group of baboons climb through the barbed wire, approach the swine and rape them. His story was dismissed as the result of Kronenbourg and too much sun. But the following day, the sentry whose rota coincided with the pigs' feeding time told a similar story. The animals, tethered and with their faces deep in troughs of swill, had been gang raped by fifteen or twenty baboons, who had queued up behind them in a very orderly fashion, elders to the front. The whole camp heard the story, and the next day legionnaire Bergquist was ready with his camera, and today in the Empire Bar in Calvi there is a photograph.

As I forced my way up the slope, I knew I had to find a place to lie-up. Reaching a curve in the tiny path I was following, I clambered up over a large rock to where a solitary thorn tree had set its roots in a deep crevice in the red ground. Dumping down my pack, I assessed the damage done to its contents during my escape. One of my plastic water bottles had been broken and I'd lost a third of a litre; my tube of Nivea and suntan cream had been crushed and I threw them away. My aftershave was unbroken. Laying my poncho in the crevice around the tree roots, I bedded myself down for the night. Hard rocks pressed into my back, and my boots constricted my feet. Lifting my head past the roots of the tree, I could see the Gulf of Tadjoura, the inland bay of the Red Sea that divides Djibouti almost in half; further to the west, at its extremity, a natural landlocked lake had been formed when an earthquake had blocked off a narrow strip of water joining it to the Gulf itself. It was reputed that this lake, known as the Pharr de Ghoubed, was the home of a giant Manta Ray, occasionally seen in photographs from the air, whose presence had been proved when Jacques Cousteau had lowered a dead camel in a cage as a sort of captive hors d'oeuvre. Apparently the cage and camel had come up with twisted bars and half-eaten occupant.

I got up early the next morning, catching the dawn. From somewhere over South Yemen the sun appeared, turning the sky from blue to red to white. Then it was day. I ate an inch of sausage, drank a mouthful of warm water and smoked a couple of Marlboros, as I wondered where to look for a hiding place for the coming day. The mountains rose and fell in a series of crisscrossing ridges, plateaux and occasional thorn trees stripped bare by wild goats. A direct march of 300 metres would involve climbing and descending five or six different precipices and slopes. The scree and red shingle would be hard going in the heat. Looking upwards, I noticed that the cliffs were scattered with caves, some of which appeared mere indentations in the rock face, while others looked as though they extended back some way into the rock. Scrambling up the scree for twenty feet, I discovered a hollow some two or three metres deep, with just enough room at its far end to lie down. The ceiling was blackened by the fires of nomadic tribesmen and set with a huge number of different shells. At some time in the preceding few million years, the whole area had been underwater. I dragged a branch and some scrub grass to the far end and lay down flat, my face inches from the roof.

I knew that back in camp the boys who had just come off their guard shifts would be describing in gynaecologically graphic detail their exploits with the prostitutes who materialised every night outside the camp. Standing on guard with a rifle and bayonet at 2.00 am one would see the *'bordel mobile'* emerge from the darkness. An old Djiboutian woman with five or six girls in tow would line up her charges outside the entrance, who then tempted the guards. *'Tiens, Johnny, viens maintenant. Fucky-fucky deux mille francs, sucky-sucky plus fucky-fucky cinq mille francs.'* A flash of skirts and a grin to set blood racing. *'Vas-y, parachutiste, l'amour c'est un grand sentiment. Donnes cinq mille.'* Five thousand Djiboutian francs, about £25, for ten minutes of sex on a rock bed, always with the prospect of nasty disease in store. The alternative was the *'Club Compagnie'*, known as the *'pouf'*, where four teenage black girls lived in a corrugated-iron hut divided into rooms. Among the girls of the village, there was much competition to be chosen to work in the *'pouf'*, as the financial rewards enabled them to enjoy a considerably higher standard of living. It was a common sight to see a mother bringing along her teenage daughters to be inspected by the Chief-Corporal, whose duties included running the club. The demands of coping with 130 paratroopers meant that there was a high turnover rate. Outside the hut was a makeshift bar, some tables and plastic chairs, and a view down to the Red Sea. In the evenings a huge tape recorder would fill the East African night with Alison Moyet and Bruce Springsteen. The procedure was simple: overcome by lust, the legionnaire would approach one of the girls who took his fancy, give her the ticket which he had purchased at the bar, and then pass medical niceties by prostrating his member to be inspected by the Duty-Medic. He was led into the girl's room, cheered on by his confederates – some of the legionnaires timed each other. Or there was Djibouti City, an old French colonial settlement, the decaying white buildings of the imperial era surrounded by the squalor and dirt of shanty towns and refugee camps. Uniforms ironed, silver parachute wings gleaming, twenty legionnaires would climb into trucks and head off for town and a weekend of Sodom. Almost every female inhabitant had her price, and consequently the choice was larger than at Camp Amilakvari.

I had come to rest one evening in the Bar de Paris, at 4.00 am, drunk and sweating. The mixture of beer, wine and Somalian gin inside me had leant softer proportions and gentler attractions to the grizzled face of the middle-aged barmaid, and I accompanied her home. The woman unlocked a door made out of metal sheeting and we entered an area of beaten earth, open to the sky, where a family of goats slept, limbs intertwined. The bedroom led off this area, and consisted of a double bed, a scrapboard table and a cassette recorder. The uneven floor was well-trodden earth, and through the gaps in the roof you could see the stars. The barmaid's mother was asleep, and complained bitterly at being turfed out to sleep with the goats merely so her daughter could entertain one drunk legionnaire.

I took off my uniform carefully, looking for a clean surface on which to lay it. Despite my partner's adept advances and wily tricks, she was no match for the effects of sixteen hours' drinking, and I passed out. Coming to an hour later I witnessed the extent to which alcohol can disrupt one's perceptions.

I lay on my back in the cave and considered my course of action for the coming days. I was restricted to moving at night, and was reluctant to attempt a tortuous 1,000 miles across country through the endless mountains. If I walked along the road at night, I would be able to detect any traffic at some distance and hide myself, and I would also avoid getting lost. I decided to try to cover thirty kilometres by sunrise the next morning. From my position beneath the branch, I could raise my head and see, 500 feet below, a path where occasionally a couple of shepherds or women on their way to market would go by.

Towards 6.00 pm the sun disappeared and dusk arrived; by 9.00 pm all was completely dark. I arose, dusted off the grime and climbed down the scree to the tiny path which led down to the main track. Guided by the moon and the stars, I followed the track until I was close to the main road. Occasionally a vehicle flashed past, headlights announcing its presence from some distance away, but otherwise the only sounds were the insects, nightjars and baboons. I walked along the road for most of the night, dashing into the rocks every time I saw the lights of an approaching vehicle; once or twice I heard voices talking Somalian or Djiboutian in the scrub, but mostly it was myself, the moon, and the tarmac.

The rumble far away on the horizon was a reminder of the bloody civil war which had been raging in Ethiopia for several years; because of the situation in Ethiopia and Eritrea, an option was to turn left at the frontier, avoid both countries and go down through Somalia towards Nairobi. Although it would mean walking another 300 miles, it might be worth it, as Addis Ababa could be inhospitable towards Legion deserters. I had another alternative – I could head for Mogadishu, the capital of Somalia, and turn myself in at the British Embassy. But two British deserters who had tried that route had been picked up by the Somalian police and thrown into jail for six months before being handed over to the British consulate; on arrival at Heathrow, they had been obliged to sign a pledge to repay not only their air fares, but also the bill for the six months' imprisonment. Another option was to give up the thought of going home, and to head towards Tigre province in Eritrea and throw in my lot with the guerrillas fighting the Ethiopian government forces; they were reputedly keen for foreign technical advice. Eventually, I decided that to head for Addis Ababa was probably the wisest choice.

I thought about these problems as I walked along, as well as worrying about my hiding place for the coming day, the urgent need to find water, and how little sausage I had left. I had seen no signs of any wells along the route, and although survival manuals told stories of collecting dew on groundsheets, and digging holes below the water-table in dried-up river beds. The reality was different: the air was so dry that the dew in the mornings was negligible, and as for digging holes, such strenuous effort was impossible. Catching food in traps made out of sharpened twigs and knotted tree bark sounded great in theory, but out in the desert things were different. I decided it would be easier to approach some of the natives and swap a couple of packets of Marlboros for some food and water.

When the sun rose I was about twenty-five kilometres further on, but thirsty, hungry and weak. I walked 200 metres up a hillside to where some thorn trees provided shade and dumped my pack, lit a cigarette and watched the ground below me for any sign of tribesmen who looked friendly. It wasn't long before the patch of shade was invaded by large numbers of small brown ants who appeared from the rocks to start climbing over my boots and up my trouser legs. Finishing the last of my water, I walked down a narrow gully to where two shepherds supervised some goats from the shade of a ramshackle shelter. Remembering training on how to deal with natives, I approached their hut and squatted down in the dust about twenty metres away, waiting for the invitation to come closer. The occupants – an old woman and her daughter – watched me, then I was beckoned over. The hut was made of goatskins stretched over a framework of thorn twigs, about five feet high at its apex, and surrounded by all sorts of junk ranging from empty tin cans and enamel cups to intricately carved sticks and bundles of animal skins. A French Army-issue water bottle sat on the ground wrapped in a homemade woollen jacket, and beside this in the dust lay an enamel oven dish containing some rice. The old woman, wearing rags and a lot of brass jewellery looked at me and motioned that I sit down next to her on a goatskin, as she fumbled behind for some water. At the side of the hut, a pile of freshly-cured animal hides covered her water container: the sewn-up skin of a newly-slaughtered goat. Taking a battered tin and emptying it of dust and grit, she upended the animal skin and poured a stream of green water from its arse. I was surprised at how cold the water was, and how for all its strange colour it tasted only of bitter weeds. Food came next. Some orange rice with pieces of flesh in it was slopped into an enamel bowl, which I accepted gratefully. However, my stomach had contracted over the past two days, and I found that I was almost unable to finish it but, as both the women and daughter were watching me, I forced it down. It turned out to be a good decision, for it was to be my last meal for some time. I took out my cigarettes and motioned that they should take a packet in return for the food. They didn't smoke, however, so I sat in silence on my patch of goatskin before standing up to fill my water bottles and leave.

I sat down in the shade of a bush on the side of a mountain and felt as if I was getting sunstroke. I stretched my poncho over the lower branches of a thorn tree, and lay underneath, totally still. With nothing to do but dream, I felt my thoughts fragmenting. The day passed slowly, and as the sun started to go down, I returned over the top of the mountain and rejoined the road, my boots slipping and sliding in the red scree. I lost two hours walking time because I skirted round a village rather than walking through it, clumping over rocks and trying not to lose sight of the road. By dawn I had almost finished the green water from that morning and was desperately thirsty, feeling sick and uncoordinated in my movements. The will to carry on was fading fast.

Clearing a bend in the road, I heard the reassuring thump and whine of a diesel engine which indicated the presence of an Artesian well closeby. Suddenly excited and filled with energy, I made new plans. I would hide for the day and fill up with water at nightfall. Ahead of me the terrain was changing and five or six miles away the volcanic rock and craggy ridges turned into desert. To continue my journey I knew that I had to cross the Grand Bara desert, which had no shade, no water and no trees. I had to try and cross its twenty miles within one night or face certain death. But I would have a go.

That day I crawled into one of the culverts that were dug underneath the road to allow the passage of the rain which came with the wet season. About three feet underground, I shared my bed of sand with the ants, a pair of scorpions and a large spider, which didn't stay very long. I was relieved about the spider, for once on patrol we had found one whose leg-span encompassed a dinner plate. One of the Corporals had kept two scorpions as pets in a large glass bowl, and staged gladiatorial contests against spiders. The spiders lost, and one was left with the strange picture of two scorpions munching their way through a carcass several times larger than themselves.

I knew that the other side of the mountains was different from the coastal strip. The inhabitants were true nomads, and had very little contact with white people: occasionally they saw a Legion patrol drive past in trucks, or watched a dawn parachute jump. They would probably kill me just for the sake of it. Adjutant Lodvic had been on a patrol in the interior in pre-Independence days, and had come across the corpse of a French deserter who had fallen into the hands of the locals. His eyes and tongue were gone, and his bloated, sun-blackened mouth contained his genitals. In those days, however, it was quite common for sentries at Camp Amilakvari to throw coins into the barbed wire in front of their positions, wait for African children to scamper in to retrieve the money and then shoot them for trying to get into the camp. Perhaps things in the interior had changed since then, but I was unwilling to find out.

I approached the well at 6.00 pm and found two buildings housing the pumping gear, and some taps which dripped invitingly. It reminded me of my recurrent fantasy of the last few days: coming across a crashed lorry carrying case upon case of pineapple milkshakes. In that temperature thirst and drinking seemed to occupy most of my thoughts. I had taken a swig of Paco Rabanne just to check if it was drinkable. It wasn't. Neither was my own urine, dribbled into a bottle top: it tasted poisoned.

The attendants of the well were Muslims and were prostrate on the ground. It was obvious that I had chosen a bad time. I stood in the shade of a huge willow and smoked, until they completed their prayers, before asking if I could fill my water bottles. They looked at me suspiciously, and I explained that I was on a survival exercise. Huge quantities of water gushed from the pipe, and I gulped down draughts of it before filling my bottles. That there should be so much water here, accessible but uncontainable, really frustrated me. I was limited to what I could carry, and my lack of foresight before my departure meant that I had to find fresh supplies every one-and-a-half litres. The Africans nodded doubtfully as I walked off towards the road that led to the desert.

I walked fast and confidently across the hard sand, the mountains disappearing behind me, and the ridges of the horizon a dull line against the night sky. I covered about nine miles before feeling too tired to go any further. Lying down, my pack under my head, the African sky above, I went to sleep.

I awoke just before dawn, wishing I was back in camp, with the certainty of breakfast and coffee ahead of me. Instead there was the sun waiting below the horizon, sand was all around and there was no water. I stood up and looked both ways, wondering what to do. Suddenly my plan of walking to Addis Ababa seemed the ludicrous idea it was; bullying Corporals and daily harassment seemed minor problems hardly compared to keeping alive in an environment like this. Pulling on my pack, I stepped on to the road, and headed back towards the coast. By 10.00 am I was off the desert and in the mountains. I sat on a rock and resolved to flag down the next car or truck heading for Djibouti City.

Nothing appeared for nearly an hour, when a small Renault approached, driven by an Indian with his wife and family crowding the seats. He had no room to give me a lift, but instead thrust two bottles at me, one containing water, and the other a grenadine and water syrup. I dashed off the road and crouched in the bottom of a dried up river for an hour, steadily sipping the warm, sticky liquid. On the other side of the river bed was a newly-built workman's hut, made from pine planks and corrugated-iron, and I could see a wheelbarrow and various tools leaning against its sides. Looking for a place to hide, I approached it and forced the door. The interior was dark and smelled of tar and paint, but was slightly cooler than outside. I settled on some planks and fell asleep.

When I emerged in the late afternoon, a curious sight greeted me. Fifteen or twenty goatherds – male, female, adults and children – were sitting in the dust. As I headed towards the road, they followed after me, scampering on emaciated legs, and waving their sticks in a hostile manner. They surrounded me as I walked along, one woman grabbing hold of my arm, and several boys attempting to tear my pack from my shoulders. At first I assumed they wanted money or cigarettes, but quickly realised they were more interested in me for bounty money. In turning back from the desert, I had accepted the ignominy of failure and the certainty of brutal punishment, yet I felt reluctant to be handed in by these scrawny natives. I was taller, stronger and tougher than them. If I attacked them, the problem lay not in their immediate numbers, but because within a kilometre radius there would be many more in their shelters of hide and branches. There would come a point when thoughts of bounty money would be replaced by thoughts of revenge. Then I would be beaten to death. I suggested in pidgin Somali that we should await the arrival of a car to take me to Djibouti City, where one of them could claim the 35,000 Djiboutian francs offered for each captured deserter by the *Deuxième Bureau*, the Legion's Military Intelligence unit.

As the light faded, a green and white taxi appeared from the direction of Ethiopia and pulled up in front of me. Three Djiboutians dressed in shirts and slacks got out and spoke to my captors before helping me into the back seat. The dusk swallowed up the group on the side of the road as the taxi pulled away. The men in the taxi seemed totally unsurprised at my presence, and apart from offering me a bottle of water and some cigarettes, all was quiet until we reached the outskirts of Djibouti City. The driver turned to me and suggested to me that the next time I wanted to desert, I should come to his house, pay him 20,000 francs, and he would drive me to the Somalian frontier. I steeled myself as we turned into the entrance of Camp

Gabode, the headquarters of the main Foreign Legion detachment in Djibouti.

Two days later, I regretted my decision made in the desert. Having been questioned, beaten up by two Spanish Corporals with bad breath, then stripped and thrown naked into a cell, I was now in solitary confinement. It was customary that deserters received at least a day in solitary for each day they had been absent; my five days were spent sweating on a concrete floor in my underpants, awaiting the arrival of my gaolers who took me for my exercise each afternoon. One of them would stroll calmly around a patch of exposed ground, and I in turn would have to run around him, thus making dizzying figure of eight patterns in the afternoon sun. When they wished, I would crawl round them, or stumble at knees bend. I was not alone one afternoon. Another captured English deserter was suspended by his hands from the branches of a willow tree. His feet barely touched the ground, which was only half a bad thing, as they were in fleshy tatters since the Military Police had made him walk five kilometres along a beach of volcanic rock in bare feet.

I had another forty days of hard labour to last out in detention. Then it was back to the unit and a return to Corsica, leave and beer.

— 8 —

Playing Scrabble with Pimps

Oswaldson swung his pick into the hard sand around the base of the tree and told me how he had come to kill his first man. I had completed my solitary confinement, and was serving out my prison time. While serving with the *2ème Régiment Étranger de Parachutistes* in 1978, he had been part of the detachment which had parachuted in to save the hostages at Kolwezi. His Company, the 2nd, had been on leave in Calvi when the alert was sounded at the camp. He had been reading *Corse Matin*, the local paper, which he had picked up to leaf through over his breakfast. The Regiment had been put on alert, and the Military Police drove round the small seaside town ordering all the legionnaires to return to camp as the unit was due to go abroad at short notice. He had caught a taxi with some others from the same company and rushed over to his barrack room to prepare his equipment and pack his rucksack. The Regiment was in a state of ordered chaos; the military attaché in Kinshasa had appealed to the French and Belgian authorities for help, and while the Belgians hesitated, the *2ème Régiment Étranger de Parachutistes* had been told to be ready to fly to Africa at noon the following day.

The small mining town of Kolwezi in Southern Zaire had been overrun by rebels from the neighbouring province, and they had started to terrorise the town, capturing white hostages and setting out on a drunken, terrifying mission of rape and destruction among the white settlers and mine workers. Ever since the Regiment had been designated in the early 1960s as a Special Intervention Force, ready to intervene anywhere in the world within forty-eight hours, this was the opportunity for which it had been waiting. Six years after Kolwezi, all of us dreamed of something similar happening, and we kept our rucksacks packed on top of our lockers ready for such an eventuality.

Oswaldson had rushed around all day, drawing rations, medical supplies, ammunition, his MAT-49 submachine gun from the armoury and his tropical uniforms. The camp was full of officers, Sergeants and Corporals dashing around, screaming at legionnaires, attending hurried briefings and thinking about all the details of an operation that involved transporting 750 men halfway across the world with their parachutes and hardware. The lorries had left Camp Raffalli in the pre-dawn chill and driven across the island to Solenzara airbase in the south of Corsica. The regiment had boarded aircraft from UTA, the airline which served France's ex-colonies in Africa. Oswaldson had slept for most of the flight to Kinshasa, the capital of Zaire. When they had landed there had been total confusion. The only parachutes available had been American T-10s, whose harnesses were incompatible with the legionnaires rucksacks. The aircraft which would deliver the paratroopers over the drop zone were C-130 Hercules, and the jump masters were Zairean. Colonel Erulin had paraded his men and told them that their mission was to jump over the town of Kolwezi and liberate it from the hands of the rebels. Oswaldson had been told by his Section Commander that the orders were to kill every single black person they encountered, regardless of whether they were rebels or not. The legionnaires put on their strange parachutes, adapting their rucksacks with pieces of string and wire, and clambered on to the planes, fully laden with all their kit on the cramped jump seats inside the fuselage. After a hot, sweltering flight, the Hercules had arrived over the drop zone, and legionnaire Oswaldson, three days without proper sleep, had tumbled out of the door into the sky over drop zone Alpha, north of the old town. He had hit the ground and extracted his submachine gun from its container. Cocking the weapon, he had rendezvoused with the rest of his Section and had come into contact with the enemy almost immediately. Oswaldson had parted a thick bunch of elephant grass and come face to face with a black man sitting behind the controls of a 20mm anti aircraft gun, traversing the barrel to left and right. He appeared incapable of handling the weapon, but Oswaldson knew he had to kill him. Standing there in the dry, waving savanna grass, he had slipped off the safety catch on his weapon, put the metal frame butt against his shoulder and taken aim at the rebel who had thrown up his hands in front of his face as though to protect himself. The weapon threw bright cartridge cases high and right as Oswaldson fired, the 9mm slugs catching the man's chest and face, pushing him back into the seat on the gun as he died, his lungs, heart and brain torn apart by the legionnaire's shooting. Oswaldson had left him there, and pushed on to Kolwezi. The following days had been spent clearing the town, freeing the grateful hostages, killing all the rebels and tidying up. The Regiment had conducted sweeping search and destroy missions in the surrounding countryside, tracking down fleeing guerrillas in huts and hamlets, questioning them and then killing them. The hostages had been liberated and the regiment had recuperated for a time in Gabon before flying home to Corsica where they took part in a victory parade in Bastia.

Oswaldson's subsequent career in the Legion had been a history of drunkenness and disobedience, so that in 1985 he was still a '*Premier Classe*' legionnaire, rather than a Sergeant or Senior Corporal like most of his friends who had been at Kolwezi with him. On his dress uniform he wore the black and red medal ribbon, which had been awarded to all those who had taken part in Operation Bonite, the action which had liberated Kolwezi. He had left the *2ème Régiment Étranger de Parachutistes* and transferred to the *13ème Demi Brigade de la Légion Étrangère* permanently based in Djibouti. He had gone out in Djibouti City two nights previously and had such a drunken time that he had been late for roll call in the morning. He told me about his evening. It sounded bloody good.

Word had got round the camp that an English female pop group were playing in the Sheraton Hotel in Djibouti City. They were called Bubbles and the three girls were pretty and young. Of most interest to Oswaldson was that they were white. Bubbles had found it difficult to secure bookings abroad, and their only Middle East tour dates were Djibouti City and Khartoum. All the legionnaires who could get leave passes that evening turned up at the Sheraton. A small stage had been put up in front of the swimming pool and bar area, and on it was the group's equipment and instruments. In front of the stage was a large crowd of civilians, regular army soldiers and legionnaires. To a man, the legionnaires were pissed. And getting more pissed. They shouted above the heads of the crowd for beer, wine and spirits, which were passed over each other's shoulders. The civilians and regular soldiers had been pushed back, and the front of the stage area had been a mass of Legion uniforms. The lights went down. Dry ice rolled across the sides of the stage. Backing music started. The legionnaires pushed forward in a wave. Two hundred soldiers who hadn't had access to white women since leaving Europe braced as the music reached a crescendo and Bubbles came on.

The Legion went barmy. The three white girls were wearing short latex skirts and boob tubes. Nobody had told them that this would excite the legionnaires out front, though they must have known. As they launched into their first number, half a company of assault pioneers tried to storm the stage. They fell back into the audience and the show continued. The legionnaires threw anything they could at the girls to show their appreciation. To shouts of 'Get 'em off' and 'Tits out for the lads' the *Mafia Anglais* danced furiously, stomping up and down in their uniform shoes, lanyards swinging, beer flowing. The group had rocked through three more numbers and then stopped, frightened at the prospect of mass rape by 200 sex-starved soldiers. To howls of anger and disapproval they had retreated, seeking refuge in the pool area. Some African waiters had tried to stop the legionnaires from following them but without success. Running across the patio, most of the legionnaires had thrown themselves into the pool as a sign of appreciation while the rest of the boys gathered round the girls' table and tried a mass pick up. Dripping men in sodden walking out uniforms climbed out of the water and grabbed at the girls. Men pushed and swilled beer, pricking each other with cocktail sticks and throwing drinks. As the girls tried to move to the lifts, everybody followed. They made their rooms and locked the doors.

Oswaldson had left at this point, uniform dry, pulse racing with alcohol and sexual excitement, and caught a cab to the best brothel in town. *L'Escalier en Bois*, or The Wooden Staircase, was set in a concrete ruined house behind the main market. Arriving in his taxi, Oswaldson had charged up the stairs, which were rickety and falling down. There were empty spaces for the windows and dirt all over the stairs. In two upstairs rooms an old woman had greeted him and taken his order. A black girl appeared from the shadows with a vodka and orange and taken his clothes, folding them neatly in a corner. They had fucked on the dusty floor, grit and concrete chips grazing the legionnaire's arse, the teenage girl simulating enjoyment as Oswaldson let out the lust inspired by the girls from Bubbles. He had had more to drink and moved on, bumping into three other English men who were clustered round the corpse of a dead donkey in the street. Two of the boys reached down and picked up its lungs and windpipe which were lying in the road. The donkey had died and been half-eaten by dogs. Piling the green tendrils of stinking, warm lung tissue into their arms, the legionnaires had put it into a carrier bag and trooped off in search of a drink. At each bar they entered, they lifted the asses guts out of the bag, and waved the mass of tubes, lungs and flesh at the barmaids. If the barmaids laughed, they stayed for a drink, and if not, the foursome moved on to somewhere with more open minded staff. They had dumped the donkey's lungs in the gutter after a taxi driver refused to pick them up.

Oswaldson had gone off to a tin shack with a girl and fallen asleep, dead drunk. The Military Police had come looking for him the following day when he missed roll call, and cruised round the bars frequented by legionnaires. Showing his photo, they had discovered the address of the whore he had last been seen with and driven over to her house in the shantytown. They burst in as he was still asleep, slammed him across the chest with a pickaxe handle, smacked him in the face twice and threw him into the jeep. Two days later he had found himself alongside me on a working party from the Regimental prison, digging holes around tree roots on the long avenue which led up to the camp gates.

After five days of solitary confinement, during which I had done little except drink water, eat dry bread and sleep in my underpants on the floor of the bare cell, I was released into the main part of the prison along with the rest of the prisoners whose offences were not serious enough to warrant 'solitary'. My periods of 'exercise' had stopped, and although I felt nauseous and my face hurt after being hit so much, the violence had ceased. The Englishman who had deserted and been suspended from the tree, was in the camp hospital with severe infections on the soles of both his feet after the treatment he had received while being made to walk along the beach.

The prison was set behind the guardroom at the entrance to the camp and contained two solitary confinement cells, a living and eating area, four lavatories and a mass dormitory with bunks and barred windows which housed the minor offenders. I had been told to prepare my kit as I was to be picked up from the prison by Adjutant Lodvic who would escort me back to Arta to face our Company Commander. As I was from the 2ème Régiment Étranger de Parachutistes, I had to return to my original unit for questioning.

The penal system in the Legion was complex. Each regiment, whether in mainland France or abroad, had a regimental prison. Offences ranged from the straightforward ones, such as being absent from 'appel' or noticeably drunk in town, to the more serious ones like being absent from duty, losing regimental equipment or damaging the unit's property. The worst crimes were theft and desertion. Once picked up by the regimental police, the offender would be locked up for the night in an isolation cell, normally being beaten up in the process, before passing for report in front of his Company Commander the following day. If the crime was serious, the Captain could order the offender to see the Colonel, as only he could administer the stiffer sentences. These ranged up to eighty days in prison. In the case of a very serious offence, the legionnaire involved could be transferred to another Regiment entirely, such as the *3ème Régiment Étranger d'Infanterie* based in South America. There the offender would find himself building roads through the Amazon jungle or clearing swamps of underwater tree roots. The incidence of disease was high due to the climate and the medieval working conditions, and many people returned home from Guyana with their health in ruins.

I returned to Arta with Lodvic, who surprisingly hadn't hit me at all. He wanted to know what it was about life in his Section that had made me desert. Apart from us new members, the Section had remained unchanged since Chad, and worked well and cohesively together. Lodvic was pissed off that I had not been able to come to him and explain my predicament, yet he knew that had I done so he would have hit me for complaining. He was furious with Garcia and Dautremont, as their behaviour had resulted in my desertion, which in turn had meant a lot of unnecessary work for everybody. Capitaine Trousseau shouted at me and referred me to the Colonel at Camp Gabode. He in turn gave me forty days inside.

I had been escorted over to the jail block by a Corporal and presented to the Sergeant-Major in charge of the prison. He was a small, slim man with metal-framed spectacles and the air of a professional dentist. He was in his white dress uniform and his chest had more medals on it than I had ever seen. He looked me up and down as I stood rigid at attention in front of him, and nodded slowly. He told me that there was a lot of hard work to be done in the next month and that should I fail in any way he would be most displeased. He spoke slowly, in articulate, perfect French, his white fingers holding a menthol king sized cigarette. I would have thought him foppish if I hadn't known otherwise. He had served in the Hitler Youth in World War Two, joining the Legion immediately afterwards. He had been one of the men who had marched down the Champs Élysées prior to embarking for Indo-China, listening to the cheers and jubilation of the Parisian crowd. Like many of his former mates from the Wehrmacht and the SS, he had found it odd that the French could cheer soldiers who two years before had been occupying their country and sending their menfolk off to die in the gas and wire of the camps in the East.

Adjutant-Major Rohtz had served in the French Foreign Legion for thirty-eight years. The prison detail ran smoothly under his supervision, and I would get up at 4.00 am to wash and shave. We slept on the floor of one of the bunk rooms on mattresses, towels spread underneath our bodies to soak up the sweat which rolled off as we dozed. It was still dark when I awoke and I smoked my first cigarette as I drank my coffee. The Corporals would inspect the living quarters and the cells, running their fingers over the surfaces to check for dust. The older Corporal would shave in the morning smoking a cigarette at the same time, which I noticed lasted him through the process of washing, shaving and having a crap. Some of the prisoners took his cigarette butts off him as they had nothing to smoke. Living, smoking, eating and sleeping in such close proximity to the other men, using the same lavatories before their water had finished flushing, borrowing their toothbrushes and using their towels was enough to make me feel sick. I sweated all the time and had the red dots and spots of prickly heat all over my torso and legs. My clothes were always damp with perspiration and even at 5.00 am before the sun rose I would feel my shaved head running free with sweat. We spent all morning on a workparty, had lunch at noon and then our siesta. We jammed together on the floor, lying on towels, lying on each other, trying to sleep, but only managing to stare at the walls and smoke. There was no air conditioning at all in the prison block and the heat of the African summer came straight in through the barred, glassless windows. It was much hotter on the coast than on the mountain at Arta, and the air was thick and dusty. The entire sky was a yellowish grey that emanated heat.

My first assignment after digging holes was to work on the garbage lorry which collected all the rubbish from the camp and took it to the municipal dump in town. After breakfast each day I reported to the dustbin Corporal, a German with a floppy, alcohol-streamed face who had served in the Legion for eleven years. He had been in Tahiti and Madagascar and had ended up driving the rusting, filthy tipper-truck. Outside the cookhouse, the stores, the barrack rooms and the dining rooms were dustbins, most containing wastepaper and floor sweepings, dirt and old clothes. The one outside the kitchen was enormous and overflowing with all the leftovers, vegetable scraps, animal and fish guts, gallons of wasted soup and cooking oil which got thrown out of the kitchen every day. African servants performed the menial tasks in the cookhouse and would throw the rubbish haphazardly into the dustbin hut, often missing the bins entirely. The convicts on the lorry emptied the bins, scooped up all the heat-rotten filth off the floor and piled it into the lorry. By the end of the round, their camouflaged fatigues were covered with a slimy mess of stale food which got into your skin and stank for days afterwards. I stood in the back of the lorry, knee deep in putrid food, used bandages from the hospital, beer bottles and pieces of paper. One of the cooks, a small man with a boil on his face, gave me cigarettes every day, but the paper and tobacco went soggy from the filth on my hands. When the lorry was full, we would drive out of the main gates and down the long drive to the main road which led to the rubbish dump at Bal-Ballah, around which an enormous shanty town had grown up. The road was edged with willow trees growing in the sparse dirty sand. There was rubbish everywhere under the trees and at intervals the green and white taxis which were the main form of transport in the area would park while their drivers made tea or drank Fanta. There was no pavement at all; the tarmac stopped and the dust began. In the dust, the Africans squatted down with their robes and sticks and stared at every person who walked past; small children would chase behind the lorry, trying to jump on so that they could feed on the rubbish. I had to stop them and push off the ones who managed to get a hold of the sides of the tipper. We drove along, me standing up with my hands on the top of the cab letting the warm breeze blow away the smell and some of the sweat.

It was more peaceful in prison than it was with the company and once you had got used to the disgusting jobs there was nothing to worry about. It was also hotter in prison and I felt sick most of the time, I didn't have enough cigarettes and I got very little sleep, but at least I wasn't being hit constantly. I didn't have to sing or iron and I didn't see Garcia or Dautremont. The *13ème Demi Brigade de la Légion Étrangère* was calmer than Arta and I felt relaxed as I stood watching the Africans around me, my legs up to the knees in cooking oil and rotting cous cous. My status as an élite soldier in the world's top Airborne regiment was slipping a bit, but I felt better as a dustman than a punchbag. We drove past the whitewashed barracks of the Regular Army which stretched along the side of the road, the washing flapping in the breeze and the conscripts strolling around bare chested as they went about their business. Across the railway line the town became more sprawling and haphazard as we went into the district of Ambouli which was out of bounds to legionnaires. The buildings were often uncompleted and the gardens overgrown, and small tin shacks had sprung up along the way offering everything from a tyre change to a can of pop. Once through Ambouli, we left the city proper and started on the road which eventually led to Arta and the Ethiopian frontier. It went through a wide, dried up river bed which had only a trickle of muddy sludge running in it, where the locals did their washing. Out beyond the river bed the road branched off, a small tarmacked track going through the shanty town to the rubbish dump beyond.

When the civil wars had started in Somalia and Ethiopia, the refugees from those countries had naturally fled to Djibouti, which was at peace. The shanty town had sprung up slowly at first, and bulldozers from the Legion camp would arrive periodically and raze it to the ground, crushing the ramshackle buildings of cardboard and corrugated iron which would then spring up again overnight, as the inhabitants dragged rubbish, scraps of metal and wood off the heaps of debris to rebuild their houses. After independence, the government had stopped trying to contain the spread of the town, and in 1985 the whole thing stretched for two miles across the dunes and sand to the right of the road. As the rubbish truck turned off the main highway, groups of small children ran after the lorry and clambered on to the sides, ignoring the danger of the turning wheels. They scrambled up into the back, where they elbowed each other out of the way as they fought for all the scraps of food. They ranged in age from five to twenty, very thin, with limbs deformed and stomachs concave; some had scars and all were malnourished. There were the twisted limbs which came from bones broken and not set properly. Accidents happened easily when you lived on a rubbish dump in a house made of cardboard and scrap metal, where your food came from the dustbins and where the only money came from a single sister who fucked drunk legionnaires. At Camp Amilakvari a lorry emptied the bins and dumped the rubbish on a tip halfway down the mountain. I was on the garbage detail one day with another Englishman, and as usual, several local children tried to climb on to the back. We pushed them off, but one child, aged about ten, had grabbed hold of the tailgate and clung on. The lorry weighed four tons and the metal tailgate of the tipper swung on retaining pins set on the side of the vehicle. It was made of steel and was the size of a bed; the child didn't realise that it was only sitting on its mountings as we had removed the retaining pins to facilitate the tipping operation. The tailgate fell away under the child's weight and the whole mass of metal fell back on top of him, its edge landing sharply across his lower legs. I saw this and called to the driver to stop. All four of us climbed down and walked back to where the boy was trapped; the sharp edge of the gate had hit his left leg below the knee, snapping the bone cleanly in half. He was grey and sweating with pain. We drove on, emptied the rubbish and swept the back clean, turning the lorry to pick up the child before putting him in the cab. His leg was swinging loosely, the edges of the bone leading out from the torn skin. We drove him up to the hospital in the village where the French doctor diagnosed a broken limb, which he treated and put in plaster before handing the child back to his mother.

Down in Djibouti, I made little effort to stop the children climbing on the lorry, as for most of them this was the only food they ate. One of them picked up a broken *képi* which lay in a pool of stale beetroot. He put it on his head but I knocked it off. Through the shanty town, more children and old women tried to get on. The track passed houses made of rubbish from the dump: everything had been put to some use – plastic sacks, old bed frames, lumps of wood and pieces of metal sheeting. Cows and goats drifted through the shambles of the dusty buildings, nosing for food amid the grime and squalor. Humans lived with the animals and foraged for food with them, the children pushing the insistent black and white sheep out of the way to get to a pile of mangled, soggy bread, while the old women, their feet wrapped in blackened and greasy rags, bent double to probe in the rubbish with their sticks. Tipping the truck, a pile of food and detritus rained down on to the eager people below, who dug and shoved in their efforts to find something to eat. Goats climbed over children who were stuffing old scraps into their shirt-fronts to take home to their families. The authorities set fire to the dump at regular intervals, and thick, acrid grey smoke drifted over the whole area. It was very hot now in the middle of the day and large black African crows hopped and jumped around the edge of the crowd. A group of shabby brown vultures were tearing up a dying cow which lay on its side halfway down the side of a pile of garbage; the animal was waving its feet feebly as it expired from starvation. The vultures were thrusting their heads up its arse and into its eyes and mouth as they looked for a way to break the skin. Some children with twisted lips and eyes weeping cataract pus asked me for cigarettes but I had none. The Corporal smoked a Gauloise, leaning against the cab as the cow died and the fires burnt. It was getting close to lunchtime, so we swept out the back of the lorry before we both climbed aboard and drove away, the metal of the tipper tray slippery and greasy with the residue from the kitchens.

After lunch and our siesta, the evening routine involved watering all the flower beds and lawns which surrounded the guardhouse and the offices of the regimental Colonel. The entrance to the camp was a mass of green lawns and ordered gardens; every evening, gallons of water were hosed over them to keep them green. The garden inside the gatepost had a flagpole in the middle flying the tricolour and the flag of the *13ème Demi Brigade dé la Légion Étrangère*; at sunrise and sunset a trumpet sounded, the guard presented arms and everybody in the camp stood to attention wherever they were and whatever they were doing. I was on a stepladder clipping a tall hedge with four other people when the trumpet sounded: as one, we smacked to attention in our positions. Some Africans watching us from the kitchens looked bemused at four grown men on ladders standing motionless in the setting sun. The guard changed, and we went off indoors for our evening meal. After supper, the Duty-Sergeant inspected us as we paraded naked outside the cells, illicit cigarettes for the night clutched between the cheeks of our arses. We were counted and then locked up; depending on the Sergeant, the air conditioning was turned on or left off. This had a direct bearing on whether or not we got any sleep as it was impossible to sleep without air conditioning.

I would lie awake smoking for an hour sometimes before falling asleep, wondering what it would be like returning to the 3rd Company and the *2ème Régiment Étranger de Parachutistes*. Despite being in prison, life in Djibouti City was so easy and untraumatising. The soldiers from the *13ème Demi Brigade de la Légion Étrangère* were laid back and relaxed, and it was rare for the Corporals or Sergeants to get over-violent. Of course, you got hit a few times a week perhaps, but nothing too much. If you switched on, then life could be fun. There were drugs, music, plenty of warm sun and the camp lay on the doorstep of the world's biggest brothel. The attitude of the Unit was epitomised by legionnaire Tino, who was serving a prison sentence with me. He had been caught with civilian clothes in his possession. Unlike some legionnaires, who had a pair of jeans or some non-regulation T-shirts, Tino had a complete wardrobe. He was a tall black man with an elegant profile and a fine sense of style. He grew drugs behind the cinema, much to the annoyance of the Military Police, who were constantly trying to catch him smoking it. He sold some of it in town, where he ventured occasionally, changing into civilian clothes in the bathroom at the Sheraton. And what civilian clothes. He had a suitcase full of silk ties, crisp cotton shirts and fine white underwear. A legionnaire had been given 100 francs by Tino one day to go and pick up a parcel from the central Post Office in town. It contained Tino's latest purchase mail order from Paris: an ankle-length silk dressing gown which he would sometimes wear for '*appel*' when he knew the Sergeant well enough. He smoked menthol cigarettes and talked about films. One of the Corporals he called '*Mademoiselle*' and he had been seen in safari jacket and white shoes talking to French civilians in town. But now he was in prison because the Military Police, unable to find his drug stash, had busted him for having Calvin Klein boxer shorts and a dressing gown next to his combats and camouflage in his locker. He had the bunk underneath me in prison, and would make up intricate sexual fantasies which he would recite to everybody.

One morning, after I had finished the dustbin lorry, Tino and I were detailed to go with a Corporal to water the flowerbeds in the Legion cemetery, which was set in a small piece of desert on the edge of the Red Sea. Towing a water cistern behind us we crossed over into a patch of desert scrub, where the dust blew over the tyre tracks as soon as we had passed. On the right hand was the African cemetery, the loosely-arranged headstones surrounded by willow and thorn trees, through which children wandered barefoot chasing each other and playing games as their parents tended the graves of their families and relatives. On towards the sea was a white-walled compound, the wrought-iron gate padlocked against intruders; its metalwork was shaped in the form of a flaming hand grenade. There were rows of neat white gravestones inside the walls, surrounded by raked gravel and ornamental shrubs and trees. At the far end was a memorial stone set in honour of all the legionnaires who had died in Djibouti; a large date palm grew to one side of it, the branches shading the white stone. Bunches of green unripe dates grew along the shoots emerging from its centre. The Corporal sat in the cab and read a porn magazine showing a black woman being pleasured by a donkey while I unwound the hosepipe and watered the shrubs. The cracked brown earth absorbed the water easily and I let the pipe gush away while Tino and I looked at the names on the gravestones. I felt melancholic and lost, surrounded by the identical stones with their names, ranks and Legion numbers. It could easily have been my remains sitting underneath the baked soil, my shrivelled corpse recovered from the wastes of the Grand Bara, thrown into a wooden box with some rocks added to make up the weight. There would have been a funeral and a service, but after that I would have stayed here for ever, the shrubs around my grave watered once weekly by prisoners whose only crime perhaps had been to wear a silk dressing gown. I smoked and looked around again, kicking myself out of my reminiscences, remembering how much of a farce my escape attempt had been. To try and cross the desert in mid summer had been absurd, as Tino told me when he asked why I was in prison.

Few of the names on the graves were French, apart from the two most recent dug three days before by a work detail from the prison. These graves housed the coffins of two legionnaires, one German and the other Yugoslavian, who had adopted French names and both of whom had died of Hepatitis B the previous week. I had been standing outside the regimental hospital as their funeral cortège had driven past, the wheels of the trucks painted white in honour of the dead. There had been an honour guard from the Regiment who had stood at the side of the grave in parade uniform, presenting arms as the wooden boxes were lowered into the ground. The Colonel of the Regiment and the Padre had both made speeches praising the exploits of the dead men. One had been a stores clerk and the other a cook, and both had died from the hepatitis contracted during a routine blood test at the hospital in Djibouti City. The names on the graves reflected the differing trends of nationalities. There were the Mullers, Krantzes and Schmidts from Germany straight after the war, Frescobaldi's and Perronelli's from Italy and the occasional Oriental name of one who had accompanied the Legion back from Indo-China. There was one Englishman. I knew his story. He was called Miller and he had been based with a combat company at Hol-Hol, a small village in the middle of the desert. He had been on leave one evening and had missed the truck back to camp. He had purchased a young camel in the market during the day and the camel had accompanied him on his evening bar crawl; realising that he had missed the homebound truck, Miller and his pet had walked through the night to Hol-Hol. Because he was late, the Sergeant-Major had punished him. The Company kept a lion as a mascot, and Miller's pet had been stuffed, protesting furiously, into the cage. The lion had eaten it while the Company looked on. Miller had died of paludism, a disease compounded by an infection of the foot resultant from shooting himself while on guard duty.

I strolled around the bushes pulling out weeds from the ground as the Corporal finished his magazine; Tino was looking over the wall at the sea, which stretched off towards the Yemen. We ate unripe dates and wondered how long it would take us to swim to South Yemen. I had no desire to try, as I was happy in prison, doing different things most days. There was a good routine, and there were all sorts of odd things that got done by the prisoners, which made each day interesting. The 3rd Company was leaving Arta on 4 August, and I wanted to work it so that I could stay away from them until then. I would be entitled to my leave in Calvi, and once that was over, Garcia and Dautremont would have left to do their Sergeant's courses, which would keep them away for four months. I felt that once they had gone, I could rediscover my enthusiasm and really get going again. I thought about England, especially when I was with Slug, but only in an abstract fashion. In prison, I drifted along, completely at the mercy of routines set by others, and I was happy to daydream and observe what was going on around me.

While I laid out the Scrabble board, the Chief-Corporal put his fingers up the prostitute's vagina, inspecting her for venereal disease. She was lying on her back with her feet in stirrups, her robes up around her middle, looking anxious as a Captain watched the inspection; the middle-aged black woman in the corner said nothing but held the young girl's hand. I set out three letter boards and distributed seven pieces on each, putting the box and the Scrabble rules on the window-sill. Moving carefully because of the bandages on my arms and head, I told the Captain that I was ready. The Corporal finished his inspection and stripped off his surgical gloves; the black girl stood down from the table and grinned weakly as the Captain signed her certificate and told the old woman that she was good enough. The old woman held out her hand to the Corporal and muttered, '*Quatre mille francs*.' The Corporal took out a roll of worn notes from his inside pocket. I went over to the fridge in the corner and took out three cold beers and some gherkins which I put on a plate; the Corporal grabbed at them immediately, saying he had a thing about gherkins. He thanked the old woman and wished her well, telling the young girl to wait in the corridor outside until he called.

We sat down to play. A Captain from the sick wing with red velvet epaulettes. A Chief Corporal, who in his role as a pimp had just bought a girl for the camp brothel. A paratrooper who had deserted from the amphibious company and was now in the infirmary covered in boils.

I started off with '*décider*'. The Captain followed with '*mechta*'. The Corporal hesitated.

None of us were French, yet we argued about the spellings, drinking our beers as the ever-decreasing supply of words squared and stamped across the board, all three of us using Legion slang and proper nouns, going against the rules. I criticised the Corporal on his spelling of '*chiotte*' but the Captain intervened, telling me that a Corporal always knew better than a legionnaire, even at Scrabble. He added, jokingly, that if I won he would cut off my supply of antibiotics in revenge. We played on until teatime, when I cleared away the board and tidied up the table; the Corporal returned to the brothel to stock the fridge with drinks, and the Captain went off to supervise the evening's medical session in the surgery. I returned to my bed, lay down in my sports shorts, and listened to 'Born in the USA' on a Walkman.

After two weeks in prison I had caught an infection from the thorns of a hedge I had been clipping; the middle finger of my right hand had swelled up so much that I couldn't move the other digits and I was driven to hospital in a jeep. The hospital in Djibouti City was staffed by white doctors but run by local nurses.

The doctor saw from my T-shirt that I was a paratrooper and felt that I didn't need an anaesthetic, so he cut open my finger with a scalpel and drained the pus from my hand; I lay there gritting my teeth, and when he had finished, the swelling had disappeared, replaced by an enormous bandage. To avoid reinfection in the filth of the prison, I was sent to the camp hospital, which was very peaceful. I spent upwards of nineteen hours a day asleep in bed, in an air conditioned ward, with white sheets on the bed and Kim Carnes playing on my headphones. The only interruptions were the thrice-daily medical inspections where I had my infections cleaned and received my antibiotic injections. Three times a day I had jabs into my backside; after ten days the medics started joking about it looking like a firing range, as they looked for a fresh area in which to place the needle. The blood infection had spread to my head, arms, legs and back manifesting itself in numerous painful boils. Three times a day the Corporal would squeeze out any pus which had collected there since my last treatment, pushing the boils, which ranged from ones the size of a pea to a golfball-like lumps on my back. Taking a sharp pair of tweezers, they would tear out the foul greenish tissue from inside the wound, before filling the hole with a mixture of iodine and brine. A clean dressing was then forced in with a pair of metal forceps. I would lie on the bench, averting my eyes from the operation, ending up watching somebody else being treated. There was a choice of ailments to observe: the legionnaire who had a groin fungus and had to stand his penis in a jar of purple tincture three times a day, half-hidden behind a screen as he hopped up and down with the burning sensation. There was a Tahitian whose leg had ballooned with the amount of pus in it, something that no amount of penicillin could control as he would go out and get drunk every night. The most interesting was another man whose back, rubbed raw by his rucksack, had become infected after jumping into the Red Sea from a chopper. He had scraped his body on a coral reef of some sort and it had reacted violently. He had the most enormous infection, like a map of the world, which meandered across his torso in a strange pustular pattern. It wasn't getting any better.

I felt that my infections, though painful, were minor in comparison, and so long as I could keep them on the go for a week or two more, I could delay returning to prison and thence to Arta. If prison had been relaxing then the sickbay was a holiday camp. There were drugs and drink smuggled in by English friends, there was Scrabble, music on my Walkman, and all I had to do was thirty minutes of '*corvée*' each day. Sometimes I would help the dentist and clean his instruments, rinsing miniature drill bits in disinfectant and scraping the cement off the probes he used for doing his fillings. We got on well together, and he told me about his motorbike and his weekends scuba diving in the sea. He had a girlfriend in Paris whom he was going to marry when he got home. I made up stories about my life in England, saying that I had been in the English army and had turned down the chance to become an Officer, preferring the Legion instead. We talked about my desertion and the effect it would have on my future in the Legion. Deserting was the most serious offence I could have committed and I had compounded my error by getting caught. I saw very little of any of the boys from the 3rd Company, as they were out on exercise in the north of the Republic, training in the forest of Auday, a prehistoric landscape of forests and mountains which had survived from thousands of years before. Trees didn't normally grow in the extremes of heat encountered in Djibouti because there was so little water. At Auday there were chestnuts and eucalyptuses, rhododendrons and palm trees. The boys had been there for three weeks and I only saw them when they came down to the camp to go to the sickbay or the hospital. I missed Slug and Marius, and felt slightly out of things in Djibouti City, although anything that kept me away from Garcia was welcome.

The Section was split between those who thought I deserved to be punished for having deserted, and those who disliked Garcia and Dautremont so much that they were understanding and sympathetic towards me. When Adjutant Lodvic had picked me up from prison, he had refrained from hitting me because he knew that something major lay at the heart of my escape attempt. I felt that I had let him down and tried to explain this to him. He was interested and impressed with my escape attempt because of the way in which I had carried it out, which he regarded as adventurous and pioneering, as well as potentially suicidal.

The Colonel in Djibouti City, who had interrogated me and sent me to prison, had asked me what I had intended to do if I had reached Ethiopia. I had had jolly hopes of walking over the frontier, hitching a ride to Addis Ababa on the back of some lorry, and then presenting myself at the British Embassy there so that they could fly me home. This simplistic view of current affairs and diplomacy would have got me shot. I had been happy to leave behind the security and safety of Camp Amilakvari for the rigours of the desert, safe in the self delusion that I was on my way to something better. As it turned out, it was better that I should have been caught, as it meant that I would be leaving Africa alive and in one piece, rather than existing in people's memories as somebody who had done something stupid one evening and walked off into the desert never to be seen again.

There was a huge difference between the way in which the Legion was seen objectively by outsiders and the way it appeared to us. To the rest of the world, the Legion was *Beau Geste*, white *képis* with flaps down the back, Fort Zinderneuf and nameless people fleeing failed love affairs. I had realised by the middle of July 1985 that the reality was different. Any hint of romance and glamour was crushed by the hard work and physical effort required to complete the daily round of exercise, discipline and military training. I was so tired at the end of each day that all I wanted to do was sleep and retreat from the clamourings and shoutings of those around me. Privacy and independence came from having the unoccupied time in which to think and reflect; it wasn't dependent on being physically alone. As long as I was within the Legion, none of my aspirations to anything outside of it meant anything. For every night that I lay awake, pushing away tiredness and exhaustion so that I could give myself time to think, was in effect a waste of time, because in the morning I would be faced with the daily round of cleaning and bullshit, which became steadily worse the more I tried to escape from it. The physical side of our existence was the easiest one to rationalise; all of us, whether former soldiers or beginners such as myself, gained confidence and enjoyment from straightforward actions such as jumping out of helicopters into the sea or running ten miles before breakfast. It was for this that I had become a paratrooper in the Legion; the possibility of conflict with the Armed Forces of somebody else's country was something most people looked forward to. We all buoyed each other up with stories of professionalism and time under fire. I just sat and listened, as I had done in the Territorial Army when the Sergeant-Major who had been in the Falklands lectured us.

My abcesses and boils were healing quickly as a result of the clean, antiseptic environment of the camp hospital. Each day the Captain in charge would look at them and decide if I should be readmitted to prison. I wanted to stay in the sickbay for a little longer, so I took a piece of cotton wool and wiped it deeply and thoroughly around the rim of one of the lavatory bowls, and then into the corners on the floor behind it. With the help of the English Corporal who was duty medic that week, we stuffed small pieces of the filthy dressing into each of my wounds and bound them up. It was like waiting for nasturtium seedlings to grow: both myself and the Corporal were curious to see what would happen and when we changed the dressings, we pulled out the small pieces of lint, scanning each hole hopefully for the greenish pus and rotten tissue which would herald streptoccocal infection. However, I had obviously developed some superior resistance to illness as nothing happened at all. So, two days later, I put everything into my small backpack, put my bush hat on and walked back over to the prison for the last five days of my sentence.

I got back to Camp Amilakvari two days before the unit left for Europe; I reported in to Corporal Garcia at the company office; he didn't hit me. Feeling like a stranger, I walked into our barrack block to dump my kit and to say hello to all the boys. There was a lot of laughter at my loss of weight. Slug rose off his bed and strode over, slapping me on the arm and pumping my hand, rattling away with all the details and gossip of what had been happening since we last saw each other. Marius came in, blond hair shaved right off, and laughed and teased me about my time in prison, and that afternoon the three of us packed up all our kit. We had two weeks in Calvi together on leave coming up. Two days later in the sweltering heat of the coast, we trooped on to a civilian aircraft at Djibouti City; after a short wait on the tarmac while two Mirages screamed into the sky, we took off, banking over the Red Sea before turning north west towards Europe.

— 9 —

MORE FUN WITH TERRIERS

The Military Policeman upended my kit bag onto the floor of the gymnasium as he looked for diamonds or drugs. He kicked my clothes and possessions around, rifled through my wash kit and underwear, burrowed in my sleeping bag and stood upright, satisfied that I hadn't tried to smuggle any contraband in my luggage. All around me, the other members of the Company watched as their belongings were taken apart in a thorough search.

The Officers and Sergeants, immune by virtue of their rank from such interference, stood at the side of the sports hall and watched, waiting for somebody to be caught with something irregular in their possession. It had been possible to buy anything in Djibouti City, from drugs to fake Kelim rugs. As in Saigon at the end of the American occupation, there was an air of commercial desperation, and for those who had enough Djiboutian currency, or, even better, Swiss francs or German deutschmarks, anything was available. A lot of people had returned from Africa with the normal souvenirs of intricately faked tribal carvings, but nobody had been foolhardy enough to smuggle in an Uzi sub machine gun or a fistful of uncut diamonds. Crawling out of the *Escalier en Bois* one evening, I had been approached by a Djiboutian who had asked me if I wanted to buy some rare and valuable swords. My interest aroused, I followed him to the flat of a friend of his, who had pulled out from under the bed a bundle wrapped in flour sacks. He had shown me two curved scimitars whose handles, though encrusted in shining, coloured stones, looked as though they were made of Bakelite. I had enough money to buy them but thought that I would have little use for them in Corsica. I didn't regret this, for the Military Police had passed on to the next legionnaire, leaving me to repack my belongings.

We had flown to Bastia from Djibouti City and paraded in front of an inspecting General who congratulated us on having fulfilled our mission in Djibouti so successfully. The air in Corsica was much clearer than in Africa; gone was the thick yellow heat haze, and in its place was the pure, mountain air of a Mediterranean island. None of us were very tanned after spending four months in the third hottest country in the world; our skins had a nasty creamy-olive pallor, looking dirty, greasy and unhealthy. My arms were covered in the freshly-healed scars of the boils I had suffered. It was good to be back from Africa in one piece, and I was glad that I hadn't left my bones in a sun-bleached pile to the west of the Grand Bara desert. Several times while in Africa, I had felt that I was at the complete limit of human existence, and that at no other point in my life would I be so far from any point of human or social reference. It was very easy to allow the four month tour to blow itself out of proportion into a heady pioneering adventure, yet all the time we had been carefully supervised. Had we fallen ill while on patrol, or tumbled off a cliff face abseiling, there would have been immediate medical backup available. At no point had we been left to be totally self reliant and make decisions which could have resulted in our own deaths. The element of risk was surprisingly minimal in the Legion. Any man who is healthy and mentally sound could parachute out of an aeroplane or march fifty miles across the desert; it only took extreme physical fitness and advanced professional masochism. The one element which inspires people to push themselves beyond their mental or physical limits was missing. That of risk.

In joining the Legion, all of us had taken a risk because we were unaware of the nature of the organisation we were becoming a part of. Once we had arrived, excelled at our basic training and been posted to the élite of the organisation, the life had become ordered in every way. Friends who had served with the British Special Air Service had told me of an inscription on a monument at their barracks in Hereford. In the middle of the parade ground was a clock tower, inscribed with the names of the members of the regiment who had been killed on active service and had failed to 'Beat the Clock'. Underneath this list of names was a quotation from a poem called 'The Golden Road to Samarkand'.

> We are the pilgrims, Master, we shall go
> Always a little further: it may be
> Beyond that last blue mountain barred with snow,
> Across that angry or that shimmering sea . . .

I had pushed myself out into the desert completely unprepared for it, gambling my health, and possibly my life, on my own innate ability to look after myself. Once the road had become difficult, I had thrown it all up for the physically arduous yet mentally safe environment of the Regimental prison. If I compared the élite status of the *2ème Régiment Étranger de Parachutistes* with that of the Special Air Service, taking the SAS as a role model for military élitism and perfection then in SAS terms I had certainly failed. I hadn't made it as a 'pilgrim' for I had taken the easy and unadventurous option.

Ahead of me lay two weeks in Calvi, followed by a return to the 3rd Company for further training and a possible underwater warfare course. This course would be physically demanding and would give me a chance to rediscover a bit of enthusiasm in my soldiering and in myself. For the next two weeks, however, we were on leave, in uniform, in Calvi, in summer. It was a chance to pose a little and to try and impress the tourists. All the days of boredom and bullshit were forgotten as we looked forward to our holiday. We would be able to lie in in the mornings, drink beer, sunbathe, get prohibitively drunk and perhaps even get fucked without paying. We were all in an expansive mood as we laid out our uniforms for the break. For those of us who had more than eighteen months' service in the Legion, leave could be taken on the French mainland. Most of the English legionnaires were looking forward to slipping over to Great Britain for a fortnight of drinking and partying with their friends and with each other. There was a lot of talk of going to Romford, driving down to Aldershot to see the lads from the Paras, staying at Mum's house, shopping in London and rolling their cases.

For the rest of us, there was the *Centre de Repos*, the Legion's hotel in the citadel. In Calvi, we had to wear our walking out uniforms, we had to salute the Military Police and we had to behave in an exemplary manner towards the tourists. Slug, Marius and myself were among those driven off to the citadel in a coach. Our rooms overlooked the bay and the beach. The rest centre was a yellowish building with green shutters, set in a small garden with a courtyard where one of the Corporals grew tomato plants against the wall. We were not allowed out of the town of Calvi, and could only visit the beach if dressed in our '*tenue de plage*'. This consisted of white tennis shirts with matching logos on the chests, white shorts with a crease ironed down the front and identical Adidas trainers worn with white socks. Sunglasses were left to our discretion. I had paid 360 francs for a pair which covered half my face like the eyes of a tropical insect. With a bundle of francs in the pockets of our shorts and our hair freshly cut into Mohican crops, we were ready for the assault on the tourists. Reports had come in from some of the boys who had stayed behind while we were in Djibouti who had already been out on the beach. Conditions were great, they said, and there were lots of Scandinavians around who were trapping well.

Slug explained the theory of 'trapping', as perfected by the Royal Marines. There were essentially two kinds of evening out, or 'run ashore' as it was known in Marine terms. There was the one where the aim was to get totally pissed by drinking as much as possible, perhaps at 3.00 am ending up in the arms of a girl who hadn't been lucky enough to get picked up. These evenings consisted of throwing drink over each other and any girls in the vicinity, and watching fat girls perform tricks with shit and beer glasses, and dancing *en masse* at the Plymouth discos patronised by the Marines. 'Trapping' evenings were for chasing women and getting fucked. You trapped by yourself, away from your mates, who would be liable to spoil things if they could. Slug told me about the activities of the Alpha Company anti-trapping team. It was winter 1981 in Plymouth and things were bad. None of the boys were getting fucked. So the boys who had no chance, either because they were too bored to try or too interested in getting pissed, formed the anti-trapping team. When somebody was noticed in the barrack rooms getting dressed up for an evening out, obviously on his own or with a girl, everybody else would take note. He would meet her in a quiet, secluded pub or restaurant, where there was no chance of bumping into his mates, who might throw up over her or abuse her. So you would be sitting in your pub, with your girl, telling her wild tales about daring and macho achievements, hoping that you hadn't been followed or noticed by any of the others. Suddenly, three or four of the boys from your company would waltz into the pub, buy drinks, throw some noise around and then walk over to where you were sitting. Having noticed from your preparations in the barrack room with deodorant and clean clothes that you were off trapping, they would have combed the town in groups of three or four, until they found you. The girl you were with would be subjected to a few insults and a bit of drink throwing, perhaps, or if the situation warranted it, four of your mates would sit round you in complete silence and watch as you talked to her. You could do nothing. They were your mates. Your evening was ruined so you joined the anti-trapping team, out to spoil anybody else's chances of getting fucked. By late December 1981 the situation was desperate. The team contained nearly every member of the company and eventually there was one member who hadn't had his evening spoiled. All 130 Marines of Alpha Company went out looking for him one evening, combing every bar, pub and restaurant in the town, which had been described by Slug as somewhere where 'you would have to have two heads not to be able to trap successfully'. The search revealed nothing. He couldn't be found. It looked as though somebody might make it to penetration. The boys made it back to the barracks. The following morning, the guy in question returned to the barracks, his evening having been a complete disaster. He had made it to the pub and on to the restaurant without being spotted and had been climbing into a cab with the girl at the end of the evening on the way to her flat. Suddenly one of the boys appeared at the taxi rank, drunk, and spotted them in the cab; the bloke inside screamed 'Drive!' at the cabbie, who hesitated a minute too long. The hapless Royal Marine watched helplessly as his mate leant in through the passenger window and puked all over his girlfriend's head. It was appalling – the bloke's evening was ruined and the two men had to share a taxi back together. They left the girl on the pavement and went off. The Alpha Company anti-trapping team was complete.

On the beach in Calvi, we walked abreast, towels rolled under our arms as we strode along subconsciously in step with each other. The island attracted a lot of tourists in the summer, although few were English; Italians and Germans were in a majority and the remainder were mostly Scandinavians. Most of the middle class European families were lodged in the hotels and guest houses in the town of Calvi or on the outskirts. The backpackers camped in the dozens of sites which lay behind the beach in the pine trees. The beach followed the curve of the bay, extending from the edge of the town at its western extremity, round past the amphibious warfare centre to where the rocks began at the far end of the bay. There was fine sand and the water only deepened very gradually over a distance of 200 metres, as the sea went from light turquoise to mid blue where it got deeper. There were numerous bars set along the sand, selling beer, pizzas, sandwiches and meals. These bars ranged in décor from the smallest ones, which were no more than a terrace with an awning and a blackboard advertising the prices, to two-storey buildings with matching sunshades and smart white tables, where the waiters served expensive food to orange-bronzed European families decked out in the latest beach wear. Middle-aged women in long white T-shirts covered in swirling appliqué designs of gold and silver stared through their horn-rimmed sunglasses as we sat down at the tables next to them, pulling out large amounts of cash from our pockets and demanding champagne and oysters. Rows of sunbeds lay in front of these bars, and we would spend the days lying on them gazing at the topless tourists.

We would arrive about noon, having woken to the reverberations of the hangover from the night before. We would walk down to the beach and take up our positions on our sunbeds, manoeuvring this way and that as we got comfortable and anointed ourselves with sun oil. A swim was followed by two or three hours' sleep, dripping sweat in the hot afternoon sun, reading Frederick Forsyth and smoking, or dozing away the heat of the day. We would swim again at teatime, clambering through the waves in our regimental black swimming trunks, splashing around in the surf. As the sun started to go down, we rejoined our towels and beach bags, got dressed and headed back into town. There we would shower, iron our uniforms, and sit around in each other's rooms smoking and chatting before getting dressed and walking down into the town. Shirts ironed with their fifteen different creases, metal parachute wings shining, we stepped carefully through the dust, passing the staring tourists.

Every evening followed a strict pattern. We would go to a bar where we would sit on the terrace and drink Pastis while we chose the restaurant in which we would eat dinner that evening. There were twenty different restaurants in Calvi, from basic pizza restaurants to the latest in *cuisine nouvelle*. All we had to do was enjoy ourselves. This was quite hard after four months in Africa in a strictly disciplined environment. Our own enjoyment was left to our imagination, which meant that each evening we would try and have the most expensive meal possible before going out and drinking ourselves stupid. One evening, we went to an expensive brasserie on the waterfront called *Comme Chez Soi*. We sat down and I started to translate the menu for Slug and Marius. There was an unspoken rivalry between the three of us. Slug had been in the Royal Marines, Marius the Swedish Army and myself the Parachute Regiment of the Territorial Army. Although I could speak better French than both of them, they were proficient soldiers in a way that I was not. They were critical of the Legion and its training methods, and the lifestyle which it imposed, but within the confines of these restrictions they were extremely professional. Both were fit and organised in their habits, and managed to keep their lives in order and still have fun. It was the same with John, the legionnaire who had enjoyed reading *Brideshead Revisited*. He could run faster than me, was in line for a Corporal's course, had a good sense of humour and could strip a .50 calibre machine gun without fault. He had been in the Legion long enough to be allowed leave on the French mainland while we were stuck in Calvi.

The restaurant in which we were sitting faced out to sea, and in common with all the other establishments along the front it had tables on the pavement. The table cloths and napkins were cream linen and the cutlery shone. Rich European tourists sat around studying the menus and lounging in their seats. We drank our beers straight out of the bottles as usual. This wasn't a display of bad manners as we behaved like that everywhere. It went unsaid that our standards of behaviour centred totally around the Legion, and there was no need for us to adapt them for the sake of other people's gratification. The way we saw ourselves in comparison to the way others saw us was well illustrated by the behaviour of an English family who were on holiday in Calvi at the same time. As in all holiday centres, people bumped into the same couples and families all the time. We had first come across this family one evening in a restaurant. The three of us and a Swiss man called Tommy were sitting at a table in a waterfront restaurant called *L'Espadon*. We were perusing the menu, chatting about our day's sunbathing and ordering a second round of drinks when a man and woman with their three children sat down at the table next to us. We turned and stared with interest, as they were talking English loudly. The father was remonstrating with his children in a strident upperclass voice.

'Charlotte, you sit there. Laura, stop playing under that table and help your mother with the chair. Charles, you sit next to me no, not there, here! No, of course you can't have an ice cream, they're nine francs, that's nearly a week's pocket money; darling, do pass my sweater.'

His wife was a silent woman in a floral skirt and white blouse, who looked as though her enthusiasm for marriage had long since disappeared. She sat down in complete silence, occasionally answering 'Yes, darling' or 'No, darling' with tired resignation. Amid a flurry of scraped glasses and banged chairs they sat down. The small boy leant over and looked at Slug with frank curiosity.

'Don't look at those men, Charles, you don't know who they are. They're probably all murderers. Help your mother with the menu.'

We had stopped talking, so that the family would not realise that we were English and thereby modify their conversation. It got worse.

'Darling, it's quite dreadful. I didn't know that they had all these Foreign Legion people in this town – I thought that they were all locked away in Algeria or something. They shouldn't be here, upsetting all the tourists.'

'Yes, darling.'

'I bet none of them would last a minute in the British Army. I had some chap in the Guards who ran off to the Foreign Legion. A right shirker, he was, always in trouble, always drunk and getting into fights.'

We gave the husband another five minutes in which to finish digging his grave, then nailed down his coffin by talking loudly about our times in the British Army. He didn't appear put out at all.

We saw them on the beach the following day. The flustered mother was oiling her children's shoulderblades in a resigned way while the husband directed the children to the exact area of sea in which they would be allowed to swim.

Slug and myself went out later on through the waves to where the son was treading water. We popped up beside him and asked him where he was at school and what he wanted to do when he grew up. He was about to go to public school at Radley and wanted to join the Guards like his father. We told him that we had both been to public schools, Slug adding with a howl of amusement that, 'Mine was so bloody public everybody went there.' On hearing this, the boy burrowed back through the waves and announced to his father that there were two public school boys from the Army swimming in the sea.

The father refused to talk to us, but got his come-uppance the following day when he was bitten by a dog on the harbour wall. Prompted by us, two Military Policemen told him that it almost certainly had rabies.

We didn't go out of our way to intimidate people, our behaviour normally being a model of politeness – we were so restricted in our freetime because we were in uniform and therefore represented the public face of the Foreign Legion. The Military Police nabbed anybody who didn't salute them or who appeared drunk or ill-disciplined.

Marius's girlfriend arrived in the middle of our leave. Tall and thin, she had bleached blonde hair of an almost industrial whiteness. She spoke English and was pleased to meet Slug and myself, having heard so much about us from Marius's letters. She was a quiet girl who lowered her eyes when she talked and it was obvious that she was very fond of Marius. He found it difficult being with us and with her at the same time, for she made demands on the softer, more human side of his nature which was a part of his personality which we had never seen before. All four of us went out to supper where we ate crabs and *Coquilles St Jacques*, along with four bottles of Corsican rosé wine. The bill came to over 1,000 francs, which was slightly above average, but as we normally spent £150 each in an evening we could well afford it; I had bought 2,700 francs with me at the start of my leave, and it looked as though it would hold out. Marius and Carina went off for a walk after supper, to have coffee before going back to her hotel which was in a cobbled square in the middle of town. Slug and myself kissed her goodnight and strolled up the waterfront in the middle of the road feeling very full and a bit drunk. We stepped aside to allow a Military Police jeep to pass and saluted the Corporal at the wheel.

We turned into the *Bar des Bons Amis*, which was run by Romy and Marie, two men who had had sex changes and who were both in different stages of femininity. Romy had a husky voice and rugger-player's hands, favouring high heels and basques over her suspenders and stockings. Slasher Moulton had a crush on Romy, and when we arrived he was talking to her at the bar, occasionally leaning over to kiss her or stroke her chest. Marie was considerably further advanced and had had the entire course of surgery, involving complicated incisions where the penis was turned inside out to form a vagina. I wasn't quite sure what her operations involved but she had been explaining it to Slug and myself for the past ten days. She had a high sex drive and was very keen on having her large brown nipples bitten and nuzzled by the legionnaires as she talked. Two nights before Slug had got her half undressed in wild curiosity to see what lay between her legs, but an Officer had come in looking for a drink, so he had then desisted. We both sat down and had a quiet beer, Marie leaning over the bar towards us, her tits slipping out of the side of her dress; I bent down and shoved my head between them as she stroked my hair and talked to Slug about her boyfriend who was in Djibouti. Slasher was well away with Romy, intertwining tongues with pink ferocity; he was also drunk, which meant that he would be wetting his bed later. He didn't mind wetting his bed, he said, as it proved that he had been decently pissed the night before. The real test of a good night, he believed, was when you shat yourself as well.

Slug and I got bored very quickly of any one bar, so telling Marie that we would be back later on, we went over to the Empire bar for a drinking competition. We settled down, primed the jukebox with Bonnie Tyler, Bruce Springsteen and Dire Straits and started to 'do the rainbow'. Above the zinc metal bar were rows of different spirit bottles, containing drinks from gin and Scotch to every sort of liqueur. It being Corsica, these ranged in colour from the Fairy Liquid green of pine cordial through the yellows of créme de banane to the pink of rhubarb brandy. Including the cassis and the cordials, there must have been twenty-five different colours which we could drink. 'Doing the rainbow' involved having a shot from every bottle, starting in the top left hand corner. Once we had finished the selection in the Empire bar, the contest moved on elsewhere. Listening to 'Twisting by the Pool' on the jukebox, I moved from raspberry brandy on to Jack Daniels via crème de cacao and orange Bols. Things got rough around the three malt whiskies, but I made the bottom of the second shelf with no problems. Slug was next to me gargling down a tumbler of Cointreau, five or six bottles ahead of me, and still in control. I hit the cassis without throwing up, chased it with pine cone brandy called 'myrrth' and finished with two shots of warm neat gin. I had done it.

I sat still on the barstool, letting everything settle in my stomach. Slug was asking for a couple of beers to chase things down with as we considered the next venue. I felt drunk but still in control. Standing up carefully, I put on my *képi* and walked out of the door with Slug. We returned to the *Bar des Bons Amis*, where Slasher was unconscious across a table, a warm trickle of vomit coming from his mouth. The contest moved on to a champagne basis. Each round consisted of a bottle each, half of which we swigged down and half of which was spilt on the floor. We listened to my favourite single of that summer, a French record called '*Paradis mi Amour*'. Half way through the song, I knew that I was finished. I grabbed my *képi*, slid out of the firedoor and threw up into a corner of the alley outside. I fell asleep in the *Centre de Repos*.

Slug, Carina, Marius and myself recovered on the beach the following day. Slug told us he had moved on to the nicest bar in Calvi, a plush haven of potted palms and leather chesterfield banquettes called *Les Palmiers* which was set on the waterfront. It was owned by Emil, a camp figure who made legionnaires especially welcome, not closing his bar until the last one left. We had seen him that morning as we walked down to the beach. He was walking his dogs, a huge great dane and a pekinese, and was wearing a green satin jumpsuit and high heeled Victorian laceup boots. He had violet horn-rimmed glasses and waved as we passed, admonishing us for having drunk so much the night before as alcohol wasn't, he said, good for sex. Not that any of us had been in any form for that.

As we oiled ourselves up and considered the day's tanning which lay ahead, Slug told us of a sighting we had had. There were three Swedish girls in town, he said, out on their own each night, eager to talk to legionnaires and make friends. I asked for descriptions. Apparently one was blonde and pretty, but didn't speak any English, the second spoke some English but had bad teeth, and the third was rounder and larger and spoke three languages fluently. Slug smeared Ambre Solaire over his tattoos and announced that it was trapping time.

Our relationships with women were strange. We had all been cooped up in Africa for four months and hadn't seen any white women during the entire period. Thirty of us were housed in the same barracks together and it was rare, even in Corsica, for us to have the time or the wherewithal to meet any girls. As we lay on the beach, heads shaved in our Mohican haircuts, wearing our black regulation swimming trunks and expensive sunglasses, there was little about us that could have been attractive to the opposite sex. I also had two missing front teeth which didn't make things any easier. There were plenty of tourists around who would probably have found the French Foreign Legion an interesting subject of conversation, but we were socially and physically tongue-tied by our complete inarticulacy. This inarticulacy went further than an inability to converse in foreign languages, and manifested itself in the shining desperation which we exuded whenever we tried to talk to women. For most of the time in the *2ème Régiment Étranger de Parachutistes*, marksmanship, physical fitness and soldiering prowess were enough to get by on. However, when faced with the problem of asking a topless Italian tourist if she wanted to join you in an ice cream or a swim, one's ability with a rocket launcher is of little use. We were surrounded by attractive women on holiday, with little else to do but sunbathe and enjoy themselves. Or so we saw it. But it was difficult to reassure girls that we were not going to steal their passports or rape them – and it got harder the more and more times we were turned down. Rejection made us resort to resentment, and this in turn led to hostility. Thus a lot of legionnaires preferred the asexual approach to intercourse offered by whores. It was certainly cheaper, if one considered that a meal and drinks involved in persuading a girl to remove her clothes on the beach at 4.00 am was often more expensive than two hours with a prostitute.

The ultimate sexual dream of a lot of soldiers was a steady relationship with a girl who drank a lot, could play pool and who liked being buggered. The comment of 'I bet she takes it up the arse' was one of praise for a girl who looked ready for anything and overtly sexually adventurous; who displayed, in fact, a lot of 'airborne' characteristics.

Buggery reduced sex from a pleasurable, emotive act to one of punishment where the girl's face was hidden and the only orifice available was her backside. As far as I was concerned, anal sex was out, but I was fascinated to find out the attraction it held for the other blokes. 'Going up the chutney tunnel' was the real end to a good evening out, and it was considered dead airborne to do it. In the Parachute Regiment in England, we had had a large parade in the summer of 1983, when new Colours, or flags, had been presented to the 10th Battalion by Prince Charles. After the parade, there had been a lunch set around a different number of marquees set up on the grass. Towards 3.00 pm when everybody was pissed, Prince Charles had walked around the tent where the Privates and Corporals were having their celebrations. Accompanied by the Colonel and the Regimental Sergeant-Major, the Prince had strolled round in his role as Colonel-in-Chief of the Regiment, chatting here and there to the lads and meeting the wives. Suddenly, from the back of the crowd came the voice of a drunken paratrooper.

''Ere, Charlie, does your wife take it up the shitter?'

Slug and I had an argument one evening about sodomy. The conversation had got round to it as we were discussing various post combat practices from Vietnam and elsewhere, such as the cutting off of ears and buggering of prisoners before shooting them. Underneath the documented and verified truth about soldiering and warfare in the twentieth century, there were lots of rumours and myths of things that happened in action and under fire that were never confirmed, but which were the subject of various apocryphal tales. I suspected that a lot of them were true, but had been denied because if, for instance, it became public knowledge that British paratroopers had sodomised Argentinian prisoners before cutting their throats in the mist and snow of a Falklands battle, then the acceptable and essentially chivalrous image of the British Army would be tarnished. I knew from people who had done it that there had been prisoners shot rather than taken captive, and within the confines and peculiar demands of battle then this was perhaps understandable. I could comprehend that a young soldier, such as myself, hyped up by his training and by the pressure of his more experienced peers could resort to levels of brutality which he wouldn't normally consider. The firepower at your disposal in a modern firefight was such that you were keen to try it out. A man who had been in prison in Djibouti City with me had served in the Falklands with the Parachute Regiment, and on Wireless Ridge had stuffed seven Argentinian soldiers into a small cave and fired a 66mm rocket into it, just, so he said 'to see what would happen'. The results had been predictable, with dismembered Argentinians smeared all over the rocks. I had never killed anybody, and prior to immersing myself in the airborne creed had never dreamed of doing so. But I could understand the enormous curiosity about one's weapons and their capabilities.

Slug wasn't very forthcoming about such brutal practices, so we had switched the conversation to sex. I ventured that because most soldiers wanted to bugger girls, treating them as sexless fuck-objects, then most soldiers were in fact into having sex with their alter egos, and were therefore homosexual. Slug denied this categorically, saying that soldiers were sexually and emotionally conservative, keen on their mothers and their mates, wanting only to have a nice time. I wasn't so sure.

In Calvi that evening we headed into town to look for the Swedish girls. We found them in one of the bars, clustered in a corner by the jukebox. I started talking to the largest of the three, who Slug described as a 'Sumo wrestler in drag'. She had worked in Calvi the previous summer as a waitress and had been having an affair with a legionnaire. The other love in her life had been her terrier, but the legionnaire had felt that he was being superseded in the girl's affections so he had thrown the dog underneath the propellers of the Calvi–Nice car ferry. Because of this she was ill disposed towards members of the Legion, and was reluctant to talk to me. I told her that just because I wore the same uniform, it didn't mean that I had the same attitude towards small furry animals. We peeled off from the others and went out to supper where she told me how she came to be working in Corsica, where she was from in Sweden and where she was now staying. We went out to the Calypso disco which was full of uniformed legionnaires dancing with tourists and with each other. Our walking out uniforms made dancing hazardous, as the metal tips of our lanyards would fly around and catch the other dancers in the eyes. Occasionally a piece of our uniforms would fall off and get lost in the crowd, but the old woman who ran the disco kept a supply of different badges behind the bar so that no legionnaire went home improperly dressed. Arriving back at the camp after an evening out it was essential to be able to walk through the gate and salute the Sergeant, thus demonstrating your sobriety.

The Swedish girl, whose name was Uta, and myself found a place on the dance floor and started twisting energetically to a song by a French rock and roll group called *Les Forbans*. I whirled her around the floor in an inexpert display of jitterbugging, bumping into friends and careering off fellow dancers. The walls were lined with seats where couples sat drinking or kissing each other with open-mouthed abandon. There was nowhere to take a girl after the disco closed apart from the beach, so last thing in the evening the front and the path along the sand was occupied by legionnaires kissing girls on benches or manoeuvring out of their uniforms on the sand, placing their carefully-folded shirts and trousers in neat piles before subsiding on top of the girls for their sex. Uta told me that she felt sad so I bought her a treble Scotch and Coke at the bar and squeezed in beside her at one of the plastic seats. Marius walked past on the arm of Carina, who looked tanned and stunning. Slug was over in another corner engaged in a heated discussion with two English Corporals about the merits of the Entebbe hostage rescue operation. Two Tahitians started a fight, but there was no room to swing their fists so a Sergeant intervened and called the Military Police. The waitresses balanced their way around with trays of glasses, and every half hour went in to mop the floor of the unisex toilet in the corner, sometimes having to push in the door against the weight of an unconscious legionnaire who had passed out while squatting down, or who had fallen dead drunk in the puddles of urine and spilt beer on the tiled floor. The bar was three deep with drinkers, paying £4 or £5 a go and the waitresses were working like stokers; the bar stools were long since occupied, and every minute the door would open and another party of legionnaires would arrive, take off their *képis* and pass them to the barmaids. With so many legionnaires around, all wearing white *képis*, it was surprising that nobody picked up the wrong one. A clever system had been devised whereby it was easy to identify your own: inside the crown of each *képi*, the legionnaire would place a sticker or a photograph of himself, his girlfriend, or some other subject. One person had a picture of a skull from Chad, another his dog at home, and somebody else their child. I had cut out a picture of Charlotte Birkin, the thirteen-year-old daughter of a French film actress, who I thought was pretty.

Uta felt the Scotch take hold and snuggled up; I looked round at the bar, feeling domestic and complete. Adjutant Lodvic winked at me and gave the thumbs-up signal, smiling his sloppy, dog-faced grin as he put his hands on his girlfriend's knees. She was sitting across from him smiling at the legionnaires around her, all of whom behaved with immense courtesy towards her as she was Lodvic's fiancée. The atmosphere in the bar was great – it was like going to a party where everybody knew each other and where everybody looked after each other. I pulled Uta towards me and slipped my arms around her shoulders, realising that she was a great deal wider than I. She was staying with two friends in a tent on a campsite a kilometre outside Calvi, on the road which led to the shooting range at Punta Bianca. Swallowing my Malibu and Coke, I stood up and suggested that I could walk her back to her campsite; she agreed, stressing that it was quite some way there and that if I came back there would be no room for me to stay in the tent as her friend was already there. I shrugged and said that I only wanted to make sure that she got back all right. We walked up the road holding hands, looking at the citadel on its rock and listening to the sea. I felt romantic and happy, enjoying the presence of somebody completely different from all the male soldiers by whom I was normally surrounded. I kissed her on the road to the *boules* pitch and again where the road passed by the police station. I stopped for a longer kiss in a layby overlooking the Mediterranean, feeling the power of her arms as she hugged me. It was great. We walked onto the campsite and past a lot of tents where large German motorbikes were parked on the concrete. Down past some trees we found her tent. It was chest height and looked as though it might comfortably sleep one person. Uta unzipped the flap and we crawled inside, across the mess of damp bikinis and empty rucksacks. Her friend was asleep in a blue sleeping bag curled up against the edge of the tent. We both undressed, her taking off her T-shirt to reveal a pink bra, myself taking off my *képi* and uniform shirt. She really was very big. I stacked my clothes on top of my shoes and slipped down on the top of her sleeping bag as she took off her shorts and white knickers, stretching out naked with her back to me. She whispered that we shouldn't do anything as her friend was asleep four inches behind me. We lay quietly for a bit longer as her breathing deepened and she started to sleep. I gave her five minutes before I started running my hands and fingers down her back and down the cleft of her backside. She murmured and protested that we shouldn't wake up her friend (who would have had to be clinically deaf to be still asleep). Uta turned over and whispered that it was all right so long as we were very quiet. We faced each other as she ran her arms over the scars on my back, feeling the raised skin of my old infections.

'What happened here?' she asked stroking my lower back, as I pushed five months' worth of hard-on into her upper leg.

'Oh, you know, combat . . . I don't like to talk about it really . . . it brings back too many bad memories.'

'Was it very terrible?'

'You can get used to it in the end, I suppose, but it always stays with you.'

I silenced her by pushing my tongue into her mouth and running it over her fillings; she opened her legs. I suddenly felt the zip of the sleeping bag press into my back, so I shifted position, lying on top of her with my hands behind her head, looking into her eyes at the point of maximum interest. She stroked the hair on my chest with her fingers, running her hands across my shaven scalp. I wanted to prolong the moment so I suggested that we stop while I had a cigarette; lighting up a Rothmans I blew the first stream of smoke over the back of her friend next to me. We murmured about the Legion and kissed whilst I drew on my fag, tapping out the ash on top of somebody's bikini at the side of the tent. Feeling my scars again, she asked where I had been in combat.

'All over the place . . . Africa mostly . . . always with the Legion . . . I just found that I got used to the killing after a while and the smell on the battlefield first thing in the morning . . . well . . . I suppose its addictive . . .'

She stiffened as I said this and looked away, over her shoulder at my pile of clothes behind her. Moving her legs apart with one hand and stubbing out my Rothmans on her ground sheet with the other, I moved into her, feeling my groin swallowed up by the expanse of her upper legs as our pelvises rubbed together in the scritch-scratch of pubic hair. She turned on her back and wrapped her legs about me as I thrust backwards and forwards into her, feeling myself getting more and more excited. She gripped my back, digging her fingernails into my skin as she moved towards orgasm. Her tits flopped out, running over the sides of her chest and jiggling around as we fucked on. Suddenly she tautened and blew out very fast about five times. Feeling her grip and pull I let go, the moment of intense pleasure dulling immediately as we both came to a squidgy uncomfortable climax. Her breathing softened and I let my head drop forward into her shoulder, my erection disappearing in a trice, feeling wet and limp inside her.

I had a fleeting thought: if I left immediately, I would be able to get back to Calvi before everybody left the bars, and so be in time for another drink. I had to persuade Uta that I needed to be back at the barracks before 5.00 am so that it wouldn't look as though it was hump and dump. I lay on top of her for a while longer before saying that I had to go; she held on to me saying that as I was on leave couldn't I just stay with her for an hour or two. I dressed carefully, worried that my uniform might be creased, but it still looked smart enough. Giving my shoes a quick wipe with her T-shirt, I made to leave the tent when she held my hand and turned towards me.

'Christian, you said that those scars on your back came from being in combat with the Legion?'

'Yes, that's right.'

'And you've only been in action with the Legion?'

'Yeah. Chad was the worst, though Zaire was rough at times.'

'But that's impossible, isn't it?'

I suddenly remembered with a sick lurch of embarrassment that of course, she would know all about the Legion and the *2ème Régiment Étranger de Parachutistes*. She had lived with the bloke from the 2nd Company for ages before he killed her dog.

'Surely if you had been in action in Zaire you would have the red and black medal like my boyfriend Johnny had on his shirt. You have no medals at all.'

I was up and moving away, pulling my shoes on as I leant out of the tent to move off; thank Christ it was dark, I thought, otherwise she would see how red I had gone. This was terrible. I had to get away. Would she tell my friends? I had waffled my way into the sleeping bag of some girl on false pretences.

She giggled as she spoke, 'Christian, I think you tell me little lies about being a big brave soldier. I know you have only been in the Legion one year – your Swedish friend, Marius, he told my friend last night when he fucked her.'

She burst out laughing, her naked bulk rocking in the darkness of the damp tent as I pissed for it up the slope towards the road.

I hit *Les Palmiers* forty minutes later to find it still crowded and busy. I threaded my way past the tables, saying hello here and there to friends and other people from the company, before pushing through to the U-shaped bar at the far end of the room. I was sweating and thinking fast. On my moonlit walk back from the campsite, I had considered the implications of what Uta had said.

I ordered a Jack Daniels and Coke and leant over to whisper to Emil, who was wearing a black dinner jacket, bow tie with a white shirt and black fishnet stockings with high-heeled shoes. He kissed me on both cheeks and offered me a glass of champagne. He had already heard about my exploits with Uta from one of the other boys who had been at the *Calypso* and he shook his head at me in disapproval.

Every time I ended up in his bar he would get me drunk and try to persuade me to sleep with him. I hadn't succumbed so far but it didn't put him off trying. One evening we had had a leisurely snog over the bar but nothing more had happened since then. His bar was the nicest in town and everybody ended up there as he stayed open all night. When it was full, as it was this evening, he would dance and perform to the legionnaires, prancing along the top of the bar and dipping the heels of his stilettoes into people's drinks. It was the one bar in town where Officers, legionnaires and Sergeants gathered irrespective of rank, and where one could have a conversation with somebody to whom it would normally be impossible to talk.

I went and sat outside at a pavement table with six other members of the 3rd Company who were drinking vodka and orange and talking about the relative merits of 5.56mm ammunition over 7.62mm. The sun was coming up over the bay and the mountains behind our camp were lit up in the early morning light. It was 29 August 1985.

We had all been out drinking and dancing for at least twelve hours, and felt sober. It was comfortable and relaxed sitting round the table, each of us paying for our rounds of drinks which came to nearly £30 each. Looking across at the other people around me, with their different scars, medal ribbons and tattoos, I felt part of the group for the first time in ages. Life had hit a low point in Africa when I had deserted, but I was now beginning to feel a participant in what I was doing, rather than just a mere observer. I was accustoming myself to the moral codes of the *2ème Régiment Étranger de Parachutistes*, and was starting to fit in. This was enhanced by the amount of alcohol that we had all consumed, but sitting there watching the early morning sun on the sea, I felt happy. If I had adopted the behaviour and ways of thinking of the people I was with then that was well and good – it had seemed stand-offish and affected to consider myself any better than them on account of my background. All of them were much better soldiers than I was, and on that morning, at that time, that was what counted. We started talking about a tattoo I could get.

People expressed their self image in a hundred different ways with a number of different tattoos. I was working on a design for one that I hoped to have done when I got some leave on the continent, when I hoped to be able to visit a tattoo artist in Marseilles who specialised in Legion designs. I wanted to find one that hadn't been done before. I had decided on a one-colour ink drawing of the Grim Reaper, complete with a scythe and cloak, galloping on a horse across a field of skulls with parachutes in the sky behind him. The caption was to go in Roman capitals above and below it, 'Dreaming of love in a life of pain'. This captured the essential masochism of the French Foreign Legion, which expressed itself in the idea of glory through death and pain. The skulls signified those of my Legion predecessors who had already perished, and the Grim Reaper was the omnipresent, semi-human face of death. The sun in the sky behind was happiness and light, and the parachutes were the central vein of the airborne spirit. The caption hinted at the future possibility of happiness earned through suffering, as in the words of the Legion song, '*Mais un jour dans notre vie, le printemps refleurira* . . .' (But one day in our life, spring will flower again . . .)

There were different schools of thought on the subject of tattoo design, varying from the religiously masochistic to the militarily romantic. You could start on the bicep or the forearm, and then move on to the chest, back and hands. The English people went for the combinations of daggers, skulls, roses and girlfriend's names, along with parachute wings and regimental crests. There were tigers crawling over shoulders, swallows flying along the backs of hands and loads of eagles. The eagle signified strength to the American Indian, and had long been a tattoo implying virility and fighting prowess. The American Indians and the Zulus were two of the most influential exponents of the warrior creed in the preceding 300 years, and lots of people emulated them, in the way they applied their camouflage cream to their choice of war cry. The Royal Marines tended towards the Zulu in their mentality, and the age-old soldier's song of 'Get 'em down, you Zulu warrior', which accompanied somebody stripping and shoving a lighted newspaper up their arse, carried on this tradition. Personally, I was ambivalent about war cries. Although I had never had need to shout one in the Territorials or opening tins of pâté in Africa, I thought they would probably be a good idea when the time came. French tattoos were one-colour line drawings, involving pictures of legionnaire's heads, the Horsemen of the Apocalypse and lines from marching songs. A cook in the British Army who had long yearned to be a paratrooper had tried to glamorise his situation with a hefty tattoo on his forearm; a skull being transfixed by a dagger, accompanied by the words, 'Pain is a purifier; for the right to kill, one must first suffer'.

Becoming a paratrooper in the French Foreign Legion meant a new image for most people, and for the younger soldiers like myself, it seemed natural to brand oneself with evidence of this identity. It helped you to see yourself clearly if you could look at your forearm and be reminded by a picture and a caption that you were an 'Airborne Warrior' or that you 'Belonged to a Warrior creed'. The ideals and beliefs behind the Legion were well illustrated by the various tattoos, and it could help you to understand why some people had joined up in the first place. The reasons why people had joined the Legion were often more interesting than the characters themselves. A French Sergeant had his entire life history tattooed on his arms; he had obviously lived in California at some point since he had the address of a girl from Santa Monica emblazoned on his arm. Above that was a picture of her, and crawling above that an enormous tattoo executed in green and black which showed a legionnaire in uniform cradling a machine gun, his shoulders draped with belts of ammunition, and a malevolent grin on his face. Scratched above this were the words 'Living by chance, soldiering by profession, killing for fun'. The wearer suited the tattoo: he was a hard bastard who had been thrown out of the French Regular Paratroopers for stealing explosives. He had a reputation for being reckless and impulsive and I had heard snatches of a story about him in Beirut, involving an RPG-7 rocket launcher and a few Palestinians; this was while on duty with the United Nations peace keeping force. The theme of fighting and conquering continued on the back of a Frenchman: Jesus on a parachute, surrounded by angels firing bows and arrows into the sky as he cries tears of blood, surmounted by the caption, 'For my ancestors it was Dien Biên Phu; for me it will be Moscow'.

Religion was popular amongst the South Americans and Latins, and the feeling of suffering as a route to self discovery and self glorification was expressed through the figure of Christ. As most of the South Americans, Italians and Spaniards were Roman Catholic, it was natural that they should use his image to portray what they most revered and respected. Faces of Christ, again crying tears of blood, were accompanied by the words, 'Like him I have loved, like him I have suffered'.

From these tattoos it was easy to imagine that life in the Legion essentially consisted of having a bad time. It didn't. It consisted of being able to thrive and feel fulfilled in an environment which was devoid of all the normal clutter and padding which accompanied a civilian existence. We lived our life in and for the present, and our only worries were getting enough to eat, enough sleep and keeping out of trouble. We would get as drunk as we possibly could whenever we could and sometimes spent an entire month's pay in one night. There were no emotional worries because we hardly saw any women apart from prostitutes, no financial problems because we were all paid the same amount on the same day every month. The orders posted on the Section notice board every morning told us what to wear and where to be at any given time, we had no civilian clothes as they were forbidden, and we all looked identical with our shaved heads. We had signed our contracts, had no control over the rhythm or routine of our lives and were not consulted over what we wanted to do. There was nothing to read and a practically nonexistent social life. We spent all day and sometimes all night training in a varied and uncompromising way to be the best airborne soldiers in the world and all our possessions, apart from our watches and our Walkmans, were the property of the Legion. It was futile to dream and plan, and little we said or did outside of the camp had any effect on our lives.

I realised sitting outside of *Les Palmiers* that this was what my life was about, and continuing my newly-discovered enthusiasm, it was going to be the basis of my continued existence both within the 3rd Company, the *2ème Régiment Étranger de Parachutistes* and any other regiment I happened to be posted to. I had stalled and stumbled along for the first year, and I was interested to see if I could manage to adhere to the principles of life as a legionnaire from then on. If I did manage, then I could regain some of the respect I had lost through deserting and become a participating and contributing member of the unit. If I didn't, then I was going to be consigned to an existence of feeble menial tasks for the rest of my contract, unless I chose to desert and leave it all behind.

Summer was finishing and the tourists were going home. After the national feast day on 15 August, there were fewer and fewer people on the beach during the day, and each evening we sat in Emil's bar watching the car ferries disappear round the hook of the bay with another load of departing holiday makers. The cafés were emptier every night. There was nothing to do and our drinking became more intense as the end of leave approached. We would normally stay out all night, wandering back to the hotel as the sun came up. I met a French woman one evening and took her out to supper in a restaurant on the outskirts of town where we ate fried peppers and talked of her broken marriage. Thinking that I was the first legionnaire that she had met and believing that she would be fascinated to hear my personal philosophy, I sat with her in a waterfront bar expounding at length on the nature of life. Waving my arm in a wide sweep across the bay towards the mountains, I leant towards her and said drunkenly, 'There's a huge world out there: you've got to get out and find it'.

She was a close friend of Adjutant Lodvic.

Our last days of leave were spent getting very, very drunk. There was a large fight in Emil's bar one evening, when some senior Sergeants from the reconnaissance platoon, who specialised in high altitude parachuting, smashed up the bar in the *Bons Amis* café, frightening Romy and Marie and tipping Slasher off his regular bar stool as he was trying to pass out undisturbed. They picked on a French legionnaire and ripped his uniform to shreds. They were all unarmed combat instructors and specialists in Commando techniques and one of them headbutted the French legionnaire several times for a joke. I was drinking at the bar next to them and kept quiet, safe in the knowledge that as an Englishman like them I was OK. I moved off to Emil's after they chucked the hat stand through a plate glass window. Slug was down there having an argument with Marius about Carina, who had left on the ferry two days before after being unfaithful to Marius with several different people, including three small Greeks from the dog handling section. Pissed, I joined in the argument, and all three of us started screaming at each other. Slug and I were in the middle of a long standing argument about the relative merits of the Royal Marines versus the Parachute Regiment, a disagreement which had been the original cause of our drinking contest in the Empire bar. It moved on to a new phase of challenges, involving disgusting behaviour and unnatural practices. Slug was talking vaguely about pissing in my drink or eating somebody else's shit, when I went down on my knees, undid his flies and gave him a ten-second blow job, the dick which had fucked the ugliest girls in Plymouth finding a brief lodging place between the gaps in my teeth.

The following day there was an inquiry into the fight in the bar, but I didn't count as a witness because in the vital ten seconds in question when an Officer had been hit I had been on my knees.

We listened to Simon and Garfunkel playing their concert in Central Park and drank vodka and orange. On the last morning of leave, there was a party in *Les Palmiers*, then we gathered our possessions, humped our bags into taxis and returned to camp. The summer was done.

— 10 —

BOILS IN THE SNOW

We put on our parachutes at Reims airport and flew off towards the drop zone at Haricot de Vadenay, an army training area set fifty kilometres from the Luxembourg border. Two C-160 Transalls with the whole of the 3rd Company were off for a fortnight under canvas in the freezing winter of northern France. My world was reduced to the area between my legs, as I had a boil in between the cheeks of my arse which lay directly underneath the buckle of my leg strap where it passed between my legs. Shortly after take off the white-hot pain and the rigid pressure eased as the boil burst. Across the fuselage from me were Slug and Marius who, along with several other members of the Company, had decided to use the visit to the mainland as an opportunity to desert. One bloke had put on civilian clothes underneath his combats, planning to make a break for it into the woods as soon as he hit the ground. Slug, Marius, two new men who had just arrived in the Section, and Slasher were all set to run for the Luxembourg border.

Coming in at 800 feet over the heathland of Haricot de Vadenay we jumped in tight groups into the dusk, our parachutes spreading out in the evening sky. I hit the ground, jettisoned my chute, and picked up my container with its attached rocket launcher and jogged off towards the rendezvous area. It was very cold, and there were patches of snow lying in hollows on the ground. The trees and bushes were covered with little crusts of ice in some places and the grass was stiff and half frozen. We lay in a tight circle while Adjutant Lodvic checked the map. We were due to move off the drop zone and march to our campsite situated in a pine forest fifteen kilometres away. The plan was to base ourselves around a tented camp and to conduct winter training and anti tank warfare in the woods and plains surrounding the drop zone. I had forgotten what it was like to be cold. Sixteen months spent in Corsica and Africa, sleeping under sheets, sweating constantly, worrying about tropical disease and wearing thin summer clothes had become the norm. For our exercise in northern France we had been issued with winter clothing – overboots, gloves and furry hats. I had been lumbered with the rocket launcher again and had brought along every piece of extra clothing I had. Most of my possessions were in my rucksack, along with the money I had saved since coming back from leave in Calvi three months earlier. I had enjoyed the amphibious warfare course in October, when I regained my physical fitness, cut down on my drinking and mastered the techniques of driving and controlling Zodiac rubber assault boats well enough to be awarded seventh place on the course. Over three weeks we had learnt everything there was to know about outboard motors and the sea. In true Legion style, we had been lectured on the intricacies of engines by a German Sergeant, speaking French to a group of people of nine different nationalities. Typically, there were now those who could name all the parts of a Yamaha outboard but who couldn't ask for the time correctly.

I had done quite well, although I had been a very slow learner and had displayed a deep-seated fear and misunderstanding of mechanical things. I had capsized my boat in front of a watching group of Officers, tipping a Sergeant into the sea, as I misjudged the strength and power of a wave which was rolling towards me. I had been run over, if such a thing is possible at sea, by another trainee on the course, who had piled his boat on top of the one I was controlling. I had fallen into the water and had watched the propellers of his engine turning feet in front of my face. The blades had grazed my watchstrap before a Sergeant had pushed the other boat away and dragged me, half-conscious, out of the water. We were out on the Mediterranean one night, and the sea was rough. I had eight men in the Zodiac I was piloting and the waves were splashing over the front of the rubber boat. I had picked the men up from a deserted beach three miles around the headland of Calvi bay, and was dropping them off at another beach closer to the amphibious warfare centre. I had waited on the beach for the men for three hours, curled up beside my Zodiac which I had dragged up beside me; while I waited in the rain, I forgot to check that the boat was properly inflated, and by the time we put to sea it was too late.

On board I had Sergeant Rodrigue, a bad-tempered Spaniard, and his group of men, who had just completed a cross-country route march through the night. It was pouring and they were all soaking wet and cold. The trip in my boat was the final leg of the exercise, after which they could march home to the camp. Two miles out at sea, the Zodiac started to feel sluggish and was slow to respond to the motor; we were sitting low in the water because the boat was full of men and equipment. The rubber sides felt soft and spongy, rather than hard and resilient as they were when properly inflated. We were slowly sinking. It was a long way to the shore and Sergeant Rodrigue realised what was happening. We all had lifejackets on and could swim but if the boat went down we would lose our equipment, the boat itself, the outboard motor, all the men's rucksacks and possibly their weapons. I would have to pay for the lot which would mean signing on for another fifteen years at least. Rodrigue picked up the wooden oar and started hitting me on the head with it, slowly, not too hard, but rhythmically and constantly, swearing and calling me a different name with each blow. The boat got slower and slower, the water level came closer and closer to the sides, and we were close to going down. As a desperate, last-minute gesture, I aimed the prow towards a patch of surf where it broke over an underwater rock. Beaching the Zodiac on the rock which lay a foot under the surface, I made the others get out and stand in the freezing sea as I extracted my foot pump and inflated the boat correctly. The others got in, swearing and mumbling at me, and we moved off, the boat handling correctly and moving properly. When we arrived at the beach, an hour late, soaking wet and cross, Rodrigue picked up the oar and made me bend down whilst he thwacked me across the arse with the flat blade.

For three weeks we had lived in a tent at the amphibious centre, our clothes and equipment constantly soaked and stained by salt. We had been running every morning and had done a lot of unarmed combat on the beach, throwing each other onto the stones and sand as we improved our techniques for disarming sentries and cutting people's throats. There had been a lot of kicking and strangling and as much of the training was carried out on the stones and rocks of the beach, there were some very bruised bodies. Without question, I was the worst when it came to unarmed combat and fighting in general. We would stand in groups on the sand or the stones and the Adjutant in charge would decide which technique we would practise that day. I was normally the dummy, and would stand with my back turned as somebody crept up on me from behind. Suddenly there would be a tearing, choking feeling as a piece of cord was thrown around my neck, a knee was thrust into the small of my back and I was twisted into a pile on the ground. There were techniques for stabbing people so that they died without making a sound, for strangling them using their helmet straps or for breaking their necks using a twisting, jerking motion. One hand on the back of the head, the other under the chin, then rotate the head and push up under the jaw before twisting savagely to snap the spinal column. It was all tiring and physically numbing, but it was very useful to know how to disembowel somebody silently or disarm four attackers simultaneously.

In the evenings I would go down and sit on the beach just over the sand dunes and drink beer, looking at the lights of Calvi across the bay. All the tourists had left and it was deserted, the only occupants the groups of legionnaires drifting from bar to bar looking for pleasure. The shops were shut and the town had a desolate, melancholy feel. We would go out occasionally hoping to find some of the excitement and fun which we had experienced during the summer, but the blinds were down on most of the bars and the beach was deserted. Getting drunk was unenjoyable and mechanical, and I felt that there was little to be seen or done. There were the tired whores at the Dolce Vita with their leotards and dying eyes, or the barmaids in town who would feign interest in amphibious warfare for as long as I was prepared to buy them champagne. So I stuck in most evenings, lying on my camp bed and scratching the scabs on my face which were recurring from my African infections.

We finished our course and returned to the routine of guard duty, ironing and training. There was Christmas to look forward to, and then 1986 held another visit to Africa, a possible war in Chad, and eight months in Calvi. I could apply to go abroad to one of the foreign Regiments, either in Tahiti or French Guyana. I had decided that I didn't want to stay in the *2ème Régiment Étranger de Parachutistes*, feeling that I had been precluded from promotion or preferment because I had tried to desert. I had been dreading going to northern France for some time, for the cold, the bullshit and the organisation that would be required to keep myself together, were daunting.

We marched from the drop zone to our tents set in the middle of the pine forest. It was 2.00 am and we were tired and cold from marching fast across the frozen roads. I wanted to dump my rocket launcher and rucksack and climb into my sleeping bag, but two of the Sergeants insisted that we make coffee, build a fire, organise the camp site and make neat lines of our rucksacks. I was exhausted, cross, irritated and cold. Why the Sergeants were incapable of making their own coffee was beyond me; they took the delegation of orders to an art form. We had to do absolutely everything for them apart from brush their teeth. So we built the fire and duly sat around until we were allowed to sleep at 3.00 am. I wrapped my parka over my uniform, kept my boots on and cuddled my rocket launcher until I fell asleep. The fire was almost out when we woke up the following morning. I dragged through the nightmare of shaving in cold water, making coffee for the group and brushing my teeth. I went for a shit and peeled my underpants down, the pus from my burst boil caking my trousers and backside. When I came to wipe my arse, I smeared shit into the open wound, infecting it again. I didn't realise this until several days later.

The wood in which we were camped was crisscrossed and marked by old trenches from World War One, which had been fought all around the area where we were. I was sure that if we had dug deep enough in the soil we would have found old helmets and pieces of twisted metal. Although the war had ended seventy years before, something of the atmosphere, of all the thousands of men who had died there, pervaded the forest. The trenches wound their way through the woods in a complex pattern, with no fixed itinerary, twisting back upon each other. I supposed that they had been the communications trenches which had been dug behind the front line. It must have been a bloody cold, depressing place in which to live and fight for five years.

We spent several nights out in the open over the next ten days, digging holes in the frozen ground and crouching down with our rifles and infra red viewing devices, as we watched for tanks moving in front of us. We were practising our anti tank warfare which consisted of patrolling through the pine forests in the darkness until we came across the huge shapes of tanks lying in camouflage; we would announce our presence by dropping a smoke grenade through the turret or grabbing one of the sentries. For the rest of the time we had lectures in the small camp, gathered firewood, cleaned our weapons and went on map reading exercises.

The Padre from Corsica had come along, parachuting in with everybody else, and taking part in the marches across the ice and snow of the training area. One afternoon he held an impromptu mass in the area between the trees and I went along. He had built an altar from a camp table, and over his mud-stained combats had draped a strip of ecclesiastical cloth which transformed him in one move from paratrooper to priest. There was ration-bread to eat for Holy Communion, and wine from a plastic container. There were two German Corporals, myself, Capitaine Trousseau, one of the French Lieutenants and three or four Italians and Spaniards. There was nothing odd in our attending mass in the Legion. The link between the military and the religious was strong, and underneath the macho posturing was often an innate fear of God. For many people, especially the Latins and the South Americans, their faith was too long standing an affair to be shaken by donning a uniform; the Legion encouraged the adherence to a stronger belief and a higher authority. We stood in the small clearing around a fire, lit to keep us from freezing while we listened to the Eucharistic prayers, and clasped our hands together and shuffled our feet to keep warm. Memories of going to church at school came back to me, and it did not feel out of place to be listening to the same prayers, albeit in French, that I had heard weekly from the ages of six to sixteen. Each of us queued up to receive a small piece of bread, then the Padre said the final prayers, blessed us and we went back to our individual sections, some to eat their late lunches, others to gather wood, the 3rd Section to prepare for a march, and myself to have my boil cleaned and dressed.

I lay on the ground a few yards from the rest of the section, who were gathered round the fire smoking and toasting pieces of bacon in the ashes. Face down on my poncho, I placed a piece of wood between my teeth as Max, the section Medic, knelt behind me and pulled my trousers down. Pulling away my filthy underpants in one movement, he swore and tutted as he surveyed the mess. I hadn't washed for a week, apart from minimal shaves each morning, and the result was disgusting to look at. Max held a huge wad of lint in both hands and tested the area round the infection. I had been incapable of sitting down properly for three or four days and the pain on my backside had become intolerable. I bit on a piece of wood and squawked with pain as he prodded the boil; suddenly he forced down hard with both hands and a week's worth of scab, shit and pus forced itself in a stinking rush into the bandage. I closed my eyes and arched my back, hammering the toes of my combat boots into the forest floor as he carried on squeezing and emptying the wound. The section gathered round the fire looked at me with interest, and Lodvic told one person not to laugh. Max wiped the whole area, covered it with antiseptic cream, and taped on a huge dressing which made me feel as though I had a cushion in my trousers.

Slug and Marius walked off into a snowstorm that night.

They had saved all their money for three months and had civilian clothes in their rucksacks. They walked away from the group of tents at 3.00 am, avoiding the guards, and slipped away into the darkness and the snow. The following night three others deserted as well. This put Lodvic in a foul mood, for it reflected on him personally when people from his section deserted. No search parties went out to look for the missing men, as everybody believed that they would be picked up long before they reached the frontier with Luxembourg or Switzerland.

I didn't go with them, despite their invitation, for it was so cold and the prospect of walking for three days in a blizzard was unappealing. Not that I didn't want to leave as well, because with Slug and Marius gone, there was nobody to whom I could complain or moan. The bullshit over the ten days of the exercise had got worse, and the atmosphere in the section had changed completely. All the new people who had arrived meant that the older hands had left to go off on courses or moved to other sections. With so many new people around, the Sergeants and Corporals could not relax, because there were too few experienced people among us to make sure that things got done without any trouble. I had started getting sloppy again, and the enthusiasm which I had felt at the end of leave had disappeared. My infections kept recurring because I was drinking too much again, which meant that every morning in Calvi I would have a hangover and would thus be incapable of operating properly. Things were tolerable enough if one kept switched on, but if the edges of one's concentration and fitness were being eroded by hangover and drink, then life became tense and worried.

When most people deserted, they subjected themselves to a much worse experience than the one they had left behind. Slug and Marius had chosen to walk off into the middle of a snowstorm, facing hunger and cold, sleeping in woods and ditches until they got to the border. From there they would make their way back across Europe to Plymouth and Sweden. Two people had deserted from Corsica by swimming across the straits of Bonifacio to Sardinia. This was across miles of rough sea, where the currents which swept around the sides of the two islands met in a jumble of waves and confusing currents. From Sardinia, they would have to make their way on to mainland Italy, leaving behind wetsuits and flippers on a remote beach, changing into the civilian clothes they had brought with them in their waterproof bundles. In Djibouti or Guyana, the methods of escape were even more dramatic. Two legionnaires had stolen a jeep, stuck the badges of rank of a Captain on their chests, and simply driven out of the front gates and into the desert. They had dumped the jeep when it ran out of fuel, and from there had headed off into Ethiopia, eventually arriving in the Sudan. They had caught a plane home to London, arriving broke and suntanned at Heathrow on a rainy autumn afternoon. In Guyana, two legionnaires had worked their way through the Amazon jungle, across the border into Suriname and on to the West Indies in a stolen fishing boat.

In deserting, the method of escape was always the most dramatic part. What people left behind was uncomfortable, violent and nerve-racking, yet secure. When they got home to their own countries they were normally broke, and had shut off one more option behind them. After deserting from the Legion, the need to succeed and do well were imperative. While working in London, I had always had the consolation that the Legion was waiting if things went wrong. It had made civilian life easier to tolerate because there was an alternative. But to come home in the middle of a contract with the Foreign Legion meant that the escape route was shut for ever.

The adventure and risk of setting sail in a fishing boat from a mangrove swamp on the South American coast, or of roaring across the desert at night in a stolen jeep were almost ends in themselves. The adventure was exclusive. It had little to do with anything which had preceded it or anything which would come after it. It combined all the risks and physical daring which people had been looking forward to in joining up, but which had been absent because, like any other armed force in the 1980s, the French Foreign Legion was an organised peacetime outfit. Within its confines of brutality, discipline and curious tradition, it was almost sedentary. There was total security, élitism and self respect which came from being part of a professional organisation and no worry about the taxing and compromising decisions required in civilian life. For everybody who had run away to France, leaving behind broken marriages or failed civilian jobs, the challenges they would have to face in the Legion were purely physical ones, more straightforward than the daily demands of electricity bills, failed marriages, crying children and unemployment. What they stood to lose in France were life, limb and blood. Healthy male attributes. At home in Britain, Texas, Sri Lanka or Paraguay, there were only the nagging weevils of poverty and social disintegration. Within the ranks of the armed forces, there was always the option of falling back on to the corporate identity provided by the unit and the uniform. Hence the tattoos proclaiming their status; 'Airborne Motherfucker', 'Legion Para'. To those who had been professional soldiers before joining, the Legion was another army, with its successes and failings. Soldiers would complain bitterly about their equipment, uniforms, tactics and living conditions to each other, yet professional solidarity took hold immediately upon attack from outside. Legionnaires and Corporals would criticise their leaders and their units, comparing them to other armies in which they had served. Yet, as the French always replied when the others complained about the Legion, nobody had asked us to join.

Most people who joined up, trained keenly and were posted to a good regiment, yet still deserted, were victims of the Legion misinformation service. They had believed everything they had heard and had been taken in by it. Like Slug, Marius and myself. Slug was one of the most professional soldiers I ever met, yet he had found the contradictions and boredom of it all to be too much. The attractions of sunglasses in the desert and night para drops in Corsica to a man who has got a few problems at home were obvious. I suspected that many people had been like myself when they joined – a shambling, drunken mess. Things had come full circle. As I fell out of the jump door of the Transall C-160 over Haricot de Vadenay, pus running down my arse and my uniform in shit order, things were falling out of place. I had got back a little enthusiasm during leave and on my amphibious course, but it was fast disappearing. Physical disintegration signalled worse inside. My uniforms were in a mess, I was constantly in debt, I fell behind on the morning runs and my rifle was always manky at inspections. I countered all this by retreating into my own self satisfaction and sense of superiority, cutting myself off from those around me. Reading Evelyn Waugh in the desert or going to mass in a French forest meant nothing. What counted in the circumstances were basic qualities of self respect and self discipline. I had none. I could not even be bothered to desert again because I preferred the comfort of my sleeping bag to the trials of running across frozen fields in the middle of the night.

I was wandering around in the wood behind the Officer's portable lavatory when I heard that Slug and Marius had been recaptured. I had been collecting wood in a desultory manner, using it as an excuse to steer clear of the camp for a while, but I dropped my armful of branches and rushed over to the tents where Carver told me what had happened. The two of them had been found in a forest close to the Luxembourg border. Marius had gone into a little village to buy food and had of course been noticed. The police had been called, and the two of them arrested with the aid of police dogs. They had been taken to the local Gendarmerie and locked up. A Captain from the Support Company of the *2ème Régiment Étranger de Parachutistes*, who had been on exercise with us, went over to pick them up. This Captain liked boys and had a habit of finding drunk legionnaires on the town in Calvi and offering them lifts home. While they were slumped in the front seat of his car he would proposition them, gliding a soft hand up the leg of their uniform trousers. He had driven to the Gendarmerie to fetch the two deserters, and on the way back they had stopped at a hardware store where Capitaine Dognau-Banco had decided that the prisoners needed restraining. He had gone into the shop and bought two pairs of handcuffs which he attached to Slug and Marius with more than professional interest.

The snow fell again that night as we prepared to break camp and head for home. In the morning we took down the tents, leaving only a flattened patch of grass and earth where we had camped. I filled in the latrine trench, shovelling earth and pine needles over it all, before packing my kit. We were going to parachute back onto Corsica, so we put on our parachutes again at Reims airport.

Slug was standing in the corner of the hangar, waving his hand-cuffed arms over his head, singing, 'I shall be released.'

— 11 —

TO WAR ... NEARLY

One day in the middle of March we had been promised that we would be able to have the day off, but last thing the night before the regiment was put on alert to fly to Chad. Throughout the months of January and February the Regiment had carried out a lengthy and monotonous preparation for an inspection of all the mechanical installations at Camp Raffalli, from typewriters and telescopic sights to lorries and jeeps. I had been detached from the 3rd Company to the 1st Company to help them clean all of their weapons. The 1st Company was away in Djibouti for four months and had left behind a small rear party who lived in their barrack block and took charge of the armoury and installations there. In preparation for the coming inspection, due to be carried out by a technical team from Paris, men were detached from each of the companies to give the rear party a hand. When asked by Capitaine Trousseau who he considered to be spare and dispensable from the first Section, Lodvic had not hesitated in suggesting my name.

Thus each morning I missed sport and parades, and trudged over to the other end of the camp to spend a dull day oiling lorries or polishing crossbows. I would go out in the evening and drift round a deserted Calvi, drinking solidly and alone. Each morning there was a hangover and the sweating tightness of working with a headache. I didn't do any more parachuting or exercise, since I was never with Lodvic or the rest of the boys, and I drifted off into a self contained blur, walking round the camp by myself in the middle of the day, saluting amiably, often being found in the foyer at 11.00 am drinking Kronenbourg with French mechanics.

We had returned from France and had had the normal preparations for a Legion Christmas. When it came round it was forced and unexciting; I had been so drunk for two days that I remembered little of it, apart from collapsing against the lavatory in Emil's one night and smashing the cistern as I fell against it. On boxing day morning, a group of us had driven across the island to Borgo, to perform guard duty at a camp there. I had lain on the floor of the open truck as we drove across the mountains of the Corsican interior, my head rocketing with two days' Malibu and wine as I clutched a machine gun to my chest and tried to get to sleep.

The inspection had been completed and the Colonel, pleased with the reactions and comments of the technical inspectors, had given the whole Regiment a day off. I was back with the Company and was trying to re-establish myself. Five or six of us had been in the Company bar playing conkers with our watches when we had heard about Chad. Conkers meant dangling your watch by its strap in front of you while your opponent smashed its face with his own watch. Mine was doing well. I had an ordinary Timex which had already been mangled by the propeller blades of the Zodiac's outboard motor. When the Sergeant walked in and told us to prepare for an alert, Carver's slim gold Piaget, with its pigskin strap, had just been splintered by someone's digital job. The face of mine was starred and cracked but had meted out serious damage to Josh's Rolex.

While we had been damaging each other's possessions, Colonel Gadaffi's Libyan instructors had moved their pro-Libyan rebels further south into Chad, across the demarcation line which had been agreed upon at the end of Operation Manta in 1984. Hissene Habre and his Chadian government forces had moved up into the desert north of N'Djamena to meet them. The *2ème Régiment Étranger de Parachutistes* was put on alert to help them. We were off to war.

Going onto an alert status with the Regiment involved a nightmare of personal and administrative organisation, entailing complex lists of equipment and weapons which, supposedly, each member of the unit had prepared in anticipation of such an event. While the channels of international diplomacy and military bureaucracy were jammed with telexes and radio signals, I left the bar to make sure that I had my three white regulation handkerchiefs and two pairs of khaki shorts which were among the items needed to go abroad on active service. My personal kit and my rucksack was a mess of empty beer bottles and old sachets of tomato sauce which I hadn't bothered to clear out since we had been on exercise in France at the end of the previous year. I stood at the end of my bed and tried to think straight. An English Corporal, a veteran of Chad and Beirut, told me that the most important things were spare Walkman batteries and a good supply of books. I had just bought a great tape by Dire Straits called 'Brothers in Arms' so I walked off to the foyer to buy some batteries before the shop sold out.

The Regiment was busy. The effort required to take 1,000 men to another continent in a fit state to perform peace keeping duties or to fight a war were immense. At each level, from that of the Colonel down to the legionnaires like myself, there were closely ordered tasks which went together to make up a composite whole. Whereas my tasks were concerned with ordering my personal equipment and making sure that I was ready, mentally and physically, to serve France and her foreign policy, the Colonel had to deal with the huge task of supplying 1,000 battle-ready paratroopers for a foreign war. We had trained for this moment for a long time. All the evenings and early mornings when we had been confined to barracks or engaged in training missions were geared to this. For each of us in the Regiment the hours and weeks of frustration and boredom spent in Africa and Corsica were validated by the prospect of going into action and carrying out the job for which we had originally enrolled in the French Foreign Legion.

I started to think about killing people.

If we got to Chad, I would be carrying the LRAC 89mm rocket launcher for my group along with four explosive anti tank rockets. The legionnaire detailed to act as my loader would back me up with another four, and the other members of the group would have one apiece. In addition to the fibreglass tube, I would carry a 9mm pistol and two magazines which I would use to defend myself at close quarters. We would be facing, if attacked, soft-skinned Toyota jeeps and possibly Russian-made tanks. My high explosive rockets could destroy a jeep at 600 metres, and, if aimed properly, could penetrate the frontal armour of a tank at 300. The results of a successful strike would incapacitate an armoured vehicle, blowing off its turret or destroying its tracks, killing the occupants, as the exploding warhead sent shards of metal flying around inside the hull. At close quarters I would use my automatic pistol or combat knife. Apart from the unarmed combat classes on the beach at Calvi, I had never thought through the mechanics of killing or dismembering another person. I had spoken at length to friends of mine who had killed people in the South Atlantic or Rhodesia. I did not know whether the thought of killing filled me with horror or interest. I suspected both. Within the confines of the *2ème Régiment Étranger de Parachutistes*, killing and the use of extreme physical violence was treated as a necessary means to the end of defeating the enemy. There was a kudos derived from having been in action, and the more gory tales of death and wounding from Vietnam, the Falklands and Africa were picked up and embellished.

I had only seen death at one remove: a corpse underneath a blanket on the pavement of the Mall during the Royal Wedding, my grandfather's coffin, an old woman dying of a heart attack in a shop in Islington. I had never actively contributed to somebody else's demise, yet here I was, poised to go to Africa loaded to the teeth with modern overkill, trained and prepared for it. We had had all the lectures about close quarter battle, fighting in built-up areas, house clearing and hand-to-hand fighting. I knew how to keep the belts of ammunition flowing through the FM-52 machine gun, I knew about back-taping my FA-MAS magazines so that I could change them with a quick wrist flick; I had practised firing my pistol at targets and could blow the testicles off a paper target at twenty yards. I knew where to stick my knife so that the victim choked in his own blood and I could hit a man hard enough to stun him. I knew all the techniques of using white phosphorus grenades, and had listened attentively to Parachute Regiment Sergeants explaining about 'white-saucing' people. (This involved lining prisoners up on the ground underneath a poncho or groundsheet, and throwing a white phosphorus grenade under the material, which contained the explosion and spread the hot liquid lumps of burning phosphorus over the victims' bodies.)

I, who had been described by one of the English Corporals as 'being frightened of his own shadow', was off to fight in somebody else's war in a country I had never visited. I knew that if it were necessary, I would do my best to destroy the enemy. I did not know how I would feel in doing so, presumably little at the time as it would happen very fast, but I knew that afterwards things would be different. I had been told that you never reacted as fast or thought as swiftly as when you were under fire, but I knew how impossible it was to appreciate the sickening nature of death in a modern firefight unless one had taken part. It was very easy to verge towards the gung ho, but soldiers who had killed in the Falklands seemed to have learnt to deal with the experience through themselves and their own mental mechanisms rather than through their training. I knew that it was not necessary to perform an action before realising that it was wrong, but I felt nervous and unsure about criticising those around me who had killed in and out of battle. It would have been profoundly hypocritical, as I waited to go off to Chad, to criticise another man for killing. The soldiers who knew themselves best were those who had been in the position of destroying others; only they could appreciate the true nature of warfare, for only they knew the powers and strengths of their weapons and the reality of fighting. It appeared that the best thing to do was to move very fast and instinctively, killing to protect yourself and your mates in as swift, ruthless and effective a manner as possible, and to suffer the mental consequences afterwards, when the rounds had stopped coming in and the position had been won. In the same way that our unarmed combat instructors had taught us that once you had put a man on the ground, it was vital never to let him get up again, so the moral dilemma of reducing another human to his component parts was something you thought about afterwards.

I had taken part in 'interrogation' exercises in the Territorial Army where 'prisoners' had been reduced to babbling wrecks through long hours of sensory deprivation, exposure to 'white noise', and verbally confusing interrogations conducted after the victim had been made to crouch on the floor for seven hours. And that had just been in the part time army. One afternoon in a deserted barrack building in Tewkesbury, myself and ten other part time paras had watched interrogators from the Joint Services Interrogation Wing 'question' members of another unit who had been acting as the enemy to us on an Escape and Evasion exercise through the fields and lanes of Worcestershire. When we had caught them they had been marching two days and nights, and were filthy and hungry. Forcing them to the ground, we had blindfolded them and taken them to this barrack block, where they had been forced to crouch motionless on the floor for seven hours in total silence. With blindfolds on, they were taken into a room and questioned cunningly and dexterously by the interrogators, all of whom wore civilian clothes and looked like retired prep-school Maths masters. Every single one of those questioned had broken down, although some of them had had to be handcuffed and slapped around a bit.

The interrogation exercises that took place in the Regular Parachute Regiment were more realistic. The para who had been in prison in Djibouti City with me had taken part in one such exercise. After three days adrift in the snow of a Norfolk training area at Thetford, he had not been caught by the 'hunter' force, but was starving and freezing. He had ambushed one of the people chasing him and taken his rifle, running off into the gorse. He had walked until he came to the edge of the training area, where he found a small, isolated holiday cottage. A retired doctor and his wife were spending the weekend there and the para burst through the door and forced them to make him bacon and eggs at gunpoint. After he had eaten, they had made him a cup of tea, and he had explained what he was doing, so they had given him some scones and jam, before he left apologising profusely for having disturbed their weekend break. When he had been captured, the para's interrogators had shown him a carefully mocked-up photograph of his wife which had been taken from his locker and superimposed in a faultless manner. It showed her being buggered by one man while another tattooed brute shoved his cock in her mouth. This was intended to make him break down and answer the questioning, but instead he answered, 'Normal Friday night for the missus.'

We stood in the queue in the foyer waiting to be served, talking of weapons. Outwardly, I was a walking advertisement for different techniques on killing. Inside, I felt that I had only adopted a superficial sheen of brutality which barely covered the core of my upbringing. However, it would be too late to think about all this when a Russian-made tank bore down on my trench, with only myself and my rocket launcher between it and the rest of the group. So I bought my Walkman batteries and thought about lines and angles of fire.

We never went to Chad.

The politicians in Paris decided that they could work things out better without the presence of the *2ème Régiment Étranger de Parachutistes* and so we stayed in Calvi, and prepared for a big exercise in the South of France which was coming up at the end of the month. Almost the entire Regiment was off to the area round Tarbes in the Pyrenees for a ten day manoeuvre involving other Regiments of tanks, artillery and engineers. It would be cold and wet, and Slug and Marius, who had come out of prison by now, were moaning about the weather and how the manoeuvre was going to be hell. Their time in prison had been considerably worse than mine, for they had spent it in Calvi, under the watchful eye of the Military Police, who were a load of bastards. Twice I had seen Slug running round the perimeter of the drop zone with a rucksack full of damp sand on his back and Corporals egging him on with sticks and dogs. Meal times had been nasty, as they had had to run around the table in the prison block, eating as they ran. Prison life in Corsica had softened considerably since the closure of Fort Charley, up behind the town, where one prisoner had died in custody after being beaten senseless and left in a roofless, windowless cell soaked with water in mid winter. The Corporal responsible had been sent to Guyana for two years, but had now returned and spent his time cooking pizzas in the foyer.

At the beginning of the 1980s, there had been considerably fewer English legionnaires. A great deal of the Englishmen had joined after the Falklands conflict and a lot of people had joined after a specific documentary on British TV. This had been directed and presented by an English legionnaire called Simon Murray who had served in the 3rd Company of the *2ème Régiment Étranger de Parachutistes* at the beginning of the sixties in Algeria. He had actually made a parachute jump on the day I was born, a fact I had discovered by looking up the old log books of the Company. He had come home to England, married his girlfriend and some years later written his memoirs in a book called *Legionnaire*. His documentary had portrayed the Legion in a glamorous way, and as a result, a lot of Englishmen had joined up. These were known as SMSs or Simon Murray Specials.

Before the arrival of these men, the *Mafia Anglais* had been a tiny group of five or six legendary figures, who had behaved in such an 'airborne' manner, behaving appallingly, that the Colonel of the Regiment had sent them abroad. Most of them were ex-Paras from England; one of them was from the Special Boat Section, and another was from the Royal Irish Rangers. You had to behave badly in those days to get thrown out of the Regiment, and they did. One of them shat on top of the *Monument aux Morts* statue outside of the Colonel's office, and one of them attacked the Duty-Officer with an axe. Four of them stole a Zodiac from the amphibious centre, loaded it down with beer, and tried to sail to England. They got as far as the outskirts of the bay before running out of petrol so, pissed, they had to row their way back. They behaved as badly as possible as often as possible, and most of them spent virtually their entire time in prison. They were role models for bad behaviour. Eventually the Colonel decided to embark them abroad, so before they left, they had one last fling, The Last Stand of the *Mafia Anglais*. After two or three days drinking, they had been banned from going out on the town and so were holed up on the top floor of one of the barrack blocks at Camp Raffalli. They were all pissed and making a lot of noise, when the Military Police were called, arriving in four or five jeeps with alsatians to have a showdown with '*Les Johnnie fuckings*'. The Military Police stormed up the stairs of the block, only to be beaten back with pick handles and fire extinguishers by the six mad-drunk English soldiers at the top. The Military Police decided what to do. None of them relished being beaten stupid by some pissed lunatic who had learnt his soldiering in the Special Boat Section, so they sent up the alsatians, who, noses snuffling and bodies straining at their leads, dashed up the stairs. There was the sound of a furry struggle, a yelp or two, a couple of thuds, and then silence. One of the Military Policemen poked his head round the corner of the stairs. Nothing. Suddenly, turning over gently in the air in floppy arcs of tawny hair and lifeless limbs, three alsatians fell from the banisters two floors up, thumping into the tiled floor in a pile of deadness. Their necks were all broken.

The *Mafia Anglais* had been split up and sent abroad, to Tahiti, Djibouti and French Guyana.

In 1986 things were a bit different. We had to iron and clean a new combat uniform for the forthcoming exercise in France because at the end we would parade in front of a General. We had known about this exercise for three months and had had plenty of time to prepare the uniforms. Everybody had done so, except me, who as usual had left it too late. Garcia and Dautremont had arrived back in the Section as Sergeants, and were letting it be known that things were going to smarten up a bit. I was so traumatised by them that I tried never to be sober. My powers of disorganisation were awesome. When we had gone to Borgo after Christmas for guard duty, I had packed my kit with my post-Xmas hangover. I had unpacked on the other side of the island, finding in my rucksack one sports shoe, no underpants, two helmets, a rifle cleaning kit that I had lost in Djibouti, some sachets of tomato sauce, half a roll of loo paper and twelve separate white socks.

When Sergeant Garcia came round to inspect the uniforms, mine was inadmissibly cruddy and creased. I had tried to iron it while drunk and had succeeded in putting in two diagonal railway lines straight across the back of my combat jacket. I also realised that I had no trousers to show so I slipped into the next room and borrowed those belonging to somebody who was in town for the day. Garcia, in a fit of charity, passed my uniform as fit to wear and left the room. So relieved was I that I forgot to replace the other bloke's trousers.

That was the afternoon I went to the dentist. Since my fight at the Parachute Regiment Christmas party, I had been walking around with two missing front teeth. A dentist in England had extracted the roots and so I had a blank space in the front of my mouth. This didn't worry me, but the Colonel of the Regiment had three times told me that he didn't want a Regiment that looked like Dracula. So I had an appointment booked in with an orthodontic surgeon at the military hospital at La Veran near Marseilles. This would tie in with my first period of leave since I had left Aubagne fourteen months before. Before leaving for Marseilles, there was some preliminary surgery to be carried out on my mouth by a Legion dentist at the camp. So, forgetting the trousers, I went off across the area of sand and pine trees in front of the infirmary and took my place in the Armed Forces Issue dentist's chair. The dentist himself, a plump Commandant with wine on his breath and a friendly chairside manner gave me an injection. He had been the dentist at Calvi for two years, his predecessor dying in front of the entire Regiment. He had been free falling over the drop zone in a standard jump, when both his main and reserve parachutes had failed to open. His wife had been watching him sky dive and so was present as his body plunged into the earth from 11,000 feet. As was the strict protocol on such occasions, the Regiment stood to attention during his last seconds in the air, anybody outside in the camp who had been watching jumping ramrod straight and saluting. His successor, also a man of the sky, cut out the nerves and a chunk of my gum. When he had finished, I stuck a pad of cotton wool on my mouth and walked over to the Section building to lie down on my bed, as was my entitlement after an operation.

The bloke, whose trousers I had borrowed and not returned, came into the room ten minutes later looking for me. He had returned from town half-drunk to find Sergeant Garcia chasing him for not having had his uniform inspected. He couldn't find his trousers and after Garcia had hit him two or three times they found them on my hanger.

In Algeria, thieves had been nailed to tables with bayonets through their hands and feet. But Garcia and the Englishman were more restrained. When they found me on my bed, the Briton walked over, ignored my comatose post-anaesthetised state and bleeding mouth, and started to systematically beat the shit out of me. He swung his fists into my mouth, eyes and jaw, kicking me on the ground and shouting at me. Other members of the Section watched from the doorway. He finished by picking up a stool and hitting me across the chest with it. Garcia then told me that when I recovered from my dental treatment there was another beating coming from him too.

I wished I was somewhere else. My face hurt and in one move I had completely and justifiably lost any sympathy I might have had from the rest of the group. My face swelled up dramatically, my eyes yellow and purple, my lips cut and my cheeks bruised. I was admitted to the sick-wing that evening and so could only watch from my bed as the Regiment took off in nine Transalls for the exercise on the mainland. Marius had joined me briefly in the infirmary, having been beaten up for refusing to sweep the floor but, together with Slug, had left with the rest of the Company. They, at least, had sympathised and stuck by me, as all three of us talked of little but desertion.

I started having blackouts and couldn't stand up straight. The doctor gave me an X-ray of my face and found nothing broken. He conducted a series of blood tests and investigated the state of my liver, deducing that I was in the throes of chronic alcoholism, and that the lining of my lower intestine was damaged and soured by all the alcohol which I had consumed. I was thus prone to infections. I had more boils on my back which were treated twice daily and consequently I smelt of infection and stale sweat through my pores. The others left me alone and after four days I was out of bed and helping the Sergeant who was in charge of the medical stores. He was easy going and I stacked boxes of pills and swept the floor. To my delight, I found some foil-wrapped packets of tablets on the shelves which were described on the box as powerful amphetamines. I could speed myself out of my misery and forget what was going on. My French vocabulary had let me down. They weren't speed. They were laxatives. I only discovered this after I had taken eight in one morning. The doctor thought my bowels had collapsed and was very worried. I wasn't allowed to eat and for two days kept diving through the doors of the toilet, ripping my shorts down in a flurry. Just before I was released from the infirmary, Adjutant Lodvic came to see me. The Section was back from France. Helpful and sympathetic for a year and a half, he prodded my chest with his huge fist and told me that I was a hopeless little shit.

When, two days later, an Irish Corporal came round the Section asking if anybody wanted to be put down for a transfer abroad, I stuck up my hand and asked to be sent to French Cuyana. I left Calvi three days later, quietly at 5.00 am along with another group of people who were going to the hospital on the mainland. Capitaine Trousseau had arranged my leave, allowing me to spend seventeen days in Paris after I had finished at the dentist. After that I had to report to Aubagne before being sent to Guyana.

I walked around the Section before I left, everybody knowing that they would never see me again. I shook hands with Meunier, Carver and Thierry, with whom I had spent so much time in Djibouti, and said goodbye to the others. Marius reminded me of an appointment we had joked about in London in summer 1987, after which we would be able to go abroad again, somewhere new, and be soldiers again. He was to desert shortly after. Slug wished me well, shaking my hand, and we confirmed our old plan to meet in England and earn some money to go back to Africa, where some friends of his were fighting in Uganda. It was sad to say goodbye to them, and I knew that at some point in my life I would see them again. Slug was to make it to war in Chad the following year. I had a cup of coffee in the Company bar looking round at the photographs of parachuting on the walls. I walked down to the guard house to join the rest of the party bound for Marseilles, and on the way bumped into Lodvic.

He shook my hand, which, coming from an Adjutant to a legionnaire was awesomely rare. Standing in the darkness on the gravel of the parade ground, I snapped to attention and gave him the smartest salute I had ever given. Turning away, I waved over my shoulder in a way I hoped looked positive.

Standing on the station platform, I smoked a Winston and waited under the eucalyptus tree for the train. I felt I was leaving in a shabby, undignified way. It was a poor end to an almost great adventure.

DESERTION

I approached the Customs barrier at Boulogne, walking along with my head down, smoking a cigarette and trying not to look apprehensive. The Irish girls with whom I was travelling giggled next to me, and one of them passed me her suitcase to carry. There were two uniformed Gendarmes checking passports, flicking through the pages and looking at the photographs. They were only stopping every third or fourth person in the line, waving the others through to where the ferry lay on its moorings. Bright lights filled the inside of the Customs shed, and the flagstones outside were shiny and slick in the rain. The policemen looked bored and disinterested. If I made it past them and on to the ferry, I would have left French soil, and once the ferry cast off I would be on my way to England. I didn't have a passport as it had been taken away from me at Aubagne two years before; my Military Identity card showed me to be a legionnaire, and the policemen would know that I was categorically forbidden to leave France. My leave pass which I had in my pocket had expired the day before.

If I was picked up now, it would be as a soldier who had outstayed his leave, and as I was trying to get through Customs at one of the Channel ports, my intention to desert would be plain.

I had left Calvi and travelled to Aubagne and thence to Marseilles, visiting the dentist. I had taken the train to Paris and spent two weeks drunk with other legionnaires before the date on my leave pass expired. I had known as soon as I left Corsica that I wouldn't be returning to Aubagne to go to French Guyana, and my fortnight in Paris had been spent trying to obliterate the realities of my impending desertion from my mind. On the day after my leave ended, I had taken a train to Boulogne where the journey had started two years before. I had got talking to a pair of Irish girls, hoping that by mixing in with two civilians I would look less conspicuous. As I got off the train I turned to look at the hill behind the town, with the cemetery where I had slept and the Gendarmerie; it was night and all I could see was a darker shadow where the slope began behind the town. I had my ferry ticket and nearly four francs in my pocket; my black jeans were shiny and greasy with filth, and my shoes were worn down at the heels from walking around Paris constantly after my money had run out. I hadn't washed for a week and I was still drunk from my last bottle of wine begged off a shopkeeper. I had a huge open infection on my back which ran pus into the two table napkins I had stuffed on to it, attached by sellotape. I was going home.

I dragged furiously on my cigarette as the Gendarmes cast an eye over me, looking me up and down from head to toe. Their 9mm pistols sat in their holsters and their patent leather belts shone in the electric lights; their hair was short. They leant forward over the table in front of them and motioned the queue forward. Suddenly, I turned to one of the Irish girls, laughed out loud and started to kiss and hug her furiously; she struggled but I forced my mouth into her neck as the Gendarmes looked away, embarrassed. I walked through and on to the boat.

We cast off twenty minutes later and just before 1.00 am I stood on the deck and watched the lights of Dover come into view.

It was 4 April 1986, and I had deserted, this time successfully.

Epilogue

Marius deserted in May 1987. After spending two weeks on leave in Paris he returned to Sweden where he attended a military academy, before being commissioned as an Officer in the Swedish Army.

Mike deserted also, and now lives in Texas.

Slug went to Chad in summer 1986 with the *2ème Régiment Étranger de Parachutistes*, where, to the best of the author's knowledge, he remains.

Adjutant Lodvic is still serving in the French Foreign Legion after eighteen years of service.

At the time of writing Englishmen make up the largest percentage of the new recruits to the *2ème Régiment Étranger de Parachutistes*.

One month after the author returned to England, he appeared at Knightsbridge Crown Court on seventeen criminal charges, ranging from theft and burglary to fraud and deception. During his nine-month prison sentence, he was instrumental in saving the life of a fellow prisoner and was granted a fourteen-day reprieve on his sentence by the Home Secretary. On release from prison he attempted to join the Special Air Service but was rejected. He now works in publishing, lives in Brixton and has had an Aids test.